ILLEGALS

THE IMMINENT THREAT POSED BY OUR UNSECURED U.S.-MEXICO BORDER

JON E. DOUGHERTY

WND BOOKS

Nashville

www.WNDBooks.com

Published in Nashville, Tennessee, by WND Books.

Library of Congress Cataloging-in-Publication Data

Dougherty, Jon E.
    Illegals : the imminent threat posed by our unsecured U.S.-Mexico border /
Jon E. Dougherty.
        p. cm.
    Includes bibliographical references and index.
    ISBN 0-7852-6236-9
    1. Illegal aliens—United States. 2. United States—Emigration and immigration.
3. United States—Emigration and immigration—Government policy. 4. Mexico—
Emigration and immigration. I. Title.
JV6483.D684 2003
325.73—dc22   2003025418

Printed in the United States of America
03 04 05 06 07 BVG 5 4 3 2 1

CONTENTS

INTRODUCTION

"America is a nation of immigrants." Throughout the debate over immigration, inevitably supporters of continued mass immigration will use that excuse to justify it.

To be fair, the statement does have a ring of truth. America was born a nation of immigrants, and because of its tremendous economic, military and political success, our country will likely always attract the world's "tired . . . poor . . . huddled masses."

That said, it has been generations since our nation was "settled." And while America may consist of many ethnic groups, as a whole we are truly unique in that we are *Americans*.

In the words of J. Hector St. John Crevecouer, author of *Letters From an American Farmer*, an emigrant French aristocrat-turned-farmer:

> What then is the American, this new man? . . . He is an American, who, leaving behind him all his ancient prejudices and manners, receives new ones from the new mode of life he has embraced, the new government

he obeys, and the new rank he holds. He has become an American by being received in the broad lap of our great Alma Mater. Here individuals of all races are melted into a new race of man, whose labors and posterity will one day cause great changes in the world. Americans are the western pilgrims.

Despite ethnic diversity, most Americans can trace their roots to America, and America alone, for several generations. We've never lived anywhere else. Our parents have never lived anywhere else. Many of our grandparents didn't, either. As such, most of us have deep cultural, spiritual and social ties to this nation—despite a desire by certain quarters to hyphenate us along ethnic lines.

Immigrants, however, have no such ties. And these days, many immigrants—especially those from south of the border—have no desire to develop such ties. But every rule has exceptions, and the general rule of immigration is no different. There are those who are coming to America to become *American* citizens. They want to share in the dream. They want to contribute. They want to prosper in ways only possible here. They want to put down roots. They want to be the first generation in a new line of Americans.

An increasing number of immigrants, however, come merely to clamor for opportunities and benefits not available to them in their home countries—and not ones they necessarily earn for themselves. Worse, there is a growing faction in America assisting them, knowing all along these immigrants aren't interested in enriching American society, but rather to take what they can from it.

There is also a change in mindset among elements of the political establishment and among the U.S. population in terms of immigration. In years past, gaining access to America so one could share in its promise was treated as a privilege, not a right to be granted automatically just because you could make it over the border. Today, however, the process of immigration—indeed, the requirement that our immigrants assimilate into our society—has changed dramatically.

Many lawmakers, for example, pander to certain ethic groups known to attract many immigrants, in hopes of garnering votes, at the expense of generational Americans who are being asked more and more to foot the bill. Many companies are now dependent upon the cheap labor supplied by immigrants—though it is illegal to hire "undocumented" aliens. The government makes a showy effort to curb illegal immigration and the hiring of undocumented workers by American companies, but as this book will demonstrate, the effort is haphazard and spotty at best.

In the end, the borders remain wide open. Most of the 2,000-odd miles of California, Arizona, New Mexico and Texas borders are unmanned, unmonitored and unprotected. Though the men and women charged with protecting our borders largely are dedicated professionals trying to do a tough job, there are not enough of them to be effective. And, few politicians and business leaders seem seriously interested in providing the resources necessary to maintain U.S. territorial integrity and national security, even as they spend billions annually to protect the borders of other countries, other regions.

The immigration problem isn't a new one. America has had laws governing immigration and naturalization since its earliest days when, on March 26, 1790, Congress established a uniform rule for naturalization by setting the residence requirement at two years. But it is certainly one of the most politically charged issues, especially at a time when America is fighting a global terror enemy bent on wreaking havoc and destruction here at home.

How the problem is solved—or not solved—ultimately may decide the fate of this nation.

CRISIS APPROACHING

Perhaps the White House is finally getting the message. It's about time they realize that the people of this country justifiably feel that the U.S. border is a sieve.

—REP. TOM TANCREDO (R-COLORADO), SEPTEMBER 14, 2002

On September 13, 2002, FBI agents Sergio Barrio, 39, and Samantha Mikeska, 38, were aboard a freight train traversing the rolling hills of Mount Cristo Rey near the U.S.-Mexico border in Texas. They were riding the rail for much the same reason agents from Wells Fargo, Pinkerton's and other frontier-era security companies in the Old West rode rails—to thwart a rash of train robberies that had been taking place on that line for months.

According to federal officials, robbers in these remote areas of the U.S.-Mexico border operate by waiting for American freight trains to slow, perhaps from a steep incline, in a desolate area of track—areas which are still inside the United States but just yards from Mexico and escape. As the slow-moving cars creep around corners and bend in the track, robbers jump aboard unseen, then open the rail cars and begin to toss out their contents. Sometimes, says the FBI, the robbers actually unhitch entire rail cars—usually those located at the end of long, winding trains—so they can take their time removing the stolen goods later.

But on this particular day, Agents Barrio and Mikeska, who were accompanied by a third agent located in another part of the train, were hiding in one car when they noticed a suspected train robber on the roof. The two agents alerted the third agent, who then sneaked into position and managed to pull the suspect from the roof. But, according to reports, by the time he had restrained the rooftop suspect, he noticed that Barrio and Mikeska were off the train and on the ground, staggering back onto U.S. soil with other suspects in pursuit.

Agents Barrio and Mikeska, the third agent soon discovered, had been beaten nearly to death by several other suspected train robbers—suspects who had boarded the train undetected by the American agents. Barrio and Mikeska were kicked and beaten and struck with large rocks, FBI officials said, noting that Barrio had suffered a severe injury over his right eye and had to undergo surgery to relieve pressure on his brain. Mikeska, meanwhile, also suffered from brain swelling and had to have surgery. Both would live, but neither would be the same.

Expanse of U.S.-Mexico border in Arizona. The dust-blown barbed wire fence shown is "the" border fence. Feel safe?

The suspects? They were Mexican nationals, and they had been routinely crossing into the U.S. just to rob the slow-moving trains.[1] What had been a relatively victimless crime—border hopping—had now turned violent, but it was an incident border policy experts and others concerned about reforming immigration issues had seen coming.

———————

By June 1997, violence along the 2,200-mile U.S.-Mexico border, which had been escalating for years, had become so intolerable that U.S. Rep. Duncan Hunter (R-California) said from the House floor that portions of the border were more dangerous than Bosnia. He also said that American law enforcement officials and U.S. soldiers had been fired upon by Mexico-based assailants at least ten times in the previous ten weeks. "There have been more firefights on the border in recent weeks than there have been in Bosnia," Hunter said before a congressional vote authorizing President Bill Clinton to dispatch up to ten thousand troops to the border to help curb some of the violence, which stemmed mostly from illegal immigration and drug trafficking.[2]

An outbreak of border fracases has led other expert observers to compare the border to a war zone.

On April 18, 1997, a pair of U.S. Customs Service inspectors were wounded in a gun battle at the Calexico border station. Agents managed to kill the Mexican attacker, but this outbreak of violence was followed later in the day by a bomb threat to a tunnel linking Calexico and Mexicali. Meanwhile, an illegal alien smuggler attempted to run down a Border Patrol officer with twenty-five illegal immigrants stuffed into his van; the incident resulted in a televised chase along California freeways that ended in suburban West Covina.[3]

Then, on May 11, Border Patrol agents and sheriff's deputies in San Diego were fired upon after a deputy attempted to stop a vehicle for speeding. That incident was followed by another on May 17, when a Border Patrol officer was wounded by a sniper firing an AK-47 assault rifle near the San Ysidro border-crossing station. The agent was just sitting in his Ford Bronco when he was attacked; he was struck in the face and endured a lengthy medical recovery.[4]

On May 20, a four-man Marine unit providing surveillance assistance to the Border Patrol was reportedly fired upon by a Mexican-American boy on the U.S. side of the border near Big Bend National Park in Texas. The Marines returned fire, killing the assailant and causing a national uproar because the attacker turned out to be an 18-year-old U.S. citizen who was reportedly tending his family's goats. In January of the same year, a Green Beret soldier shot and wounded another assailant who the military said had first fired upon U.S. soldiers.[5]

On May 23, a pair of Border Patrol agents working near Border Field State Park in southern California came under sniper fire again. The agents defended themselves, firing some fifty to sixty shots back into Mexico, from where the sniper fire originated. Another attack was reported the next day, and at least two other gun battles between Border Patrol agents in Naco, Arizona, and assailants on the Mexican side of the border took place that same month.[6]

Then, on June 1, Border Patrol agents were again fired upon west of the San Ysidro, California, Port of Entry. Shots were also fired at Border Patrol officers—again from Mexico—in separate incidents June 17 and 18 in the same vicinity. And a Border Patrol agent was killed June 14 when he fell down a ravine while pursuing suspects.[7]

"These shootings coming from south of the border aimed north are something that we haven't experienced until just about a month or so ago," explained Border Patrol spokesman Jim Pilkington.[8] Also unprecedented was the type of weapon being used: AK-47 rifles equipped with special telescopes and laser range-finders normally restricted to the Mexican army.

The problems—and the danger to American citizens and law enforcement personnel—have only worsened. By March 2000, Border Patrol and Immigration and Naturalization Service (INS) agents began to voice what many believed were legitimate concerns about "armed incursions" into the United States from Mexico-based assailants; they reported that heavily armed Mexican army units and federal police, called *federales*, had infiltrated U.S. territory and fired upon them, in some cases because—

federal agents would later discover—Mexican drug lords had put prices on the heads of American law enforcement agents along the border.

The National Border Patrol Council, a nationwide union that represents all of the roughly nine thousand non-supervisory Border Patrol employees, said that on March 14, 2000, shortly after 10 P.M. local time, two Mexican army Humvees carrying about sixteen armed soldiers drove across the international boundary and into the United States near Santa Teresa, New Mexico. There the vehicles pursued a Border Patrol vehicle, which was "outfitted with decals and emergency lights (that were activated for much of the pursuit) over a mile into the United States," according to a statement issued by the council.[9]

The lead Mexican army vehicle, the council said, contained nine soldiers "armed with seven automatic assault rifles, one submachine gun, and two .45 caliber pistols," and was eventually apprehended by other Border Patrol units. The second Humvee, however, "pursued a Border Patrol agent on horseback and fired a shot at him. The soldiers then disembarked their vehicle, fired upon one more Border Patrol agent and chased another agent before fleeing [back] to Mexico in their vehicle."

At the time the council said the incident was the most serious of its kind, adding "it is but one of hundreds of incursions that have been reported over the past several years."

Why would Mexican army units intentionally pursue Border Patrol agents, U.S. Drug Enforcement Agency officers, Customs officials and INS agents? Some federal border and law enforcement agents believe it was because of bounties up to $200,000 placed on their heads by a few of Mexico's rich and powerful drug cartels. Border Patrol officials in March 2000 confirmed that at least one drug gang—the Juarez cartel, until recently one of Mexico's largest—had implemented a bounty on U.S. lawmen.[10]

"A good trafficking organization has a larger budget than we do," said DEA agent Bernie Minarik, one of six hundred U.S. agents working the southwestern border. "They know who we are," he said, adding that more drug busts along the border usually means more attention from drug lords.

The attention can be deadly, he noted. The drug lords "consider it a cost of doing business," but, of course, every business wants to cut its costs, he added.[11]

In June 2000, Fox News reported that the violent assaults against federal agents along the southwest border increased from 156 in 1994 to 500 by 1999. By October 24, 2000, another border shooting occurred—the second such shooting incident that year. Mexican army soldiers reportedly crossed into the United States and fired on U.S. Border Patrol agents, according to L. Keith Weeks, vice president of the National Border Patrol Union Local 1613 in San Diego, California, which is separate from the national council. Weeks said two border patrolmen who had just disembarked from a "clearly marked Border Patrol helicopter" immediately came under fire from a ten-man unit of what appeared to be soldiers with the Mexican army. Weeks said the incident occurred in Copper Canyon, about eight miles east of the Otay Mesa Port of Entry.[12]

"It happened," he said. "These agents departed their helicopter and were immediately fired upon." He said about eight shots were fired, and described the assailants as a Mexican military unit dressed in military-style uniforms with tactical vests and carrying "high-powered military rifles with bayonets."

As they began to receive fire, Weeks said the BP agents identified themselves in Spanish, but "were nonetheless pursued by some of the soldiers," who crossed into the United States by entering through a barbed-wire fence. As the Mexican soldiers pursued the border agents, other soldiers set up a pair of sniper positions—one inside Mexico and the other inside the U.S., "pointing their weapons in the direction of the [agents]," said Weeks. The soldiers, in Spanish, ordered the agents out of the brush, but they refused. Instead, the agents re-identified themselves and ordered the soldiers to return to Mexico. "Once other Border Patrol agents neared the scene," Weeks said, "the soldiers retreated to Mexico and drove off. . . ."[13]

In March 2002, a Border Patrol officer near San Diego once again encountered four men who appeared to be Mexican soldiers. They were all dressed in camoflauge fatigues, armed with three submachine guns and one M-16 rifle, and crossed the border near Tecate, Mexico. The Border Patrol agent, who was not identified in press reports, said he was following footsteps left by the Mexican patrol. When he encountered them, one of the Mexican soldiers had his sidearm unholstered. The agent then unholstered his sidearm and identified himself. He told superiors the Mexican troopers then realized they were inside the U.S. and cooperated with the Border Patrol agent, who took them to a nearby Border Patrol station.[14]

In May 2002, Tancredo demanded an in-depth investigation after yet another incident in Arizona in which at least one shot was fired at a Border Patrol agent. In what Tancredo labeled "another Mexican military incursion," and what the Border Patrol agent on the scene called "an act of war," the incident was serious enough to cause the INS to issue a statement indicating the U.S. government had asked Mexico City to explain what happened.[15]

This attack occurred along the U.S.-Mexico border near Ajo, Arizona. According to Border Patrol sources, the Tohono O'odham Indian Reservation Police Department encountered a Mexican army unit about 8:30 P.M. local time, along the Santa Cruz trail inside the Papago Farms border patrol area, just south of Forest Road 21. The area is between five and 10 miles inside Arizona.

"Everyone keeps claiming that these 'incursions' don't take place, that people are just getting lost, and the whole idea of incursions is erroneous," Tancredo complained. "Unless we open our eyes and recognize that what's happening along the U.S.-Mexico border is real, one of our guys is going to get killed."[16] Three months later, that's just what happened.

In early August 2002, 28-year-old U.S. Park Ranger Kris Eggle (pronounced *egg-lee*) was patrolling in the Organ Pipe Cactus National Monument near Tucson, Arizona, when he was called to assist U.S. Border

Patrol and other federal agents who were closing in on two suspected gunmen with ties to drug cartels. Mexican authorities were in pursuit of the fugitives and had alerted U.S. officers the pair had crossed into the United States.

Mexican cops continued to give as a Border Patrol helicopter spotted the car the two men were driving. The chopper crew relayed the car's location to ground agents, then moved into position and hovered over the vehicle as agents closed in. The vehicle stopped, and one suspect tried to run but was captured. The second suspect, however, took out an assault rifle and shot and killed Eggle, striking him just below his bulletproof vest. "He probably didn't live more than five to ten minutes," said Park Ranger Dale Thompson.[17]

Reports said the second gunman was shot and killed as he tried to make it back to Mexico, but no Border Patrol agents or other authorities reported firing their weapons. That means Mexican authorities likely shot the suspect from their side of the border.

"This is very much a combat zone," says Robert Eggle, Kris's father. "This scenario . . . is every bit as dangerous an element of combat as anything that I faced in Vietnam."[18]

Fortunately, it isn't every day that a U.S. agent or, for that matter, Mexican authorities, are killed by incidents that occur along the southwest border. But as history indicates, violence is becoming a regular occurrence there, and the likelihood that more will die is increasing.

In fact, in May 2003, the Border Patrol reported an upsurge in alien smuggling arrests, particularly in just a small section of the Texas-Mexico border.[19] And while the Department of Homeland Security—which absorbed the INS and Border Patrol in March 2003—says the uptick in arrests indicates that newer high-tech surveillance is working, others suggest it is because alien smuggling is getting to be big business. And as long as big profits are involved, the harder the crackdown in the United States, the more likely smuggling rings will take extreme measures to protect their "business," say some experienced immigration law enforcement officers.

But the danger is not all related to human smuggling. Much of it is drug-related. And in a September 25, 2002 report, the *Washington Times* said most of the drug smuggling along the border is occurring within the boundaries of the Tohono O'odham Nation. The paper said the one-hundred-mile stretch of wild desert between the Organ Pipe Cactus National Monument and Coronado National Forest, has become one of America's newest drug corridors.[20]

"Mexican drug lords, backed by corrupt Mexican military officers and police officials, will move tons of marijuana, cocaine and heroin this year over rugged desert trails to accomplices in Phoenix and Tucson for shipment to willing buyers throughout the United States," said the paper.

Meanwhile, few politicians in Washington have gotten serious about employing more manpower and the latest technology to try to stem the epidemic flow of people, drugs and—some say—terrorists, despite Homeland Security Department claims to the contrary. One side of the political aisle seems too eager to cater to illegal immigrants and their families for votes, while the other wants to exploit them for cheap labor as favors to corporate donors and sponsors. In fact, recent surveys and studies report a huge disconnect between government and academic elites and ordinary Americans on the issue of immigration reform.

"The elite are not like you and me. They think globally. They value diversity. They have maids and nannies and people to mow their lawns and clean their pools," says Brian Mitchell, a columnist for Investor's Business Daily. "All of which might explain the gap on immigration between John Q. Public and Thurston Howell III. It's been growing since 9-11."[21]

Mitchell's column focused on a study by the Chicago Council on Foreign Relations, which found that 60 percent of Americans believe the current levels of immigration pose a "critical threat to the vital interests" of the U.S., while only 14 percent of the nation's elite believe so.[22] "That's a 46-point gap in 2002—up from the 37-point gap four years ago,"

Mitchell wrote. "In 1998, 55 percent of Americans thought immigration posed a 'critical threat' to the country compared with 18 percent of opinion leaders." In 2002, 41 percent of the elite said high immigration is "not important," while just 8 percent of the general public agreed. Elites also said global warming and world population growth are more critical than immigration, but not the public.

In other words, as the specter of new and dangerous outside threats became more real to the public on 9-11, most Americans also became more concerned that rampant, uncontrolled immigration could be a catalyst for new attacks. But the nation's elite—which included members of Congress, senior government officials, journalists, academics, religious leaders and the heads of Fortune 1000 firms, labor unions, public interest groups, think tanks and colleges—became less concerned.

"What surprises me most is that the opinion leaders didn't seem to be budged by 9-11," commented Roy Beck, executive director of the policy group NumbersUSA, and co-author of a study on the poll. "Sept. 11 was caused in part by our huge illegal immigration system, our system of allowing and encouraging and winking at illegal immigration, and yet the opinion elite started off unconcerned [about immigration] and they didn't get any more concerned."[23]

For the public, immigration ranked sixth out of sixty-nine foreign policy issues; for the elites, it ranked twenty-sixth. Asked whether immigration levels should be raised, lowered or kept the same, 55 percent of the public said they should be lowered, compared to 18 percent of elites (60 percent of elites said the levels should be kept the same). Finally, 70 percent of the public said reducing immigration should be a "very important" foreign policy goal for the U.S., compared to just 22 percent of elites—a sizable forty-eight-point difference.

Beck says he believes the reason why the disconnect between elites and the general public is so vast is because elites are largely insulated from the rest of society and from the ill effects mass immigration is having on many parts of the country.

"These people's jobs are ones that place the highest premium on the mastery of the language and culture of America; therefore they are the least susceptible to competition from the immigrant coming in," he said. "They're the least likely to have their schools overcrowded. They're also least likely to have their neighborhood deal with special problems whenever you have high levels of immigration." He also believes the elite have a tendency toward multiculturalism. "For the way they want to change America, immigration is a tool to fundamentally change America from what it's been and fundamentally change it against what the American people want it to be."

Co-author of the study, Steven Camarota, said the poll results stem from the political realities surrounding immigration. He hinted that it may explain why border enforcement has been enhanced in the past decade but internal policies regarding immigration have remained lax.

"[The results explain] why border enforcement increased in the 1990s, but at the same time enforcement within the United States was phased out," said Camarota—who is head of research for the Center for Immigration Studies (CIS). "More recently, it explains why broad interest-group support for illegal alien amnesty, including the business community and labor unions, has not translated into the passage of an amnesty."[24]

"The results of the survey indicate that the gap between the opinions of the American people on immigration and those of their leaders is enormous," said a separate analysis of the poll by CIS. The results also "indicate that there is no other foreign policy-related issue on which the American people and their leaders disagreed more profoundly than immigration."[25]

CIS noted that President George W. Bush's call for the extension of a new amnesty for illegal aliens hurts him politically. In late 2002, the public's overall favorability rating for his handling of foreign policy was a healthy 53 percent, but that figure fell to 27 percent favorable on immigration. Indeed, 70 percent "rated Bush as poor or fair on immigration," CIS said.

Though Congress authorized more money to hire additional Border Patrol, Immigration and U.S. Customs Service agents in the wake of 9-11, seasoned field personnel say hiring additional manpower often accomplishes little because the attrition rate is so high and the policies hampering their border control efforts don't change—two factors they say are often intertwined. Not only that, say immigration enforcement officers, but the sheer numbers of illegal immigrants trying to get into the U.S. is staggering, as evidenced by the thousands of beaten trails leading into the country from Mexico.

"Each year the Border Patrol is making more than a million apprehensions of persons who flagrantly violate our nation's laws by unlawfully crossing U.S. borders to work and to receive public assistance, usually with the aid of fraudulent documents," said one immigration reform analysis.[26] "The INS estimated in 1996 that about 60 percent of the then estimated five million illegal immigrants were EWI [entry without inspection] and 40 percent were overstayers. Both types of illegal immigrants are deportable under Immigration and Nationality Act Section 237 (a)(1)(B) which says: 'Any alien who is present in the United States in violation of this Act or any other law of the United States is deportable,'" the analysis said.

Experienced border agents especially are a premium in some patrol sectors, which worsens the pending crisis. But even in sectors where such agents are prevalent, they are still too few in comparison to the sheer length and remoteness of the American border. Agents are most often stationed miles apart, but even those deployed within sight of each other cannot intercept dozens of border jumpers who are hurrying across perhaps no more than a hundred yards away.

To counteract that kind of traffic, agents say they would need to be stationed "in depth," or at various distances inland from the border, to apprehend illegal aliens who were able to make it past agents deployed directly on the border. In instances where that tactic has been employed, rates of capture are much higher, say seasoned agents. Often, however, whether agents are prevalent or lacking along the border makes little difference because political considerations have a hampering effect on their ability to do their jobs.

Another idea gaining some momentum is to employ the U.S. military as a back-up to existing federal law enforcement agencies, by treating the illegal immigration issue as the crisis it is. But that idea has met with stiff resistance and bad publicity, much of it coming from an incident in 1997, when critics had a field day after Texas teenager Esequiel Hernandez was shot and killed by Marines. Though the Pentagon claimed that Hernandez fired first, in the end it didn't matter because the Clinton administration backed off further deployments of the military in conjunction with federal border enforcement duties.

The tide of opinion, however, could be changing again, in no small part because of the September 11, 2001, attacks and due to continued escalating violence along the border. Indeed, as early as 1997, a Scripps-Howard Texas Poll of one thousand residents found that 55 percent of Anglo-Saxons favored dispatching troops to secure the border, compared to 36 percent of Hispanics.[27] And by June 2002, less than a year after terrorist attacks in Washington DC and New York City killed nearly three thousands people, 68 percent of Americans agreed with the statement, "the U.S. should deploy military troops on the border as a temporary measure to help the U.S. Border Patrol curb illegal immigration," according to a Zogby International survey.[28] Zogby also reported on September 27, 2002, that 70 percent of Hispanics believe a dramatic increase in border security in the U.S. is needed.[29]

The popularity in Congress of putting troops on the border, however, is nowhere near the level of popularity among constituents. Congressman Tancredo, head of the House Immigration Reform Caucus, is one of the few supporters and the most vocal of the idea, though in November 2002, Sen. Trent Lott (R-Mississippi) came out in support of using U.S. troops along the border.

"The time is right to call for the deployment of military assets on the border in order to protect our national security interests," Tancredo said during an October 8, 2002, press conference on Capitol Hill. "As long as our borders remain undefended, we cannot claim that we are doing everything possible to protect the nation."[30]

"Most politicians run around worried about civil libertarians and being sued by the ACLU," Lott said in a televised interview. "This is not only a porous border in terms of illegal aliens, it's also a porous border with regard to crime and drugs."[31]

Tancredo says retired Border Patrol agents and others experienced in enforcing the nation's border control policies estimate twenty to thirty thousand U.S. troops would be needed to adequately augment the current number of federal agents deployed along the Mexican and Canadian borders.

Other lawmakers, backed by some Pentagon and White House officials, say the costs would be too high for the nation to afford, however. "We need to be aware of threats to our security, but the answer is not closing our borders at a cost that would divert huge resources from what the real need is," said Rep. Chris Cannon (R-Utah) in a June 19, 2002, interview with the *Denver Post*.[32]

Yet, nearly a quarter-million U.S. military personnel currently are stationed in other nations protecting their borders from dangerous foreign incursions. According to the December 2002 issue of *Reason* magazine, over 112,000 American soldiers and airmen are stationed in Europe alone, followed by 79,800 in the Pacific region and South Korea; nearly 16,000 troops are in Bosnia and other United Nations-related peacekeeping operations, with 11,500 troops stationed in the Middle East, and another 5,000 or so in South America. But deploying up to 30,000 troops along America's troubled, increasingly porous borders is too costly, say critics, and would likely take resources away from the nation's *real* needs—though, presumably, national security would be one such need.

"I need the president of the United States to understand the severity of this problem, and to focus not just attention but resources on it—and not just some public show of support and effort on one area of the border," Tancredo said after Eggle's death. "We have to put the military down here; we have to help these people."[33]

The White House and most of Congress are not alone in opposing the deployment of troops along the border. "We really don't want to have military forces on the border. They are borders with friendly countries," a

Pentagon official said in March 2002.[34] The Department of Defense was also concerned about arming soldiers for what was a six-month special tour of duty to bolster national security following the September 11 terrorist attacks in New York City and Washington DC. An armed deployment "raised the possibility of an 'unlawful and potentially lethal use of force incident'—the accidental killing of an innocent traveler by a soldier not trained in law enforcement," according to a March 11 letter from the Pentagon to Sen. Patrick Leahy (D-Vermont). The letter also said the DOD was worried about mission creep and that it did not want to include border security as part of its objectives.[35]

———————————

While America is being overrun by illegal immigrants it can't absorb, it is also being swamped by a sea of drugs for the same reason: Because, critics contend, the will does not exist in Washington to enforce America's legitimate borders. And the problem is getting much worse: Mexican drug lords spent in excess of $500 million in 2002 alone in bribes and payoffs to a cadre of Mexican military generals and police officials to ensure that illicit drugs reach their destination.[36] Four years earlier, in 1998, the Drug Enforcement Administration reported that drug traffickers in Mexico had cozy relationships with elements of the Mexican military.[37]

In ordinary times, a vast border with a friendly nation would be a huge asset to any government—the United States, arguably the wealthiest and freest nation on earth and infinitely capable of defending itself, being no exception. But Washington can no longer be assured of a largely hostile-free environment along its southern border with Mexico. These are not ordinary times, and, in some parts of the U.S. Southwest, many Americans feel as though they are engaged in a war of sorts with armies of illegal immigrants, drug smugglers and potential terrorists. Worse, they feel as though nobody in their own government is listening to them. They wonder how many more will die needlessly—on both sides of the border—before Congress and the White House pay attention.

Others have raised the alarm about the disasters connected to corporate elites keeping the borders propped open for cheap labor and those on the outside seeking to take advantage of that sizeable gap.

Warned Abraham Lincoln, "I see in the near future a crisis approaching that unnerves me and causes me to tremble for the safety of my country. . . . Corporations have been enthroned, an era of corruption in high places will follow, and the money-power of the country will endeavor to prolong its reign by working upon the prejudices of the people until the wealth is aggregated in a few hands and the Republic is destroyed."[38]

Similarly, Samuel Gompers, founder and first president of the American Federation of Labor, said in a 1924 letter to Congress:

> America must not be overwhelmed. Every effort to enact immigration legislation must expect to meet a number of hostile forces and, in particular, two hostile forces of considerable strength. One of these is composed of corporation employers who desire to employ physical strength (broad backs) at the lowest possible wage and who prefer a rapidly revolving labor supply at low wages to a regular supply of American wage earners at fair wages. The other is composed of racial groups in the United States who oppose all restrictive legislation because they want the doors left open for an influx of their countrymen regardless of the menace to the people of their adopted country.[39]

But others see nothing wrong with mass immigration. "Without Mexican farm workers, legal or not, the rest of us wouldn't eat. Failure to legislate and enforce fair standards for farm workers is a conscious policy that takes advantage of problems in other countries," says Alex Pulaski, Northwest Treeplanters and Farmworkers United (NFTW) union. "Why should corporations be allowed to move from place to place, seeking lower wages, while working people are prevented from moving to seek higher wages? . . . Immigration policy has not stopped the entry of undocumented workers. It raises their vulnerability, in order to keep them from standing up for their rights."[40]

Yet the reality is that today, illegal immigration—and its tolerance in high places of public, private and corporate interest—is a major component of Lincoln's dire prediction. Just as Gompers saw eighty years ago, "Aliens arriving at our shores must understand that residency in the United States is a privilege, not a right," confirmed Attorney General John Ashcroft in a May 2002 order authorizing the deportation of a Haitian nanny who was convicted of second-degree manslaughter in the beating death of a nineteen-month-old boy in 1995.

Immigration reformists, concerned Americans, border and immigration law enforcement agents, economists and policymakers galore are waiting for Ashcroft—and the rest of the federal government—to apply that axiom across the board, before the coming immigration crisis arrives. Depending upon who is already in our country and their intentions, it may already be too late.

IT'S A SIEVE

America requires a border management system that keeps pace with expanding trade while protecting the United States and its territories from the threats of terrorist attack, illegal immigration, illegal drugs and other contraband. The border of the future must integrate actions abroad to screen goods and people prior to their arrival in sovereign U.S. territory, and inspections at the border and measures within the United States to ensure compliance with entry and import permits.

—BUSH ADMINISTRATION POSITION PAPER, JANUARY 25, 2002

Before he moved his family to Whetstone, Arizona, a small community twenty minutes from the Mexican border, John F. Petrello III admits he never believed the stories about an "invasion" of illegal aliens. Like most Americans—especially those who don't live near the vast southwest border, which spans Texas, New Mexico, Arizona and southern California—John thought yarns about "the occupying hordes" were just concoctions of radical anti-immigration extremists, people who were so absorbed with nationalistic hatred and bigotry they were incapable of embracing other ethnic groups, even if they immigrated legally to America.

But within months of relocating John was not only transformed into a believer, he became a full-blown convert. And, like most of his neighbors, his concern about continued mass illegal immigration and the threats it poses to the nation, if not just his own corner of the world, came about in a personal and harrowing way.

———————

One morning as John's wife, Heather—pregnant with their second child, a son—was outside watching the couple's young daughter play on their four-acre property, she witnessed the driver of a pickup truck speed up to an adjacent property and quickly drop off twelve men, then disappear just as quickly as it had appeared. John and Heather had been living in the area long enough to know the men who had been dropped off were likely illegal aliens; in the past illegals had been dropped off without incident, but it still unnerved Heather to see them dropped off so closely this time. She began calling for John, who was working in the yard out of her view and out of the view of the band of illegals.

Upon hearing the urgency in her voice, John went for his .45 caliber sidearm just inside the house (he said he usually carries it all the time for protection, but leaves it inside if he's outside working and believes there may be a chance of knocking it around and having it accidentally discharge). After retrieving it, he immediately went back outside to find Heather, who had already grabbed up their daughter, yelling at him that a *coyote*—as immigrant smugglers are called—had just dropped off a group of men. "The coyote could have picked them up from any number of several locations nearby," John said.

But rather than move off in the opposite direction, the twelve men began moving towards the Petrello's small property, which, John realized, had been what caused his wife so much anxiety.

John instructed Heather to take their daughter to a neighbor's house, lock the doors and call "someone to come here and help me out." By that time he could see the aliens moving in nearby mesquite trees "about a hundred yards away." He said he yelled at them, "*Alto! Alto!* [Stop! Stop!]" and indicated they shouldn't come closer. He said he knew they had seen and heard him because a few members of the group had made eye contact. But they didn't stop coming towards him, and within a few moments the group breached the perimeter of his property.

As they approached, John says they could see he was armed. "I had one hand up waving them off and the other on my weapon," which was in plain view on his hip, he said. Still, they continued to advance towards him until finally, he says, he began to fear for his own safety.

Finally, in desperation he says, "I drew my weapon and laid down several rounds directly in front of the lead man's feet. It was close enough that dirt was hitting him." But the men kept advancing and it was at that point, he admits, that "I thought I may have gotten in over my head."

For one thing, John realized he had only one magazine in his pistol, and that he had just used over half the bullets in an attempt to scare the aliens away. For another, he says, he wasn't accustomed to seeing or hearing of groups of illegals that were so brazen; in the past, when confronted by armed Americans, most either ran away or quickly surrendered (though since John Petrello's incident, locals say illegals aren't as intimidated or afraid as they used to be).

"I don't care who you are or what you've been through, you know that if you're shooting at someone and they keep advancing on you, those are some serious people," said John, who had become accustomed by then to seeing and detaining illegal immigrants on his property. When they didn't respond to warning shots, he said he began to believe at least a couple of the illegals may have been armed, a phenomenon that has also been on the rise in recent years.

In a final bid to scare the intruders away, John fired a few more precious rounds at the feet of the advancing aliens, to show them he was as serious as they. With that, he said, the pack of men finally stopped in their tracks; they didn't run away, but instead began to stare John down. The man in the lead locked eyes with John in a "hateful stare," causing him to level his pistol with few remaining rounds "right at his head." The lead illegal alien was less than ten yards away.

"He was pretty damned close," John said, "but when he saw that big .45 barrel looking at him, he finally figured out I wasn't kidding."

Scared but thankful the advance stopped, John continued to keep his pistol aimed at the man. For several tense seconds, both he and the illegal kept eyes locked, staring hard at each other, watching and waiting to see if the other would make a move, show signs of fear or signal he would give up. In the end, it was the lead alien who blinked first; John says he and the other men in the small group began quietly talking among themselves in Spanish—too low for him to make out words—before the lead man turned and began running the other direction, the rest of his party in tow.

That is, "with the exception of just one guy," John Petrello said. One man further back in the group stayed and stared John down for a few more seconds, "and it was obvious he was pissed."

John explained that he has since learned that the leader of such groups—the coyote—is not usually the first man, but instead will hang back toward the middle or end of the group, probably to keep a lower profile. He believes the man who stayed behind for a few seconds and gave him the evil eye was the coyote and, if anyone were armed, it would most likely have been him.

The young Arizonan said he didn't like the way the man was looking at him, and he said he suddenly became mindful of the fact that he still had a round left in his pistol, though he was hoping he wouldn't have to use it to kill another man. "I was really scared," John said, "so I fired another round into the ground in front of him. I wanted him to get the hell out of there and go back with his group." After firing what literally was his last shot, the suspected coyote flinched, then slowly turned around and trotted back towards his group, which had fled out of sight into the desert scrub around the Petrello's property.

Relieved that the men had retreated, John said he immediately ran back to his house, reloaded his pistol and retrieved extra magazines as well. His attention then turned to his pregnant wife and daughter, who were still holed up at the neighbor's house, which was some two hundred yards away (the neighbor wasn't home but the Petrello's had a prearranged agreement that they could seek refuge there anytime of day or night if each other's home was threatened). He asked right away if she had made contact with the border authorities, but was stupefied by what his wife told him. Heather Petrello said she had indeed called "911" as he had instructed, but the central police dispatcher who answered said they couldn't help because it involved illegal aliens and "it was a civil action." That meant, said local police, it was out of their hands and jurisdiction.

"Actually," John Petrello fumed, "it was an *uncivil* action. Seriously, what happened on my property is indeed about as 'civil' as you can get, I guess. I was involved in an armed stand-off with a group of men whom I wasn't sure whether they were armed or not, and they were invading and threatening me, my family, and my property."

Heather said the police dispatcher did, however, transfer her to local [Cochise County] sheriff's authorities. Once connected, she told their dispatcher what was happening.

The closest sheriff's station was just a few miles and a few minutes away, in nearby Sierra Vista, but John and Heather both said no deputies ever showed up to help out.

"I don't know if they ever actually said they would or would not show up—and she can't remember specifically—but she says she told them there were illegal aliens on our property, and that I was involved in an armed stand-off with them," John Petrello said. "In the end they obviously didn't give a damn enough to show up to help defend a pregnant woman or a three-year-old child."

A Border Patrol agent finally did show up more than fifteen minutes later. John said Heather eventually had to telephone the Border Patrol directly. Since the illegal aliens were long gone by then, all the border agent could do was take down a report. John said the agent told him he was within his rights to defend his property and that the Border Patrol saw no legal problems for the couple, which was somewhat of a relief to the Petrellos but not something he was very concerned about at the time. "I was going to defend my family, period," he said, "regardless of whether it was, quote, right or wrong."

As for the Cochise County Sheriff's Department, its Web site claims the department "is committed to solemnly, faithfully and impartially support the Constitution of the United States, and the laws of the State of Arizona." One would assume that includes the sanctity of U.S., as well as county, borders. The statement continues, "As an organization and as individuals, we pledge to be valiant to the public trust."

A spokesman there even supported that, telling me that it is the department's policy to respond to all calls made by citizens, even if they involve suspected illegal "migrants." The spokesman said in Arizona trespassing on private property is a crime, which ranges from a misdemeanor to a felony depending upon whether the trespass was merely on private property or whether the suspects actually went into someone's home. He said that's a policy that has been adopted by a number of local law enforcement agencies in the area. The spokesman did acknowledge that while he could not remember any specific cases, there may be times when on-duty deputy sheriffs are all tied up on other calls and dispatchers will then forward calls dealing with suspected illegal aliens to the Border Patrol, though this doesn't explain why county residents reporting incidents involving illegal aliens wouldn't be told that up front.

Whether the Border Patrol eventually showed because the Petrellos called them or because the sheriff's department dispatcher called is irrelevant to the young couple, John says. The incident unnerved both of them, as well as the reality that, because of the sheer numbers of illegal crossers that come through their area every year, they may have to face a similar incident in the future—alone. Since the incident, the couple has encountered a number of other illegal immigrants on and around their property and have even detained some, but none so brazen as the twelve men who challenged John in the fall of 2001. He said it took the couple about a week before the incident "sunk in," but since then they have "educated" themselves about the border and what has been happening there.

"There's no doubt in my mind, knowing what I know now, that what I did was waste ammunition," says John. "If it happened again today, I would not shoot at the ground, I'll just say that. My kids are helpless and my wife could be easily overwhelmed; I'm defending my family here." He adds: "The Border Patrol knows as well as we do that there are some bad people that come through here. [The agents] realize that we are simply trying to defend our families, our homes and our property. They even offered to have me call them if I got into trouble by local law enforcement, and they said they'd back me."[1]

Are you serious? Sign just yards from the U.S.-Mexico border in Arizona sums up the irony, hypocrisy and otherwise sad state of border enforcement.

Supporters of immigration and open borders have a cheery view of the subject. According to the "Immigration" section on the Web site of the Washington DC–based Cato Institute's Center for Trade Policy Studies,

America was founded and shaped by immigrants seeking freedom and opportunity. Since records were first kept in 1820, our nation has absorbed more than 60 million immigrants. Those new Americans have almost universally embraced American culture and values, serving bravely in our armed forces, founding some of our most successful companies, and pioneering advances in science, technology and industry. Immigrants have been crucial to America's dominance and dynamism in the global economy.[2]

But John Petrello and other landowners who must continually endure waves of illegal aliens have a much different view of immigration. In some ways they agree with the rose-colored Cato description of immigration in general, and even support *legal* immigration to a degree. But the key term is *legal*, and to them it is obvious that a great many border jumpers have no intention of "embracing American culture." Rather, say Americans who try to live and work in border areas, many illegals are simply coming here to reap the benefits of an open, generous society that doesn't seem capable of saying "no."

Little more than a small oasis in Arizona surrounded by mesquite desert that alternates with rolling mountains stretching upward to clear, blue skies, Whetstone is the picture of quiet, rustic serenity to the naked eye, like many border communities. It has the appearance of modernity—convenience stores and smooth paved four-lane highways—mixed with a persona that has defined real and imagined impressions of the Old West for generations. It is hot and arid land, but with modern technology and engineering, it is livable and, by any measure, generally hospitable. However, unlike other communities further inland, those situated along the border like Whetstone are at the epicenter of an invasion of contraband and humanity that is virtually unrivaled throughout the western world.

As the only remaining global superpower, you might think America has technology and manpower to spare when it comes to guarding, sealing and protecting its own borders—and indeed she does. Yet, one day's trek around bucolic frontier havens like Whetstone proves otherwise. And it provides an enlightening, if unwanted, education for even the most ardent immigration supporter. Homes in these netherregions of the Southwest are sparse, but for the most part county-maintained dirt roads connect residents to one another, and to civilization in larger towns nearby.

This network of infrastructure is primitive by modern standards, but it is enough to be used by coyotes and illegals alike to get into the country and disappear. In fact, all through the border areas is evidence of the sea of humanity trekking north into the United States. There are literally hundreds

of "runs"—trails worn into the earth by tens of thousands of human travelers. There are scores of tire tracks along stretches of desert where there are
no roads, identifying the spots dozens of coyote vehicles nightly collect and
deliver groups of illegals. Oftentimes when those vehicles break down or
give out, they are simply abandoned to rot and rust where they stall, with no
thought given at all to the property owner who must then pay to have the
cars hauled off. "Designated" trails and pick-up points change daily but they
are literally everywhere, which makes it difficult to figure out which ones
will be used on any given day. The trails crisscross both public and private
lands, but when fences become obstacles, they are either cut or bent over or
torn down completely.

*Section of U.S./Mexico border fence "altered" by illegals for entrance into
the U.S.*

Trash is evident along the runs, but it is heaviest at "rally points"—
places where large groups of illegals meet before they make their way to the
coyote pick-ups. The amount is truly monumental; in many places discarded water jugs and bottles, underwear, panties, toothbrushes, diapers,
drug paraphernalia, toilet paper, backpacks, food and snack containers,
plastic shopping bags, cosmetics, shaving cream, razors, shoes and clothing
are two feet deep. In many others, it is strewn as far as the eye can see.

Blankets found rolled up one day are found laid out the next, having been slept on the night before by border jumpers. The smell in many areas is overwhelming, especially in the heat of the summer. The amount of human waste and debris is astounding—much more than could be left by a few dozen or even a few hundred people. At several rally points, aliens have constructed "nests"—tent-like dwellings made with scrub brush and tree branches—that are not generally visible from nearby roads and highways. Bands of illegal aliens begin to gather in these rally points as dusk gathers; they can be heard moving through the brush to the pre-determined areas.

Property rights activist J. Zane Walley, writing for WorldNetDaily.com, Oct. 19, 2001, also described it this way:

> The foot traffic is so heavy that the backcountry has the ambience of a garbage dump and smells like an outdoor privy. In places, the land is littered . . . deep with bottles, cans, soiled disposable diapers, sanitary napkins, panties, clothes, backpacks, human feces, used toilet paper, pharmacy bottles and syringes (the drug runners inject stimulants to keep their energy up).[3]

Mounds of trash and discarded empty water bottles litter a rally point near an Arizona highway pick-up point. This scene is in a ravine and is hidden from view from drivers.

Chilton Williamson Jr., author of *The Immigration Mystique: America's False Conscience*, and an editor and columnist for *Chronicles* magazine, noted, "Added to the smell of privy is the smell of fear. Unsolved murders and arsons are common. Citizens acting in self-defense worry about retaliation by coyotes smuggling people and narco-militarists running drugs. . . ."[4]

So heavy is the illegal smuggling traffic in some parts of the "suburbs" of the rural southwest border communities, for example, that local residents have constructed roadblocks, to force the coyotes to either drop their human cargo elsewhere or to prevent them access to swathes of private property. When asked why roadblocks are not removed or why "outsiders" shouldn't drive around them or through them, residents often reply with a question of their own: "You wanna get shot?"

––––––––––––––

The coyotes who are paid to smuggle the illegals—usually along an established trail—are paid handsomely; figures range from $1,000 to $3,000 per migrant (though a Pakistani smuggling ring in New York City, which was busted by federal authorities, was charging its "clients" $15,000 to $30,000 each[5]). It works like this: The coyote leads his group through the desert to a predetermined rally point and, depending upon when the group arrives, will "lay up" (or wait) in the brush and chaparral until it's time for them to be collected and transported to a mid-level or final destination. The illegals often have food and water waiting for them when they arrive that is left by people working for the coyote or by groups inside the U.S. who are sympathetic. Other times the illegals will pack food, water and provisions with them in backpacks, rucksacks and plastic shopping bags. This is evidenced by the amount of trash and debris found at rally points. Besides the food and water containers, personal care items and clothing, the backpacks—many of which are brand-new—are also discarded.

Other illegal immigrants don't use coyotes. They rely on sheer numbers. Residents of Douglas, Arizona, said that before the year 2000, groups of about two to four illegal aliens could be seen passing through town from the Mexican city of Agua Prieta, which is directly across the border from Douglas. Since then, however, the number of border jumpers has increased dramatically to the point where now, groups sometimes numbering a hundred or more will pour across the border in the hopes that even though some will be caught by sporadic border patrols, most will escape inland. These are called "banzai runs."

Another increasingly favorite tactic is called "port running," whereby illegal alien drivers blaze through ports of entry on the wrong side of the highway, only to immediately exit interstates on their way to disappearing. Border Patrol, Customs and Immigration authorities are usually close by, but the sheer brazenness of port-running makes it a tough act to follow.

Glynn Custred, a professor of anthropology at California State University, Hayward, describes the "banzai run" phenomenon in the *American Spectator*:

> [In 2000] the trickle swelled to a flood with groups of thirty to well over a hundred people at a time pouring across the border, hurrying through alleys, through people's yards and between their houses, climbing over roofs and clambering over graves in the cemetery. They knocked down fences, trampled flowers and shrubs, and cluttered neighborhoods with litter. They came in groups all day long and in a steady stream throughout the night while dogs in town barked till dawn. . . . No longer were the migrants just men looking for work; now there were women and children as well, whole families illegally crossing and streaming north.[6]

There have been efforts undertaken by the Border Patrol, in conjunction with other federal immigration agencies, to stem the flow of illegals into the country. Where they were most successful, in San Diego and El Paso, such efforts focused not on apprehension of illegals once they made it into the U.S., but in stopping them from making it across the border in the first place. In El Paso, under "Operation Blockade" (later renamed

"Operation Hold The Line"), begun in 1994 by then–Border Patrol sector chief Silvestre Reyes, the effort focused on utilizing technology, fences and closer monitoring by agents and resulted in a significant decline in illegal crossings. In San Diego, under "Operation Gatekeeper," the results were the same, but came with an added benefit of economic gain; because of the significant drop in both illegal border crossings and out-of-control violence originating in Tijuana, Mexico—directly across the border from San Diego—entire new suburbs and housing projects were able to be built (and are still being built). "The lesson," one Border Patrol agent told me, "is that good enforcement is a boon to the taxpayer, the economy, and the country as a whole."

The successes in the urban corridors, however, have forced the illegal alien traffic into the under-populated, under-patrolled rural sectors of the border—mostly in Arizona, but also in New Mexico and parts of Texas and California. "Cut down the flow of illegals in El Paso or San Diego, and it moves to places like Douglas and from there to ranch lands and ever deeper into the desert beyond. In other words, despite relief in the urban corridors the overall problem remains unsolved," wrote Custred.[7]

This sieve-like phenomenon is a common side-effect of stepped-up urban enforcement. Border Patrol officials in the Tuscon, Arizona, sector, for instance, reported in April 2003 that apprehensions of illegals topped 145,000 just since the previous October. In Douglas, Arizona, Border Patrol officials said they arrested an average of 150 illegals a day in 2002, or more than 54,000 in all, in a town of only 14,000.[8] Drug confiscations were also up, officials said.

––––––––––––

Just what are the numbers for the entire border? How many illegal aliens attempt to cross into the U.S. each year? How many are already here? Such figures depend largely upon whom you ask, but the data are available from a number of reputable sources, and they are staggering.

"I think it's safe to say there are more illegal aliens in the country now than at any other time in our history," says one former Border Patrol supervisor.[9] Indications are he's right. The former INS, in a report issued in January 2003, said that, according to its most recent estimates, the illegal alien population climbed to seven million in 2000, including 78,000 from countries of "special concern" due to the war on terrorism— "visitors" who are now required by the agency to register.[10] Other reports say the illegal alien population could be as high as eight or nine million. Another estimate claims the illegal immigrant population rises by 500,000 a year.[11]

The INS report said that, during much of the 1990s, around 700,000 illegal aliens entered the U.S. each year, a figure that increased to around 817,000 by 1998 and nearly 1 million by 1999. The U.S. Census Bureau, meanwhile, said the nation's population had grown to about 281 million in 2000 (that number had risen to more than 292.5 million by February 2003).[12] If current immigration trends hold, the U.S. population—which has increased 85 percent since 1950, growing from 151 million to 283 million in just fifty years—will reach 400 million by the year 2050, according to Census Bureau projections.[13] Less than half of our population—an estimated 236 million people—will be natives of America.[14] Worse, border agents say many of Washington's lawmakers and bureaucrats who are responsible for the policies that have led to these increases are more concerned about their careers than enforcing immigration laws and protecting American citizens.

For that reason and others, the invasion trend isn't likely to abate soon. According to INS sources, in the first eleven months of Fiscal Year 2002 the Border Patrol made 861,566 apprehensions along the southwest border. But the agency estimated it only apprehends about one-quarter of those trying to cross illegally. So, for every illegal immigrant caught, three more make it into the U.S. undetected.

Some independent immigration reform groups believe that estimate is too conservative. They say the ratio is more like 10:1. But using Border Patrol statistics, that means if 861,566 were caught, approximately 2,584,698 made it into the U.S. undetected, for an average of about 7,700 undetected illegals a day—a believable amount considering the vastness of the border and the light resources allotted to guard it.

"The size and scope of the illegal immigrant problem in the United States is a national scandal in more ways than one," says Dan Stein, executive director of Federation for American Immigration Reform, a national non-partisan organization that wants to see limits on immigration. Commenting on a Northwestern University study of 2000 Census and Bureau of Labor Statistics employment data, Stein said the information "places the [real illegal alien] figure at nearly double any previous estimate of the size of the illegal population, indicating gross incompetence on the part of the government agencies charged. . . The illegal alien situation in this country is a tinderbox waiting to blow up in our faces." The university study also found that eight million immigrants had joined the labor force between 1990 and 2001, accounting for half of the new wage earners.[15]

Says Steven Camarota, research director at the Center for Immigration Studies, another independent immigration reform think tank in Washington, D.C.: "These new estimates are extremely troubling and confirm what many Americans already know—the scale of illegal immigration is truly enormous. . . . Perhaps even more troubling are the implications for national security. If a Mexican day laborer can sneak across the border, so can an al Qaeda terrorist. . . . We can't protect ourselves from terrorism without dealing with illegal immigration."[16]

Much of the American public agrees. According to a survey conducted in February 2003 by Hamilton College in New York and polling firm Zogby International, most of the 1,078 randomly selected adults in the survey said while they view immigration as important to enhancing society, concerns over national security outweigh any of those perceived benefits. "Immigration policy used to focus on welfare issues, and now it focuses on terror and security," said Paul Hagstrom, a Hamilton College economics professor who designed and analyzed the survey. He said 63 percent of respondents would support a government policy that halts all immigration from nations suspected of harboring terrorists. "Over half of all Americans would feel very or somewhat uncomfortable if an immigrant from the Middle East moved into their neighborhood," said the survey, while 41 percent overall said they favored decreasing immigration levels—a figure that would likely rise if residents of border states alone were surveyed. "That to me was a very startling finding—that these sentiments run deep enough that we are not going to be willing to accept refugees," said Hagstrom.[17]

But on any number of social, cultural and political issues, elected leaders often disagree with the people who elected them, and that is certainly true of immigration, legal or otherwise. Writes syndicated columnist Paul Craig Roberts:

> Are democracies democratic? Or do elites determine political outcomes regardless of majority opinion? Elected representatives' actions to increase immigration are a slap in the face to those 82 percent of the electorate who desire the opposite. President Bush continues to favor amnesty for illegals despite the fact that 70 percent of the public give him low scores on the immigration issue.[18]

Perhaps not surprisingly, the illegal immigration problem has even reached the White House. A Mexican man who used fake documents to work on the White House grounds was arrested and indicted after he tried to illegally re-enter the U.S. in December 2002.[19] Justice Department officials said Salvador Martinez-Gonzalez, using another name, worked two years for HDO Productions Inc., a provider of tents and other items for special events.

———

Where do the illegal immigrants come from? Generally, about 94 percent of the apprehensions involve citizens from Mexico, says INS data. Most are apprehended at the borders, but others are caught well inland, and some aren't apprehended for a year or more. Forty to fifty percent of all apprehensions occur in Arizona, followed by Texas and California (about

22 percent apiece, on average, in 2002), with New Mexico generally having the fewest illegal immigrants (an average of 6 percent in 2002). But Mexican citizens are not the only ethnic group trying to get in; INS data says citizens from South and Central America, Europe, the Middle East and Asia are also entering illegally.

"These illegals aren't just Mexicans," said Henry Harvey, a retired California deputy sheriff and city manager, and longtime resident of Tombstone, Arizona, "the town too tough to die." "One portion of the desert out here is called OTM ["Other Than Mexican"] Valley, and we know that since 9/11 persons from 160 countries have been arrested coming through here."[20] OTM Valley, also called "OTM Hill" by locals, is a vast area of scrub desert filled with trails and trash. Bordering a paved road, a trained observer can find several spots in the barbed wire fence that have been "modified"—i.e., cut down, torn down or otherwise destroyed—to allow illegals to cross without getting snagged.

It's also easy—and much cheaper—to get to the U.S. via Mexico from Central America. Migrants hoping to make it to America can, for about sixty cents, bypass all government checkpoints and take a short boat ride across the Suchiate River near Tecun Uman, Guatemala, to the Mexico side. From there, say immigration activists, it takes little more than a week to make the 1,500-mile journey across Mexico to the U.S. border.[21]

The Reverend Ademar Barilli, director of Casa del Migrante, a church-run shelter in Tecun Uman, said in December 2002 that the number of migrants passing through his sanctuary had exceeded 8,500—about one thousand more than in all of 2001 and a figure that is more normal. "For a while, they started enforcing the border because all immigrants were considered terrorists," Barilli said. "Now you can reach the U.S. in eight days without a problem."[22]

Would it ever be possible to completely shut off the tide of humanity streaming into America? Most experts say no, despite what Washington and the affected states do. But there are ways to seriously impact the flow, and one idea, favored by U.S. Rep. Tom Tancredo (R-Colorado) is to deploy U.S. troops along the border, to assist federal, state and local authorities in sealing off as much border as possible. The problem with that, he says, is what he calls an institutional bias in the Bush administration—as in past administrations—against getting too serious with enforcing immigration law. He says when Tom Ridge was still heading up the White House Office of Homeland Security and had not yet been confirmed as the nation's first Cabinet-level director of Homeland Security, the former Pennsylvania Republican governor told him "cultural and political reasons" would prevent the administration from ordering troops to the border. He says Ridge would not elaborate, but most experts and analysts interpreted that to mean as long as votes and cheap labor are to be had, Washington would attempt to look the other way.

Another part of the problem contributing to the continued flow of humanity and contraband, say border enforcement personnel, is that the same "cultural and political reasons" mentioned by Ridge prevent them from doing their jobs. "[INS inspectors] are, for all purposes, asked not to enforce immigration laws," complains one Border Patrol agent, who says the inspectors and many fellow agents are little more than "Wal-Mart greeters—we're standing there to say, 'Welcome to America. Come on in.'" The agent also said several ports of entry "get port-runners everyday"—illegal aliens who blow through the checkpoints in vehicles—"but we're not allowed to pursue them. What happens to these people? What are they carrying in their vehicles? Who are the vehicles carrying—terrorists or just illegals?" When illegals are caught, they know exactly what to do, say border officials—they demand food and water, medical attention and, in some cases, legal representation, because they are "taught" to make such demands in Mexico, often with the assistance or direction of the Mexican government.[23]

"The Mexican government of President Vicente Fox has basically demanded that the United States accept and care for citizens of his country who are sneaking in illegally. Fox has become increasingly vocal in demanding that the United States create an amnesty and work-visa programs to legalize more than three million illegal Mexicans now living in the United States," says columnist Tom DeWeese, writing for the American Policy Center.[24]

Indeed, the Mexican government even keeps tabs on the number of its citizens that die trying to cross the border into the United States every year. Mexican officials keep files containing gruesome photographs and stories of illegals who have died from dehydration, drowning, car accidents and gunshot wounds. The files are kept in a computer database available in each Mexican consulate in the U.S. and to Mexican authorities in case relatives of the dead come looking for whereabouts. In 2002—the latest year in which figures are available—about one Mexican citizen died each day trying to get in (heat exposure is the number one killer, says the Border Patrol).[25]

That's tragic, but telling: The number of those who die trying to get in is just a tiny fraction of the number who not only make it to the U.S. but who cross illegally several times per year. In fact, Mexico is actually aiding and abetting the deaths of its own citizens. Instead of warning them not to try to cross illegally into the U.S., the government provides survival kits instead. Syndicated columnist Samuel Francis, in his May 21, 2001 column, wrote:

> Antiquarians may recall that [recently] two high Mexican government officials came to the United States and boasted of how much they were going to help us in controlling illegal immigration. Last week the help arrived in the shape of the Mexican government's plan to distribute some 200,000 survival kits to Mexicans who plan to sneak across our borders... "For the first time," Mexican Interior Secretary Santiago Creel said during his April visit to Washington, "the Mexican government is recognizing that we have a responsibility regarding the migratory flows" into the United States.[26]

Francis went on to say the proclamation by Creel sounded like Mexico City was prepared to "actually do something" to stem the tide of its citizens flowing north into the U.S. However, he pointed out, the decision to pass out survival kits (rather than, say, implement new job or education programs to help citizens get ahead) indicates that Mexican politicians were prepared to do what they had done for years—let their citizens make a living elsewhere. He writes, "It also confirms, once again, the ugly truth behind the self-righteous gabble the Mexicans always serve up to Americans about immigration. The truth is that the Mexican government and ruling class, unable to provide a decent economy or government for their own citizens, welcome getting rid of them by encouraging them to leave."[27] In other words, the government of Mexico is quite content to export its poverty, rather than face the difficult task of providing its citizens with the opportunity to stay at home and earn their way out of destitution. Francis also says the ruling elite is so "eager" to rid themselves of the bothersome problem of providing for the nation's poor, they'd rather hand them "survival kits" and send them north:

> The survival kits, however, are only part of the package. The kits are part of a larger program to instruct illegals in what to expect once they sneak into the United States alive, and the pre-sneak training sessions include 'tips on maintaining self-esteem and on Asian meditation techniques to combat depression, stress and anxiety in a country they have entered illegally and without speaking the language. . . .'[28]

Worse, Mexican leaders seem to want to justify the migration of their own people. For instance, in 1997, then-Mexican President Ernesto Zedillo announced: "I have proudly affirmed that the Mexican nation extends beyond the territory enclosed by its borders and that Mexican migrants are an important, a very important part of it."[29] Mexican leaders have never and, likely, would never, admit publicly that such an absurd statement can only be meant to substantiate their failure to provide for Mexican citizens. But considering the blatant falsity of the claim, what else could it mean?

In July 2001, while addressing the annual meeting of the Hispanic civil rights organization, the National Council of La Raza, Mexican President Fox appealed to the U.S. to relax immigration restrictions that can cost lives. "Current policies have failed to reduce undocumented migration from Mexico, and instead have fostered a dangerous and even deadly migration black market," he said. "The prospects for a better life on both sides of our common border will be enhanced by what we do and will be diminished by what we fail to do. The time to act is now."

Border residents counter that Mexico should do a better job of providing for its own citizens and stop relying on the generosity of its northern neighbor. Then, they say, Mexico wouldn't have a mass exodus to deal with in the first place.[30]

Hypocritically, as Mexico pushes U.S. politicians and the American public to accept more of its citizens, it seeks to crack down on illegal entrants crossing into Mexico via its *southern borders* with Central and South America. In July 2001, Mexican authorities began "clamping down on the hundreds of thousands of Central Americans crossing Mexico's southern border," according to the December 16, 2002, issue of *The New American* magazine.[31]

The publication elaborates, "The Mexican police and military stepped up patrols along the six-hundred-mile jungle-covered border with Guatemala and Belize, and threw up a similar barricade across the Isthmus of Tehuantepec, the narrowest part of Mexico. During the year 2000, Mexican officials deported 150,000 Central American immigrants." Felipe de Jesus Preciado, head of the Mexican migration service, said "the flow of Central American migrants north is a national security problem for Mexico. It wouldn't be such a big problem if they were getting through to the U.S., but they get stuck and hang around in the frontier cities making trouble, sleeping in the streets with no money."[32]

So it's okay for Mexico to roust immigrants for national security reasons but not the U.S.? That's the general idea, yes.

While Mexico remains staunchly duplicitous regarding its own immigration and security policies versus those of the U.S., pro-unlimited immigration advocates in America are a force of their own to be reckoned with. They have successfully used politicians and the media to shift the debate from the lawbreaking and national security aspects of illegal immigration to one of humanitarian concern.

They have even shamelessly used unsuspecting children—who cannot begin to grasp the gravity of an issue as complex as illegal immigration—to advance their agenda. Joe Guzzardi covered such a case on Vdare.com—a respected immigration news and commentary Web site published by Peter Brimelow's Center for American Unity. Eighth grade students at Lodi Middle School in California were assigned an essay from a given number of topics, one of which was immigration. Extra credit was promised to students who sent their essay to the local paper and had it published. Three student letters on U.S. immigration policy were subsequently published by the *Lodi News-Sentinel*, practically carbon copies of each other according to Guzzardi, whose BS detector went haywire. He called the principal who assured Guzzardi that the "exercise was intended to build critical thinking skills" and that "the teacher did not take a position." Guzzardi said the letters' similarity still left him skeptical. "Adding to my doubt is the teacher's failure to respond to a request for a phone call. . . ."[33]

So Guzzardi responded with a letter of his own:

You have urged that immigration laws be liberalized so that more people can come to the U.S. and make better lives for themselves. More jobs, you suggest, will be done if there are more people to do them. First, you should also know that there is no job that Americans have not done in the past or would not do today—especially in our depressed economy. Then, you must ask yourself why so many people are compelled to leave Mexico and come to the U.S. Providing for Mexicans is the responsibility of the Mexican government. For decades, Mexico has failed its citizens. Because of that repeated failure, Mexicans have come to the U.S. seeking opportunities that do not exist in their country. In high school, you will learn about the laws of supply and demand. For every new worker who enters America, an employee is jeopardized. An unemployed person who recently arrived in the U.S. will be delighted to, for example, paint houses for $8.00 an hour even though the going wage is $15.00. And construction foremen will be anxious to hire them. Working for a living may seem a long way away from the 8th grade but one day you will hold a job that you won't want to lose to someone willing to do it for less money. Or maybe someone in your family is employed today who needs that job to provide for you. You would be very unhappy if the wage earner in your family lost his job under those circumstances. . . .[34]

In any event, in the meantime, Washington gives "a wink and a nod" to the porous border, since "the government relies on foreign workers and their cheap labor," says Richard H. Ward, dean and director of the Center for Criminal Justice at Texas's Sam Houston State University (he's also a former NYPD detective). And so the Border Patrol, Ward said, "finds itself in the unenviable position of trying to curtail what some view as a monumental problem."[35]

Dan Stein of the Federation of Immigration Reform says: "At best, [border security] is a marginal holding action." He calls the current level of border control "unacceptable."[36]

Craig Nelson, executive director of ProjectUSA, an advocacy group that supports restrictions on current immigration levels, describes border security as "atrocious," and says current immigration bureaucracy likely isn't up to the task of closing the sieve. "I don't think [federal border enforcement agencies] are capable in the least of securing the American people."[37]

Others believe the situation is now so bad—politically, culturally and practically—that it is all but impossible to control illegal immigration. Writing in February 2001, Samuel Francis said:

Thanks to the racial solidarity of Hispanics, their willingness to use their collective racial power to force themselves into this country despite the laws and the availability of federal power to help them against real Americans, what the American people want means virtually nothing. . . . Immigration policy—who and how many people we allow to enter our country—is ceasing to lie in the hands of Americans or their legal government. Once immigration has reached a certain level, neither our laws nor the officials who make and enforce the laws are able to stop it, and power naturally passes to the immigrants and those allied with them.[38]

Indeed, there is growing evidence that both major political parties are catering to Hispanics. The leadership of neither major party is willing to get tough on illegal immigration because it mostly involves Hispanics. They fear alienating potential voters.

"Click on the Web sites of the national political parties or some of the Democratic presidential candidates and you can read their statements in Spanish," says a March 2003 report by The Associated Press. "Listen to John Kerry stumping for votes, and you might hear the Massachusetts senator speaking Spanish; he's been practicing with language tapes the last few years. Like the 2000 White House rivals George W. Bush and Al Gore, who occasionally made their appeals in Spanish, the current candidates are trying to burnish their images with Hispanic voters. Leaders in the community, however, expect more than just lip service."[39]

This is attention now expected of American politicians by Hispanics. "Both parties have to fight for the hearts and minds of Hispanic voters," says Gabriela Lemus, a policy specialist for the League of United Latin American Citizens. "It's not enough to speak Spanish to us. We're being acknowledged, but window dressing isn't going to do it."[40]

The AP report said Hispanics want concrete proposals from both Republicans and Democrats guaranteeing them better education benefits, better employment, access to health care and, of course, favorable immigration policies—favorable, meaning adoption of policies that allow mostly Mexican citizens unlimited access to the fruits of America while remaining at least partially loyal to Mexico. Hispanics want "access to quality education and the ability to get their children into college," as "about two-thirds of Hispanics in this country are twenty-five or younger; quality jobs and access to quality health care"; and "resumption of talks with Mexico about immigration policy and inclusion of other Latin

American countries in those talks, as well as access to citizenship and benefits for immigrants who are already working in this country or are in this country trying to find work."

President Bush's lack of focus on the immigration problem could be explained by his polling numbers among Hispanic voters, described as "crucial" to his success in the 2000 election, analysts say.[41] In 1996, GOP candidate Bob Dole received just 21 percent of the Hispanic vote; Bush Sr. garnered 25 percent in 1992. Perhaps because of his role as governor of a heavily Hispanic state, Texas, "Dubya" got 35 percent of the Hispanic vote in 2000, a vote that has traditionally been given to Democratic candidates.

Robert H. Goldsborough, president of the immigration think tank Americans for Immigration Reform, described the current political climate regarding immigration in 2002 in this way:

President George W. Bush and [South Dakota] Democrat [Sen.] Tom Daschle are desperately trying to outbid each other on how many millions of illegal aliens can be legalized and given U.S. citizenship. Because [former President Bill] Clinton's political operatives legalized and registered about one million immigrants (legal and illegal) in order to steal victory from almost certain defeat in the 1996 presidential election, both parties are now salivating at the thought of using immigrants to win elections. It appears that the leadership of both political parties is more than willing to sacrifice America's heritage, culture, customs, and language in this almighty quest for immigrant votes. . . . In this bidding war to sell-out America, the politicians have ignored the plight of the American people. The Democrat/Republican sellout to illegal immigrants is pure insanity.[42]

Also, according to David Schippers, the chief counsel for the House Judiciary Committee who later was chosen to prosecute President Bill Clinton during his impeachment trial, the administration in 1996—under the tutelage of Vice President Al Gore—kept pressure on the Immigration and Naturalization Service "to make sure the aliens were pushed through by September 1, the last day to register for the presidential election."[43]

Schippers, in his book *Sellout*, wrote that under the Clinton administration implemented a "blatant politicization of the [INS] took place during the 1996 presidential campaign when the White House pressured the INS into expediting its 'Citizenship USA' (CUSA) program to grant citizenship to thousands of aliens that the White House counted as likely Democratic voters."[44]

"To ensure maximum impact, the INS concentrated on aliens in key states — California, Florida, Illinois, New York, New Jersey and Texas — that hold a combined 181 electoral votes, just 89 short of the total needed to win the election," Schippers wrote.[45]

Immigration is so heavy and, some say, out of control, that entire regions of the U.S. are becoming dominated by immigrants. As WorldNetDaily.com reported in January 2002, "a radical Hispanic movement's dream to retake the southwestern United States is becoming a reality with the aid of Mexican and U.S. policies, according to some immigration watchers."[46] Glenn Spencer, head of American Patrol, a border control group advocating reduced immigration and beefed up border security, says a massive influx of illegal immigrants is "importing poverty" and growing an ethnic community with greater loyalty to Mexico than the U.S. "Unless this is shut down within [a few] years, I believe that it will be irreversible, and that it will most certainly lead to a breakup of the United States. I don't think there is any doubt about it."[47]

Prominent Chicano activist and University of California at Riverside professor Armando Navarro says he believes secession of a state or states in the U.S. is very possible if immigration levels continue at a rapid pace. "If in fifty years most of our people are subordinated, powerless, exploited and impoverished, then I will say to you that there are all kinds of possibilities for movements to develop like the ones that we've witnessed in the last few years all over the world, from Yugoslavia to Chechnya," he said. "A secessionist movement is not something that you can put away and say it is never going to happen in the United States. Time and history change."[48]

Spencer says he believes the ultimate goal for Hispanic immigrants from Mexico is to re-populate and annex "Aztlan"—the mythical birthplace of the Aztec Indians. That area is said to include much of the American Southwest: California, Arizona, Nevada, New Mexico and parts of Colorado and Texas. "I see that as the overarching goal of the Mexican government and many Mexicans who want self-determination," he says.[49]

Indeed, one group, *La Voz de Aztlan* (the Voice of Aztlan), identifies Mexicans in the U.S. as "America's Palestinians."[50] Many Mexicans see themselves as part of a transnational ethnic group known as "La Raza," the race. A May editorial on the Web site, with a dateline of Los Angeles, Alta California, declares that "both La Raza and the Palestinians have been displaced by invaders that have utilized military means to conquer and occupy our territories."[51]

"One could argue that while Mexico lost the war in 1848, it will probably win it in the 21st century, in terms of the numbers," Navarro says. "But that is not a reality based on what Mexico does, it's based on what this country does."[52]

That rings true. In fact, there are already entire sectors of America that are little more than extended enclaves of Mexico. Spanish is the primary language; "Anglos" speaking English are sometimes shunned or ignored, even in restaurants or entirely "American" businesses like Wal-Mart, K-Mart and other retail outlets. In some border towns, most billboards are in Spanish. Hispanic business owners and their employees have difficulty understanding English and often make no effort to try. The Hispanic influences of Mexican, not American, culture dominate the flavor of most American border communities. Mexican flags are often in equal prominence with U.S. flags. And, naturally, Hispanics are the dominant ethnic group, outnumbering whites, blacks and even indigenous Indians.

Such realities are difficult to accept for Americans like the Petrellos who live along the border regions and are fed up with the invasion of immigrants and the associated violence. They're tired of the costs. They're tired of the threats. They're tired of the trash. They're tired of the drugs. They're tired of being tired of it all. But most of all, they're tired of being ignored by politicians, law enforcement, bureaucrats and policymakers—most of whom criticize any effort citizens make to take care of the problem themselves.

"I have them through my property all the time, every day," Gary McBride, who ranches in Arizona about thirty miles north of the border, told the *Los Angeles Times Magazine* in a March 2003 interview. "They leave stock fences open so the cows get out. They damage water tanks. They leave behind an unbelievable amount of trash, which my cows sometimes eat and get sick. We're damned tired of it."[53]

Without the commitment of politicians—state and local, as well as national—the sieve that is our southwestern border will continue to seep humanity, bringing with it all the hardships, costs and danger irresponsible border policies entail.

ENEMY OF THE STATES

There have been more firefights on the border in recent weeks than there have been in Bosnia.

—REP. DUNCAN HUNTER (R-CALIFORNIA), JUNE 1997

Doroteo Arango, a.k.a. the notorious Pancho Villa, was born in the Mexican state of Durango in 1878 and grew up as a share-cropper peasant on a hacienda. Legend has it that the incident which launched his career as an outlaw occurred when he was sixteen; as he returned from the fields one day, he discovered that his sister had been raped by the owner of the hacienda, Don Agustin López Negrete. Arango took up his revolver, shot and killed Don Agustin, then escaped into the surrounding hills. From there he joined up with a gang of cattle rustlers led by a man named Francisco "Pancho" Villa, and in one of the gang's many fights with the *rurales* (Mexican national mounted police), Francisco was shot and killed. Arango took over the gang and assumed the name of their fallen leader— though he may have done so not to honor Francisco but to throw off those who hunted him for the murder of Don Agustin.

Villa was a natural leader and extremely successful as a *bandito*. He led several raids on Mexican towns, killing those who opposed him as well as looting goods, horses and cattle. But he was also involved in legitimate ventures, such as his work as a contractor on the Copper Canyon railroad.

But then, in 1910, the Mexican Revolution broke out and Villa was recruited by Abraham Gonzalez, the revolutionary leader. Villa formed an army of renegade cowboys and ruffians, assumed the title of general and took command of the war in Mexico's northern provinces. His allure as a former *bandito* and his victories made him an idol and hero to the peasant masses.

But in 1916, Villa became an enemy of the United States when he crossed the border and raided the town of Columbus, New Mexico. Reports are sketchy, but it is generally accepted that Villa attacked the town because American weapons dealers there had failed to deliver arms Villa had bought and paid for. One other explanation for the raid is that it was an expression of Villa's frustration with the fact that the United States was backing a rival Mexican general. But whichever version is correct—or if parts of both are correct—what is known is that Villa's forces laid waste to the town, forcing the U.S. government to quickly raise an army led by Gen. John "Black Jack" Pershing—who would later command U.S. forces during World War I—and send it into the Mexican state of Chihuahua after Villa. Pershing and his army never caught up to the Mexican revolutionary general but as it turned out they didn't have to; Villa was assassinated in 1923.

———————

Since those days, crime along the U.S.-Mexico border has not only increased but it has become more "modernized;" while Mexican revolutionaries no longer cross the border and attack American towns, Mexican drug lords—sometimes escorted by elements of the Mexican military—have attacked, on occasion, U.S. law enforcement agents (as in the case of murdered U.S. Park Ranger Kris Eggle). Also, the same drug cartels and military units daily employ, guide and protect scores of peasant "mules" who hump drugs and other contraband into the U.S.

But "normal" illegal immigrants also target law enforcement and border officials. And they have also attacked, assaulted, robbed and even killed American citizens. In fact, local residents regularly talk about the increase in violence along the border, as in the case of one woman in Duvall County, Texas (who asked she be identified only as "Mrs. Morales"). Her home has been invaded twice by illegal aliens—both times while her husband, a local county police officer, was away. And they live almost fifty miles from the border.

The first invasion took place one summer evening in 2001 around 6 P.M., and involved perhaps a half dozen illegals. Morales said her husband had just left for work when she decided to lie down for a while to rest up in the air conditioning from the day's work and heat. Shortly after she closed her eyes she said she heard the screen door to the kitchen "open and close" (the couple's bedroom is right off their kitchen) and someone walk in. She had closed her bedroom door but in the reflection of light on the floor that shown through the crack below she could see the shadows of at least two people walking around. Realizing it wasn't her husband and that her home had been invaded, Morales lay there quietly for a few moments pondering her next move when, suddenly, "all hell broke loose," she says.

Morales said the invaders began ransacking the place; they overturned her kitchen table, ran their arms the length of several shelves which held plates and glasses knocking them to the floor and tossed everything out of the couple's cupboards. When they finished destroying her kitchen, Morales—who immigrated legally to the U.S. from New Zealand—said she heard the screen door open and shut again, indicating the pair had gone back outside. "At that point, I grabbed a .22 rifle from the bedroom and went to the front door," she said. Once there, she found the men in the front yard "picking peaches off one of our trees." She said one man carried a "bag full of food and clothing."

At five feet, four inches tall and 115 pounds, Morales admits she is not very intimidating, but nonetheless—as she held the rifle—she yelled to the men and demanded, "Get off my property!" But instead of fleeing at the site of an armed American—woman or not and despite her demure physical appearance—the men only jeered at her and said in English, "No. We want water." Morales said she began to really get nervous when she noticed other Hispanic men crouching behind a fence that surrounds their home and is topped with barbed wire. "I pointed my weapon in their direction," she said, "and told them, 'Stand up!'" They just shrugged at her as if to say, "Why? What are *you* going to do?" Now as frustrated as she was frightened, Morales said she demanded once more the men get off her property. When they refused to leave once more, she went back into her home to call the police. For several more minutes the men stayed. In fact, she said, they watched her call the police through her bedroom window.

Adding to her fear, Morales says she called 911 *twice* but never even got an answer. She said she let the phone ring "at least ten times" each try. Now angry, she directly dialed a sheriff's office which was located only six miles from her home. She said a deputy there told her he could not respond because her home was located outside of his jurisdiction.

"I told them what appeared to be illegal alien men had been in my house, they had torn up the kitchen and stolen things and were still on the property," she said. "He told me, 'You're in [the neighboring] county, there's nothing I can do.' I answered, 'But the sheriff for this county is over thirty miles away. You are the closest law enforcement, and I need help.' He said, 'I guess I can call Border Patrol for you.'"

Exasperated, Morales told the deputy to call Border Patrol for her, then nervously went back to a window and noticed that a few of the men had begun to wander off into the desert. Seeing an opportunity, she decided to risk an escape, so she grabbed her rifle and bolted out the door, running the entire length of the couple's driveway—a few hundred yards—to the highway, where she waited for the Border Patrol so show up. That took forty-five minutes.

"I asked them, 'What took you so long?' and he—there was only one agent—answered, 'Well, I wasn't told this was an emergency. I was told you just saw a couple of illegals.'" She shook her head in disbelief; how could the deputy she spoke to on the phone not understand she was in dire straits?

Nonetheless, Morales showed the agent where she had seen the men, and he took some time to search the property. The agent told her he found footsteps all around the house and they were patterned in such a way as to lead him to believe at least a couple of the illegals had actually cased her home in advance. He said the fact that they remained hidden—perhaps for a few hours—until her husband left for work led him to believe they had cased the home several times and knew the couple's routine. They knew enough, the agent proffered, to wait until her police officer-husband left.

Several months later, Morales said her home was invaded again, this time around 7 A.M. when she was sound asleep. She said she was lying on her stomach and was awakened suddenly when she heard a loud "*Bang!*" at the front door. She turned over just in time to see a man grabbing for her neck. Reacting quickly, she reached over and grabbed a pistol from the nightstand next to her bed and stuck it in the man's face. Shaking, she said she yelled at the intruder—a Hispanic-looking man—to leave her home immediately. She said she was dumbfounded when "he just looked at me and said, in English, 'What?'" Morales said she repeated her demand: "I said, 'Get out of my house!' but he said, in perfect English, 'No. I just walked all the way from Mexico; get out of bed and cook something for me.'"

She was shocked—and angry—at his audacity. *He* invaded her home and was demanding *she* get up and fix him some food. But Morales—gun still in hand—refused, and instead more forcefully repeated her demand for him to get out of the house. Again he refused, and a stand-off ensued for several tense moments.

"To scare him," she said, "I pointed to my wedding ring and said, 'My husband's a police officer.' But he just looked at me and laughed and said, 'So?' I told him my husband's with Immigration, which wasn't true, but he wouldn't have known that. When I did, though, the man just began howling and belly-laughing. He said, 'They can't catch me and they don't even try.'" Morales said she was running out of options and was considering defending herself with the pistol, but then, with a dismissive flip of his hand, the man finally turned and left. She immediately called the Border Patrol, but help wasn't quick in coming. "They sent one agent out and it took him nearly an hour to get here," she said. "The station was only six miles away." Morales said the agent, when he arrived, admitted seeing who he believed was the man she reported in her home, but didn't stop him. Incredulous, she asked, "Are you going to go arrest him?" but she claims he replied, "No, he's probably long gone by now."

Morales' story is hair-raising and troublesome. It also highlights the increasingly brazen level of criminal behavior that is happening more and more frequently along the porous U.S.-Mexico border. What is much more common, however, is the level of damage being done to the private property of American citizens. For instance, the illegal alien traffic across the Moraleses' sixty-acre spread is so bad they had to install barbed wire atop the fence surrounding their yard. Other homes have installed steel gates and iron bars on windows and doors.

The Moraleses have had so many of their goats killed they finally had to stop raising them; they are considering doing the same thing with their cattle. And, the couple says, illegals have stolen horses and poisoned their dogs and other livestock. "We see them crossing our property everyday," she says, adding that before the pair of home invasions, she and her husband would either try to run the illegals off or detain them for the Border Patrol. Not anymore. Another reason why, says Morales and many other local residents, is because more and more illegals are crossing armed. "So now," she says, "we just watch them pass through." She and many other border residents also keep guns handy.

"They'll take anything," she said, noting that she and her husband cannot even leave yard implements like axes or rakes or hoes outside, lest they risk having them used against them as weapons. "I can't even guess how much money we've spent to replace things or fix our fences. . . . They've even taken our clothes right off the line. . . . I have since bought a dryer."[1]

The increase in cross-border crime is no secret to lawmakers, policy chiefs and bureaucrats in Washington (or Mexico City, for that matter). Besides the fact that much more media is covering what is going on down on the border, federal bureaucrats knew it was on the rise some years ago—years, in fact, before the September 11, 2001, terrorist attacks.

In August 1997, the Clinton administration announced it was beefing up the Border Patrol because of a dramatic increase in border-related crime. American ranchers and property owners along the border began complaining to their elected officials about the increase in crime in the 1980s, with a rising number of them making a special effort to tell lawmakers they were having to arm themselves because illegal aliens and drug mules were becoming more prevalent and more violent.

According to a *New York Times Magazine* story, Mexican drug traffickers often exploit "illegal aliens to carry the drugs." The magazine quoted a border-area U.S. police chief who said, "They're hauling drugs just down from my house. I even carry a .38 to mow my lawn, but those guys are carrying assault rifles." The magazine also quoted a border rancher, who told reporters: "It's getting worse every day, and nothing's being done about it."[2]

The rash in violence at the time led Rep. Duncan Hunter (R-California) to declare: "There is a war going on for control of our border with Mexico."[3]

In one of the most high-profile recent cases of an illegal alien committing crimes, one of the alleged snipers who terrorized the Washington DC–area in October 2002—seventeen-year-old John Lee Malvo—was not only in the country illegally, but he had been apprehended by the Border Patrol the previous year in Bellingham, Washington, with his mother, Uma Sceon James, because agents discovered they had come into the country illegally aboard a ship several months earlier in Florida. The Border Patrol had intended for Malvo and his mother to be deported—per federal law as they understood it—but INS district officials in Seattle released them both; Malvo and ex-Army soldier John Mohammad are suspected of killing ten people and wounding three others in sniper shootings in Maryland, Washington DC and Virginia. Federal law says illegal stowaways, "regardless of when encountered, are to be removed without a hearing."[4]

Even federal law enforcement professionals were angered by the Mohammad-Malvo incident. "This makes me sick to my stomach," Daryl

Schermerhorn, vice president of the Northwest regional chapter of the National Border Patrol Council, told columnist and author Michelle Malkin. "The INS is not concerned with enforcing immigration law. It's more concerned with freeing up jails and saving a few bucks than it is with protecting Americans and removing people who don't belong here."[5]

There are also concerns that some illegals may be coming here specifically to commit terrorist acts against Americans, some on the scale of the 9-11 attacks. One case that caused such concern involved a Mexican alien in Virginia who was arrested after police received a tip he was planning to poison water supplies in the winter of 2002. Virginia authorities, in conjunction with the FBI, began an investigation of Ipolito "Polo" Campos, who was living illegally near Virginia's eastern shore despite being expelled from the U.S. once before. According to court records, Campos had told an associate, who later informed authorities, that he was from an "Arabian" country and "if he did not poison the water someone would kill him." When the FBI and state authorities moved in to arrest him a gunfight ensued; a Virginia state trooper was wounded in the arm and another man holed up with Campos was shot and killed. Campos was already facing charges of using phony immigration documents and a false Social Security number; now he faces charges of attempted murder, assault of a state trooper and possession of a sawed-off shotgun. When he was taken into custody, he told authorities he was out of work and broke, with six children and a wife who also wasn't employed; taxpayers in the state of Virginia picked up the most of the costs of his incarceration.[6]

On January 23, 2003, the *Washington Times* reported that U.S. intelligence officials were concerned that al Qaeda "sleeper cells" were located inside the United States after Immigration officials caught two suspects thought to belong to the terror group attempting to enter the country. "The war in Afghanistan has proven costly to the al Qaeda network, but not fatal," one U.S. law-enforcement official, who asked not to be identified, told the paper. "They are looking for places from which they can plan new attacks without drawing a lot of attention. . . . It would be safe to say they have spread themselves globally, and the United States is not immune."[7]

Bill Gertz, the *Times'* national security correspondent, also reported in mid-September 2002 that a group of Islamic terrorists from the tri-border region of Paraguay, Argentina and Brazil—a region which is known to be a haven for extremists—was making its way to the United States.[8] The movement was reported to various law enforcement agencies; authorities said the group had planned to enter via the "porous" U.S.-Mexico border.

Illegals also commit many other serious, if not headline-grabbing, crimes. As of January 2003, 54 Mexican nationals were sitting in U.S. jails awaiting execution for capital offenses.[9,10] One, Daniel Sanchez Covarrubias, was sentenced to death in 1994 in California for the shooting deaths of two men and a young woman; he was also convicted of the attempted murder of an eleven-month-old baby girl who survived the attack. Her mother—Martha Morales—was holding the girl, her daughter, when she was gunned down.[11]

One of the numerous instances of lesser crimes committed by illegal aliens involves Antonio Miguel, a Guatemalan national in the U.S. illegally since 1988. Though the *Miami Herald* newspaper published a story that could be construed as sympathetic to his plight—he has three children, each of whom have received taxpayer-supported liver transplants—he lied to immigration officials to gain entry to the U.S., and has been arrested for carrying a concealed weapon in his car. He's also been convicted of dealing in stolen property.[12]

Sometimes the activity of illegal aliens itself is responsible for death and injury. For instance, two women were killed and fifteen others were injured—many seriously—when a pick-up truck carrying illegals crashed near Descanso, California, on January 9, 2003. Border Patrol agents gave chase—a rare occurrence, due to agency policy generally forbidding chasing fleeing illegals on the highway[13]—because the driver of the vehicle, who survived the eventual crash, attempted to run down a pair of agents as he blew through a border checkpoint. After a twenty-two-mile chase, the truck "crashed into a bridge support on Interstate 8 at state Route 79, hurling men, women and children through the air," said the *San Diego Union-Tribune*. The two women killed were among four people who were thrown over an embankment to Route 79, about thirty to forty feet below; a five-year-old boy was among those critically injured.[14]

Also, more and more illegals are falling prey to those who deal in human smuggling.[15] According to law enforcement authorities, an increasing number of smugglers are holding illegal immigrants hostage in the U.S. until they or their families pay a ransom. In addition, rival gangs of criminals also steal immigrants from their smugglers and hold them for ransom. Criminals are kidnapping illegals already settled in some states because they are confident the victims will likely not run to authorities for fear of being deported. In one case, authorities are investigating the execution-style killing of eight immigrants whose bodies were found outside Phoenix, Arizona, in 2002. Reports said one of the eight was a coyote kidnapped by men who pistol-whipped him in front of his family and demanded a $40,000 ransom. He was bound with his underwear and stabbed repeatedly. Police believe the eight could have been kidnapped for ransom or may have been drug or immigrant smugglers who infringed on rival turf.[16]

The lawlessness has even reached the international level. In January 2003, U.S. taxpayers were forced to subsidize nearly two thousand farmers in Texas to the tune of $10 million because Mexico has failed to release immigration water into the Rio Grande River, as per the terms of a 1944 treaty.[17] Mexico managed to withhold 1.5 million acre feet of water, causing an estimated $1 billion in damage to the Lower Rio Grande Valley economy since 1993, according to a Texas A&M University study.[18] (An acre foot is 325,851 gallons of water, or enough to cover an acre of land one-foot deep.) In an agreement reached with the U.S. State Department, the Mexican government agreed to repay 350,000 acre feet of what it owed by September 30, 2003—200,000 of that amount by the end of January 2003—though area farmers said they needed a minimum of 600,000 acre feet, noting the repayment amounts do not take into account conveyance and evaporative losses. In May 2002, angry Texas farmers were threatening to blockade three major international bridges if the issue wasn't settled;[19] by October farmers and state officials were pushing Washington to impose economic sanctions against Mexico for its continued failure to release water under the treaty, and there were protests by Texas farmers as well as Mexican farmers who also suffered because of the meager water releases.

Mexican troops are also involved in promoting illegal activities, according to border residents, law enforcement officials, and illegal immigrant watch groups. In February 2003, the civilian border watch group American Border Patrol videotaped a group of Mexican soldiers rounding up migrant nationals just south of the U.S.-Mexico border, then herding them to an area nearer the border where it was easier to avoid detection by American law enforcement during entry into the United States. Larry Vance, a spotter for the group, "watched as the Mexican troops moved a group of up to one hundred invaders toward a wash running north and south that offers cover for border crashers," said a description of the incident published by the group. "They probably had them wait for a shift change to make their move," Vance said, noting the Mexican troops likely waited until border enforcement personnel were at their thinnest before instructing the illegals to cross into the U.S.[20]

Despite the ready occurrence of cross-border crime, some studies suggest that it is actually underreported, and for a variety of reasons. Says the Center for Immigration Reform:

> Immigration enthusiasts might be prone to use such research as evidence that widespread fear of immigrant crime is an irrational, if understandable, response to sensationalized anecdotes. But such a view may be hasty in its own right. Many immigrant crimes are not reported, and possibly in greater proportion than the crimes that the U.S.-born commit. Many victims of immigrant criminals fear reporting crimes to the police because their victimizers are of the same nationality, and thus are more likely to retaliate in ways that would dissuade the victim from calling police. This is especially true with immigrant crime rings. . . . [21]

One reason why the underreporting occurs is because, CIS says, what Americans consider criminal activity is a traditional response on some cultures—a "'family matter' not requiring outside interference."

"In this view, police are not supposed to supplant patriarchal authority in resolving disputes, however evident that the 'conflict' in question is a case of prey needing protection from predator," said CIS.

Another reason is because some immigrants—even in this day and age—are still sold or traded into virtual slavery to people already living in the U.S. "In a bitterly ironic note," CIS discovered, "a Nigerian woman who investigated child abuse complaints for the City of New York was arrested in 1999 along with her husband and charged with forcing a Nigerian girl into servitude for nine years. Federal investigators also noted the couple and several relatives had forced two other Nigerian girls into servitude. . . . Cases such as these are far more common than imagined. Each year, according to a 1999 report by the Central Intelligence Agency, between 45,000 and 50,000 women and children are trafficked as slaves into the United States from Asia, Europe, Latin America, India, and Africa."[22]

Still another reason immigrant crime is underreported is because criminals from across the border come into the U.S. to commit their crimes, then vanish back into Mexico to avoid capture and prosecution. "Police officials in the San Diego area have complained that organized groups from Mexico cross over from Tijuana and commit robberies in middle-income neighborhoods," said CIS. "Indeed, criminal activity along the U.S.-Mexican border in San Diego County led local officials in the 1980s to conduct a study of arrest rates according to legal status. In the City of San Diego, 26 percent of all burglary arrests and 12 percent of all felony arrests involved illegal aliens, who are estimated to comprise less than 4 percent of the total city population. . . ."[23]

David Walsh, a freelance writer/photographer who writes about immigrant issues, sees another reason for the "dearth" of information involving immigrant crime:

Recently, while exploring the incidence of immigrant crime and its impact on the US, I was stymied. Not by the dearth of information: it's there if you really want it. What was troubling was the lengths to which people who rely on such statistics . . . will go to avoid discussing them.

Some officials were fearful, some indifferent, others seemed to question my motives. It all seemed to mirror the big media's tendency to skirt the issue. . . . Police, intelligence agencies, the courts, parole officers, social workers, and health professionals—as well as Americans at large—all must accustom themselves, it seems, to immigrant crime. . . . [24]

Why's the issue so touchy? Walsh interviewed Richard H. Ward, dean and director of the Center of Criminal Justice at Texas's Sam Houston State University, and his answer: No one wants to cause political and diplomatic trouble for our trading partners to the south.[25]

Immigrants have created a sort of cottage-industry crime wave. Police in California and other migrant communities report that many immigrant workers are robbed because they don't trust American banks and instead carry their "wad of cash" around with them: "Typical was an incident . . . when police said a laborer walking near his home [in Oceanside, California] was accosted by a man and a woman who punched him in the head and face. When he fell to the ground, the assailants grabbed his wallet that contained approximately $800—about two weeks' pay," the *San Diego Union-Tribune* reported.[26]

————————————

By sneaking into the U.S., illegals are violating a number of laws. There is no question some of them resort to violence and that many of them trespass with impunity on private property. Illegals have been known to kill pets (mostly barking dogs), kill cattle for meat if they are hungry, tear down fences, pollute incessantly; and the evidence points to the fact that as this cross-border crime wave continues—or is allowed to continue—it is worsening.

A case in point is Organ Pipe Cactus National Monument, which borders Mexico in west-central Arizona. Immigrants traverse there by the thousands, destroying rare foliage and vegetation. The "arms" on an Organ Pipe cactus can take up to a hundred years to grow; when one is knocked off or damaged, the cactus dies. But as disturbing as that ecological damage is, there is another fact about Organ Pipe Monument that should anger Americans. It's listed as the most dangerous park in the nation because it is rife with drug-smugglers toting drugs *and* weapons.[27]

At the monument, federal law enforcement agents say it is getting to the point where they are no longer equipped to handle the most violent cross-border offenders; the especially well-armed drug runners, like those who shot and killed Ranger Kris Eggle in August 2002 in Organ Pipe, often carry AK-47 assault rifles. Border Patrol and park service agents say the task of policing parks and monuments, where Americans go to camp and enjoy themselves, is extremely hazardous and that some agencies—especially the Park Service—are not organized or staffed to adequately protect American civilians, let alone themselves.[28]

U.S. Customs special response team. Beefed-up tactics are needed against today's increasingly sophisticated illegal alien and drug smugglers.

In these areas, the Department of Interior has most of the responsibility for law enforcement. They are areas that comprise 36 percent of the nation's border with Mexico. Park rangers are the primary law enforcement officers in these monuments and parks, but they "are not trained, they are not staffed, they are not equipped for the mission," Doug Scott, the agency's assistant inspector general, said in a 2003 interview.[29] It's not just about Smokey the Bear and campfire dousing anymore; "there are carjackings, robberies, sexual assaults, confrontations with drug runners," Scott said. In an investigative report issued early in 2002, Scott also warned that the department's law enforcement operations were devoid of leadership and poorly coordinated.

The worsening situation of crime in the nation's border-area parks and recreation centers has, for what it's worth, garnered the attention of some lawmakers. "The slow pace of law enforcement reform is putting park rangers, Interior police and park visitors at risk," Sen. Charles Grassley (R-Iowa) has warned.[30]

It has become so bad at Organ Pipe that many rangers report to work in full camouflage uniforms and tote M-16 rifles to track drug runners and illegal aliens, who far outnumber them. Up to a thousand smugglers and aliens are in the park on any given night, say park service officials.[31] Tom Clynes, writing in *National Geographic*, reported the situation this way:

Now that American immigration policy has pushed the wars on drugs and immigration into the desert wilderness, it has suddenly become the ranger's job to hold the line. Before Eggle's death, Organ Pipe's former chief ranger, Dale Thompson, realized that his rangers were outmanned and outgunned by the drug traffickers, with their growing infrastructure of communications and surveillance systems, automatic weapons, and even support from elements in the Mexican police and military. He called for reinforcements, but his requests for more resources got little more than sympathy in Washington. Budgets were frozen, and in the wake of September 11, trained rangers were being siphoned off by other federal law-enforcement agencies, who could pay more.[32]

Clynes said rangers are expected to enforce a gamut of laws. In many respects, rangers are DEA agents, Border Patrol agents and U.S. Customs Service inspectors, as well as park rangers.

"We're understaffed, our training is substandard, and we haven't developed an understanding, among management and the general public, of what today's park ranger does," said Donald Murphy, the service's deputy director, in an interview with Clynes. "This is a wonderfully complex and rewarding job. Yes, park rangers are the good guys in the Smokey Bear hats who lead hikes and campfire talks. But they also risk their lives on a daily basis."

Park rangers, says the U.S. Department of Justice, are the most assaulted of all federal law enforcement officers (and they're followed closely by Border Patrol agents). In February 2003, a Border Patrol agent was attacked by illegal border crossers near Palominas, Arizona. A local resident gave this account:

> The agent was struck in the head with a homemade blackjack, which was made with a sock filled with rocks. The agent was immediately knocked unconscious, and was out for quite a while. They believe it may have been up to a half hour. Nobody really knows for sure, though. The persons who assaulted him fled and weren't apprehended. The agent did not have his gun and radio stolen (as was reported by some news media). In fact, before he lost consciousness, he was able to press the "emergency" button that is standard on all radios now. That's how other agents were able to find him. Even though he was working alone, they knew where he was because he had radioed that he was checking a sensor. It took a while to find him, because he was a long way from his vehicle. But, at least [other agents] got there instead of worrying about where he was when he didn't show up at the office at the end of his shift.[33]

Meanwhile, scores of other civilians and local, state and federal police charged with plugging the crime-ridden sieve known as the U.S.-Mexico border also have their hands full. At Organ Pipe alone, crime has exploded. In 2001, rangers and federal law enforcement seized fourteen thousand pounds of marijuana—up 37 percent from a year earlier—and they engaged in more than thirty car chases in pursuit of suspected smugglers. As many as one thousand illegal immigrants pour through the cactus preserve each day.[34]

"Similar problems exist at all the Interior Department's law enforcement operations along the border—including the Fish and Wildlife Service, the Bureau of Indian Affairs and the Bureau of Land Management," the *Los Angeles Times* reported. In 2001, 357,000 pounds of marijuana were seized on Interior lands along the Mexican border, a four-fold increase since 1999; more than a quarter of it was seized on refuges operated by the Fish and Wildlife Service and more than half in areas controlled by the Bureau of Land Management, said the *Times*. At Coronado National Memorial in Arizona, a woman was abducted from her car at knifepoint in 1999, tied up and pushed over a hill, her car stolen. In the first weeks of 2003, over nine thousand pounds of marijuana was seized by federal officials in Big Bend National Park in Texas.[35]

"Unfortunately, it takes the death of somebody before people sit up and realize changes have to be made," said Bo Stone, an Organ Pipe ranger and close friend of Kris Eggle. "All the issues down here are bigger than the Department of the Interior. You could get a hundred park rangers down here, and it won't solve the problem. You would need a guard tower every quarter of a mile. . . . We have caught people from China, Pakistan and Yemen coming through. If a thousand illegal immigrants can walk through the desert here, so can a thousand terrorists."[36]

Cross-border crime has been allowed to proliferate, in part, because Washington hasn't placed the emphasis and importance necessary to make the border regions safer, but also because the INS often fails to do its duty to deport illegal alien criminals. According to an analysis by Cox Newspapers in late 2002, federal investigators say thousands of immigrant felons have not been deported, although no one knows precisely how many.[37] The list includes child molesters, drug dealers and robbers, many of whom were never picked up by INS after they served prison terms for their offenses. In February 2003, Cox Newspapers reported:

A 42-year-old woman, gang-raped a few days before Christmas last year, might never have faced that ordeal except for the federal government's neglect. The woman, a mother of two, had been sitting with a boyfriend on a park bench in New York City's Flushing Meadows neighborhood when the attackers surrounded the couple and dragged her away. It could have been just another horrible crime, except that the five men charged should never have been in that neighborhood. All were illegal immigrants who under federal law were subject to being deported.[38]

Four of the attackers were petty criminals, and two had done jail time. Those two remained in the United States largely because Congress and successive administrations have never provided the resources to monitor or remove tens of thousands of illegal immigrants who each year move in and out of state and local jails. That resulted in federal immigration officials—who run the deportation process—being forced to focus most resources on only the most violent illegal alien criminals in large prisons. But, Cox Newspapers reported, that's "not for lack of authority." Congress has already authorized a series of tough laws "to crack down on criminal aliens" incarcerated in local jurisdictions.[39]

As a result, the Immigration and Naturalization Service (INS), which runs the deportation process, focuses its limited staff on the most dangerous felons in large prisons. It's not for lack of authority. Congress has passed a series of tough laws to crack down on criminal aliens in local jails.

"They're supposed to deport them. Why aren't they doing it?" asks Alex Markowich, an assistant district attorney in Atlanta, Georgia, when told an illegal immigrant pedophile who molested a two-year-old girl wasn't made to leave the country after serving his four-year sentence. "Everybody, I recall, seemed to understand that he was going to do prison [and] since he was an illegal alien, when he got done with his sentence, they were going to send him back to Mexico. That's horrible. That's horrible."[40]

INS officials in Atlanta said they had no record of the pedophile case—some called that a "stock" answer—but according to the Cox Newspapers analysis, that's not the only case of criminal immigrant outrage. Since 1990, "at least eight immigrants convicted of molesting children were released from prison in Georgia but were not immediately removed from the country, records of the Georgia Corrections Department indicate," reports the *Atlanta Journal-Constitution*.[41] When reporters tried to locate the immigrants, they discovered that three were wanted by authorities—two for failing to register as sex offenders and another because he hadn't reported to his probation officer. Two of the convicts had been deported long after they served their sentences—five years in one case—and the INS had no record of the remaining three. INS officials around the country have conceded they have no fail-safe system for identifying immigrants in prisons and jails.[42]

Border crime and violence is also committed against illegal aliens, often by their own handlers. Coyotes, who are usually Mexican nationals themselves, are infinitely more responsible for killing illegal immigrants than U.S. law enforcement agents. Sometimes they kill their charges if they can't get more money from their families for smuggling them across the border. A typical case is one described by the *Arizona Republic*:

> They come into the shadow of the White Tank Mountains to kill. And then they disappear, like their namesakes, coyotes. Since March [2002], smugglers of illegal immigrants, known as "coyotes," have left behind eight bodies, each killing as brutal as the one before, investigators say. Some of the victims were coyotes themselves, while others were smuggled across the border illegally and did not have enough money to satisfy their smuggler. "This is all revolving around coyotes and the smuggling of aliens," Maricopa County sheriff's Detective Travis Anglin said. "We believe it is the coyotes who are doing the killing. When coyotes are ending up dead, it's a safe bet they are killing each other. They're

so ruthless." Adds Maricopa County Sheriff Joe Arpaio: "This is the message they want to send to everybody. . . . Pay up or get executed."[43]

Later in the article, the paper described another incident, this one involving the abduction for ransom of a known immigrant smuggler living in Phoenix. According to the paper, Luis Enrique Ybarra was sitting down to eat a late dinner in his trailer home in Phoenix July 31, 2002, with his wife, Maria, and daughter, two, when suddenly, four gunmen crashed through the front door. They pistol whipped Ybarra while his wife looked on. She later told police she was lying on the floor holding their daughter as the four suspects ransacked their home, looking for valuables such as jewelry and any cash they could find. But upon investigation, police found in Ybarra's belongings a ledger with all sorts of names, dates and amounts of money people had paid to be smuggled into the U.S. from Mexico— and the figures showed business was good. Ybarra "acted as a distributor and had a few lower-level coyotes working for him," he told police, according to *Arizona Republic*. On one of the ledgers, police found a total of more than $20,000.

The paper reported:

> The kidnappers called about an hour after Ybarra was taken, demanding $40,000 in cash. The wife, working with police, tried to negotiate for three days. Then the phone calls stopped. Nearly two months after he was abducted, Ybarra's mummified body was found in a desert wash. He was bound with the waistband of a pair of underwear. Unlike the rest of the victims, who were shot, he was stabbed to death and left in the same wash where investigators found the skeletal remains of another, unidentified victim. Ybarra's killing seemed more personal than the other seven, investigators said.

As in the case of Ybarra, more and more smugglers are holding their charges hostage while demanding more money than they have already been paid from the families of the illegal being smuggled. If the families don't—or can't—pay up, coyotes will often abandon their human cargo or worse; American law enforcement officials increasingly find them dead, either in the desert or in "safe" houses inside the U.S. Rival gangs of smugglers also steal illegal immigrants from each other to ransom them to family members; they are even taking hostage illegal immigrants who are established in communities throughout the border states.[44] Though kidnappings have been reported in border communities from El Paso to San Diego, the city of Phoenix—as of early 2003—was being hit the worst, authorities say.[45]

In January 2003, Phoenix police found sixty-one illegal immigrants being held hostage in a "stash" house while smugglers tried to extort more money from their families. Authorities said several of the men had been pistol-whipped by their smuggler-captors, and one woman had been sexually assaulted at least twice. The illegals were discovered after one of them escaped and called police. Three of the smugglers were turned over to INS. "This type of violence is commonplace during these types of operations," said Phoenix police Detective Tony Morales. "It just does not get reported. In this particular case, we were lucky."[46]

To be fair, crimes are often committed by illegal aliens unwittingly, because they don't understand and read English and, hence, cannot hope to understand and obey local laws and ordinances, many of which are posted in English in cities and towns. (Though in some heavily populated Hispanic border communities in the U.S., this is changing—some road and public service signs are being posted in Spanish *and* English.)

The Associated Press reported a case in point in Oregon.[47] Gervais police Sgt. Joe Fast pulled out of a parking lot on a foggy night in February 2003 to stop his third car in an hour. Upon approaching the vehicle, Fast discovered a young Hispanic driver, the third one in a row he'd stopped. The driver was in his late teens; his girlfriend was sitting next to him in their Honda Accord holding the couple's fifteen-month-old child. Their three-year-old son was climbing around in the back of the car, unsecured. Upon further investigation, Fast discovered the driver had a suspended license and no automobile insurance. In the eerie glow of the squad car's red and blue flashing lights, the officer told the couple it doesn't matter that they were only going down to a market a few blocks away to purchase children's medication; driving any distance with unsecured children is dangerous, especially on a night with low visibility.

"It's that drunk driver with no headlights," he explains. "He hits you at thirty or forty miles per hour and it's going to be like hitting a brick wall. Your kid's going to go right through the front window and you're going to have to live with it the rest of your life."

The encounter wasn't uncommon in Gervais, which is a small farming community about fifteen miles northeast of Salem. There is a large Russian and Hispanic population in the town; in fact, some 65 percent of the town's residents are Hispanic, 40 percent don't speak English, and one-third are not legal residents.[48]

AP continued:

In some ways, the teenager behind the wheel on this night breaks the profile because he speaks clear English and has roots in town. He isn't a citizen, but he does carry a green card. Encounters like this aren't unique to Gervais or other small towns. In July, police stopped a young couple in a Keizer parking lot and cited them for reckless child endangerment. They recently had arrived from Mexico and later told a state caseworker that they didn't know they weren't allowed to let children ride in the trunk of their car. Locals, including some Latinos, acknowledge that language barriers and a lack of understanding of Oregon laws contribute to a high rate of traffic violations, particularly among Mexican immigrants.[49]

Columnist Tom DeWeese says President Vicente Fox is using tactics similar to those used in the past by Cuban dictator Fidel Castro, merely to export his own criminal element: "In 1978, Castro purged his prisons of murderers, thieves and drug dealers and put them in an armada of boats headed for America's shore. The resulting crime wave flooded jails, overworked police and community budgets [and] made living in Miami,

Florida, almost unbearable for a time, and still inflicts the community's culture. Much the same is now happening in Mexican border states, as crime rises and quality of life diminishes. . . ."[50]

Among immigration reform activists there is increasing alarm that the ultimate cross-border "crime" could eventually take the shape of a terrorist attack, though some analysts say 9-11 should have led the government to crack down for good on the border sieve. "If Sept. 11 doesn't cause us to finally get serious about plugging our porous borders, nothing will," writes syndicated columnist and author Don Feder.[51] But it didn't. And judging by all current indications, the government won't be cracking down anytime soon. As long as Washington remains aloof, crime on the border will continue to proliferate and, many fear, grow worse.

4

IT'S THE ECONOMY, STUPID

In the American Southwest, where I happen to live, only sixty miles north of the Mexican border, the subject of illegal aliens is a touchy one—almost untouchable. Even the terminology is dangerous: the old word wetback *is now considered a racist insult by all good liberals; and the perfectly correct terms* illegal alien *and* illegal immigrant *can set off charges of xenophobia, elitism, fascism, and the ever-popular genocide against anyone careless enough to use them. The only acceptable euphemism, it now appears, is something called* undocumented worker.

—EDWARD ABBEY, AUTHOR AND COMMENTATOR

Each day during the school year scores of Mexican children bearing backpacks and textbooks trek back and forth at ports of entry into the U.S. to be educated in American public schools, all of which is subsidized by American taxpayers. Monthly, Mexican nationals using American addresses drive their well-outfitted SUVs into U.S. Post Offices to collect welfare benefits and other entitlements, which are also financed by American taxpayers. Also daily, Mexican ambulance crews transport uninsured south-of-the-border citizens to American hospitals because they know laws here forbid U.S. medical providers from turning them away—and because Mexican hospital administrators instruct them to take the uninsured north for treatment.

Meanwhile, some U.S. and Mexican politicians are plotting to merge both nations' social security systems, even as the economic impact of immigration—legal and otherwise—is dooming budgets in a number of states.[1] Add to this mix a high (and climbing) unemployment rate in the U.S., including the loss of thousands of jobs that are being filled by illegal aliens, and in many ways American taxpayers are finding they are supporting not one country but two.

Immigration—legal and otherwise—is not a zero-sum game. In fact, it costs taxpayers on a local, state and federal level *billions* of extra dollars per year in terms of services, welfare, medical care, education, crime prevention, incarceration and other things. According to a study by the Federation for American Immigration Reform (FAIR), a Washington, D.C.-based group that supports a reduction of legal migration, the cost of the inflow is enormous. "[W]e are admitting over one million mostly poor people into our society every year—a society that is already challenged to deal with the poverty of its natives," says FAIR.[2]

Based on Census Bureau data, FAIR says the costs of immigration—legal and otherwise—was $61 billion in 2000 alone. But before a chorus of immigrant rights activists counter that "even illegal immigrants pay taxes," this mammoth figure represents costs *after* immigrants' tax contributions are factored in. Indeed, *legal* immigrants are more expensive; they account for $35 billion of that figure. And these repetitive costs come from many sources—which grow more expensive every year as inflation rises (partly because American systems and programs are being abused by illegal aliens; it's a vicious circle, to some extent). "As high as the cost is now, the rising tide of immigration will lift it even higher in years to come. By the end of 2002, the annual net cost of immigration will have risen to $66 billion," says research quoted by FAIR.[3]

A separate study by Dr. Donald Huddle, Professor Emeritus of Economics at Rice University, found that immigrants cost American taxpayers $69 billion in 1997 alone, over and above the taxes they paid.[4]

For example, said Huddle's study, 1996 figures of total immigrant receipts of means-tested welfare benefits came to $180 billion, though "the real costs are probably even higher than these estimates, which do not take into account the effects of immigration in displacing American workers from their jobs and depressing wages." (A separate study showed that for every hundred illegal aliens who find jobs in the U.S. sixty-five American workers are displaced[5]). Other analysts have predicted that between 1997 and 2006, the projected total net cost to taxpayers for immigration will be $865.98 billion.[6]

And analysts say poverty-stricken immigrants will continue to be the norm. "Immigrants arriving in the past decade or so are earning less compared to native-born Americans than immigrants who arrived in earlier decades," said a 1995 National Bureau of Economic Research study, "Immigration and the Welfare State."[7]

Here are more statistics, based on 1996 estimates:

- The cost of educating legal and illegal immigrants, aged K-12, in the nation's public schools is more than $20 billion; most of this burden is borne by states bordering Mexico (one of which is California, which is teetering on economic meltdown).

- "ESL," or English as a second language, and bilingual education alone cost more than $4 billion.

- Immigrants collect more than $26 billion in Social Security benefits annually.

- The nation spends greater than $15 billion a year on immigrant-related Medicaid expenditures.

- Immigration costs local governments $20-21 billion annually.

- Nearly $7 billion is spent on immigrants annually in the form of Aid for Dependent Children (ADC) and food stamps.[8]

In all, while immigrants pay around $95 billion in taxes, they consume about $156 billion in public services. That's a net cost of around $61 billion. Economically speaking, America derives no benefit by continuing its "open borders" policy.

"Illegal immigration is about much more than fighting terrorism. The fact is, illegal Mexicans are pouring across our borders, and, as a result, American tax-paid services like education and healthcare are being pushed to the brink of collapse," says columnist Tom DeWeese. "It is an incomprehensible arrogance exercised by both Mexican and American officials who, while promoting illegal immigration, see no problem in letting U.S. taxpayers foot the bill."[9]

One study by Harvard economics Professor George J. Borjas shows immigrants to the U.S. continue to use public welfare more than native-born Americans, despite federal immigration laws that prohibit residency for aliens likely to become "a public charge." He also found that six years after a Republican-controlled Congress passed major welfare reform in 1996, the number of people on welfare has only declined slightly and is, indeed, again on the rise. "I would not be surprised if we saw after a few years that [welfare reform] had very little long-term effect," said Borjas. He found that the number of native households receiving welfare assistance declined from 15.6 percent in 1994 to 13.5 percent in 1998, but grew to 13.7 percent in 2000. At the same time, reliance on welfare by foreigners in the U.S. declined from 23.4 percent to 20 percent in 1998, but rose to 21 percent in 2000, the last year studied.[10]

Borjas believes the results show that immigration reform is needed, especially on a national level. "If we are concerned about immigrant welfare use, it would probably make sense to select immigrants who don't need welfare in the first place, rather than trying to prevent immigrants from using it after they have already been allowed into the country," he said. "We could do this by selecting immigrants based more on their education levels rather than the current system, which for the most part admits immigrants based on whether they have a relative in the U.S."

As local and state governments fight to find ways to trim services because of, in part, extra immigrant-driven costs, American citizens will continue to suffer because few of the same people seeking the budget cuts want to do much to trim immigration (in a case of bitter irony, states bear most of the costs of illegal immigration while most of the taxes paid by illegals go into the federal treasury). And most of the financial brunt of immigration is borne by the border states. In 1994 in California—where, in 2003 the state found itself in the red some $25 billion to $35 billion, depending on estimates—then-Gov. Pete Wilson said the state spent $2.3 billion in unreimbursed costs, to provide federally mandated services to illegal immigrants: $300 million for health-care, $1.7 billion for education, and $377 million for corrections.[11] That estimate had risen to $3 billion by 2002.[12]

One study co-authored by New Mexico State University government professor Nadia Rubaii-Barrett found that the cost per capita of illegal immigration to residents of New Mexico counties bordering Mexico was $23.45, while in Texas the per capita cost was $12; in Arizona it was $22; and in California it was $19. "The burden is falling on the poorest counties, which can least afford it. They either have to cut services or raise taxes to cover the costs of what we think is a federal government responsibility," said Rubaii-Barrett.[13]

"The citizens of the four border states pay a disproportionate share of [immigration] costs," wrote U.S. Senator Jon Kyl (R-Arizona), in a January 11, 2002, column to constituents. Quoting columnist and author Michelle Malkin, Kyl said, "while public funds are being used to provide care to illegal aliens, 'indigent senior citizens—American citizens—must abide by stricter limits, fewer choices, and rising prices . . . under their government health-care coverage'. . . .We are a generous people, but more and more my constituents are saying this is unfair." Kyl, along with fellow Arizona Republican Sen. John McCain, says they are working to provide more federal funding to border states to alleviate budget crunches associated with handling illegal immigrants.

"Even though illegal aliens make little use of welfare [as we've shown, legal migrants make plenty use of it also], from which they are generally barred, the costs of illegal immigration in terms of government expenditures for education, criminal justice, and emergency medical care are significant," says a cost analysis published by the Center for Immigration Studies. "The fact that states must bear the cost of federal failure turns illegal immigration, in effect, into one of the largest unfunded federal mandates."[14]

———————

Many public hospitals in the United States, especially in the Southwest, are facing major financial difficulties because of the services that they are rendering to indigent alien patients. Some have closed; others are threatening to do so. By the spring of 2003, lawmakers said seventy-seven hospitals along the border were facing a crisis. In September 2002, the U.S.-Mexico Border Counties Coalition found U.S. border hospitals spent close to $190 million in 2000 to provide health-care to illegals. The study calculated the losses at $79 million in California, $74 million in Texas, $31 million in Arizona and $6 million in New Mexico. It also said that emergency service providers incurred another $13 million in uncompensated costs.[15]

FAIR says that, according to its estimates, illegal aliens soak up $3.7 billion annually in Medicare and Medicaid benefits. "It's an enormous cost and can be very crippling, especially in border states," says David Ray, a spokesman for the group, regarding the cost of those benefits. "The federal government is the one that's dropping the ball in allowing poor immigration enforcement to [negatively affect] the states' pocketbooks."[16]

"The simple fact is, our border hospitals are struggling to remain in business because they can no longer afford to absorb the cost of providing medical care to undocumented immigrants," says McCain. "As hospitals and emergency rooms close, citizens across the state and the nation will face higher health-care costs and reduced access to care. It is time the federal government took responsibility for this problem, before the crisis worsens."[17]

Kyl sounds the same note: "Unless we act now to reimburse states and local health-care providers for the cost of federally mandated care to illegal immigrants, more hospitals will be forced to cut costs and possibly close their doors."[18]

"I've been shouting from the rooftops for a long time about this problem, but to no avail," says U.S. Representative Jim Kolbe, also a Republican from

Arizona. "No one denies that there is a moral and legal obligation to provide care, but the question remains on who is responsible for paying the bill."[19]

Under federal law, hospitals and emergency medical personnel cannot turn away anyone seeking medical help. They also cannot inquire about income or immigration status.

Haley Nolde, a columnist for *Mother Jones* magazine, describes what has become a prevalent phenomenon in hospitals along the border: "On a blistering day in May [2000]," he writes, "U.S. Border Patrol agents in southern California's Imperial County found a man collapsed in the desert. The 39-year-old had successfully sneaked across the border from Mexico, only to succumb to heat stroke. The agents called an ambulance to take him to nearby El Centro Regional Medical Center, where he spent two days in intensive care and several more in recuperation. The agents didn't come back for him, so he left with relatives bound for Los Angeles—leaving the hospital with his unpaid bill for $26,890....."[20]

No one at hospital was surprised, the magazine said. That's because the facility was losing more than $1 million annually, since they are forced by federal law to treat illegal aliens. To add insult to financial injury, many of the illegals had to be treated because they were injured trying to sneak into the U.S. either by jumping from a twenty-foot border fence in Calexico, nearly drowning by trying to swim the All-American Canal or by dying of heat stroke or dehydration in the Imperial Valley Desert. A nearby hospital, Pioneers Memorial, lost a half-million dollars in 2002, to say nothing of unpaid ambulance and physicians' fees.[21]

Writes Nolde: "The two hospitals have to cover 150,000 people in a county that already has some of the highest unemployment and poverty rates in the country. 'We're struggling to treat needy people, and the cost is bearing down on people least able to afford it,' says Ted Fox, CEO of El Centro Regional."[22]

Besides the direct cost of providing medical care, there is another issue that is driving physicians and other health-care providers away from border areas: medical liability. According to an assessment by the Texas Medical Association (TMA), insurance companies are increasingly refusing to provide coverage for physicians who work in "high-risk" places. "The Texas-Mexico border region and most of South Texas are such high-risk areas," said the assessment.[23] Why are they high-risk? Because, the TMA found, 70 percent of border physicians have medical liability claims filed against them, while another 60 percent have been sued (in Texas, 85 percent of claims are settled with no indemnity). In all, one in three border doctors had insurance providers decide to stop writing liability coverage on them, while a whopping 94 percent say they had insurance premiums "increase dramatically" (some were doubled) since 1999. Because of these astounding facts, more and more physicians are leaving border areas for "safer" work environments. Those who remain have difficulty recruiting new doctors to replace those who leave. The losses are affecting the quality of care for legal and illegal residents alike.

The TMA assessment concludes that if the border-related liability crisis doesn't ease, fewer physicians will be available to treat patients, especially high-risk patients; hospitals will be unable to fill available beds and will eventually remove them, thereby reducing capacity; hospitals will have to cease providing certain kinds of services; new medical technologies will be unaffordable; severely injured trauma patients will require transport to other facilities, often hundreds of miles away; and nursing homes will be unable to provide care "because of the lack of physician involvement."[24]

Border medicine is in severe crisis, says the TMA assessment. "The future economic stability of the region as well as the health of its residents depends on the timely availability of medical attention. Physicians must be available to provide a broad range of medical services. This can only be accomplished if liability coverage is available and affordable."[25]

Writing for the *Houston Chronicle* May 5, 2002, James Pinkerton described the situation around Harlingen, Texas:

> It is a contradiction as stark as the contrast of gleaming office developments and dusty, dilapidated colonias that line the Texas-Mexico border. In a region of 2 million people where a rate of growth—in jobs and population—continues to outpace that of the nation, a pervasive lack of

health care has mortgaged the border's future with a profound and often deadly liability. Border residents fall ill and die from disease at rates significantly higher than those of not only the United States as a whole but also the rest of Texas. An appalling example is women in the lower Rio Grande Valley and other places along the border who are dying at twice the national rate of cervical cancer, even though the disease is curable if caught in time. And rates of tuberculosis and liver disease are twice as high on the border as in other parts of the state. . . . If that were not enough, the border region is a porous frontier where diseases more prevalent in the Third World are increasingly appearing. Outbreaks of mosquito-borne dengue fever, a plague of deadly birth defects, drug-resistant strains of tuberculosis, rabies, leprosy, high rates of children with hepatitis A, and even cholera are crowding the plates of border health workers.[26]

"We've had enough," says Dr. George Benavidez, a family practitioner from Corpus Christi. "[Americans] need to know if they don't support their physicians, when Grandmother or Grandfather has a burst appendix at 3 A.M. there won't be anybody to take care of them."[27]

Joe Guzzardi, a columnist for the immigration news and commentary Web site, Vdare.com, says after he published a column in mid-January 2003 entitled, "Illegal Aliens: The Health Cost Dimension," he received a number of e-mails from readers relating their similar experiences. One reader, he wrote, "mailed me that his insurance company was billed $60,000 for an appendectomy and, on a separate visit, $12,000 for outpatient treatment . . . a hospital administrator, when confronted with the exorbitant invoice, said, "We have to charge you guys with good insurance because these patients [nodding to a room full of pregnant Mexican girls] don't pay anything. . . ."[28]

Syndicated columnist Michelle Malkin, in her February 20, 2003, tome, highlighted the costs of providing organ transplants to illegal immigrants—as well as the impropriety of providing them to illegal immigrant recipients in the U.S. before American patients:

No one can deny that the plight of Jesica Santillan, the sick teenager who mistakenly received organs at Duke University from a donor with a different blood type, is a sad one. But we cannot ignore the tough public policy questions in Jesica's case that the sob-story writers at the *New York Times* prefer to paper over: When resources are scarce, as the supply of voluntarily donated organs notoriously are, why shouldn't U.S. citizens get top priority?[29]

Malkin writes that, based on national figures, sixteen patients in the U.S. die every day waiting on long organ donation lists. Righteously, she asks some tough questions in her column: "How many American patients currently on the national organ waiting list were denied access to healthy hearts and lungs as a result of Santillan's two transplant surgeries? Who will tell their stories?"[30]

She concludes: "In a world of scarce resources, compassion must have limits. We cannot afford to be a medical welcome mat to the world."[31]

Some analysts, experts and pundits have suggested creative ways for immigrants themselves to help finance part of their own upkeep. One such idea, floated by Brenda Walker, publisher of ImmigrationsHumanCost.org, suggested taxing immigrants to support border hospitals: "There is money available to help these hospitals in crisis. Taxing remittances 10 percent to 15 percent per transaction would be fair because the cost would fall on those who benefit. What's needed is congressional leadership that can recognize this opportunity and seize it. . . ."[32]

Some states are beginning to react to the influx of costs posed by immigrants. Democrats and immigration rights activists decried Republican Gov. Bill Owens of Colorado in March 2003 for signing legislation eliminating state-paid medical benefits for documented immigrants. And in the 108th Congress, some GOP lawmakers were proposing legislation to boost federal payments to states whose hospitals were being hit the hardest economically for having to treat illegal immigrants.

In South Florida alone, more than 1,500 new students have come to the area's schools from Colombia. Almost 2,000 have come from Mexico and more than 5,000 from Haiti. Hundreds more have come from troubled Venezuela, say local officials.[33] South Florida schools are "used to such influxes," said one report. But those schools aren't alone; immigrants— legal and illegal—are flooding American schools with their children. All the while many of these immigrant families live on state– and federal-sponsored welfare and aid programs. And as it did with medical care, the Supreme Court ruled in 1982 that states cannot refuse to educate the children of illegal immigrants through the 12th grade—though some state education officials would like to end that.[34]

Since 1996, federal education spending has increased 118 percent,[35] and as mentioned, much of that increase has been caused by immigration. Best estimates say it costs taxpayers more than $20 billion annually just to provide public education benefits to legal and illegal immigrants. Add to that the cost of so-called BLE—bilingual education—courses, and the cost is more than $23 billion on the federal level alone[36] (one study suggested providing bilingual education doubles the cost of educating non-English speaking children[37]). But the costs—which climb every year (and have climbed 5.6 percent in fiscal year 2004 alone[38])—are not likely to disappear anytime soon because the Supreme Court has ruled that the nation's public schools are required to educate every child who shows up for class, regardless of their immigration status.

"I would be a bald-faced liar if I told you that 100 percent of the children enrolled in the district's schools are legal residents," said Lowell Billings, assistant superintendent of the Chula Vista, California, Elementary School District in September 2002. "But we are not the INS. Our job is education and we are focused on teaching and learning."[39] His predominantly Hispanic school district, located just three miles north of the U.S.-Mexico border, has built six schools since 1998 and is adding six hundred to eight hundred students a year.[40] Studies put the cost of educating California's 1.5-plus million "English Language Learners" at around $10 billion annually.[41]

"It is amazing that America is willing to provide free medical treatment to people who are not citizens—and even illegal aliens—while the home countries of most all of those people will not do so," writes Matt Hayes, an author and former immigration lawyer. "This occurs while our schools lack adequate money and while many of America's senior citizens scrape to pay for medicine. If you think that the problem is minor, or under control, you should think again. America is in the throws of a historically unprecedented wave of immigration, both legal and illegal, and the costs are mounting. . . . All of this takes place in the face of a federal statute that makes it a felony to facilitate an illegal alien's remaining in the United States in violation of the law."[42]

There is also some danger with providing a secondary education to immigrants from some countries. Research shows, for example, that 1,215 people from countries listed by the U.S. State Department as sponsors of terrorism—Iraq, Cuba, Iran, Libya, North Korea, Sudan and Syria—received science and engineering doctorates in the United States in the 1990s. That number includes 147 doctorates in subjects related to weapons of mass destruction, such as nuclear and organic chemistry and biotechnology research.[43]

Some education costs even border on the absurd. Because U.S. schools must "educate" all children, regardless of immigration status, that means they must also educate—or try to educate—the children of illegal immigrants from Mexico, even though most illegal immigrant children don't speak English. What a nightmare that is for teacher and school administrator alike, as well as immigrant children.

"Schools are suffering the same fate as medical care as illegal aliens fill classrooms, bloat budgets, and rob taxpayers of decent facilities for American children," says Tom DeWeese. "Moreover, state run colleges and universities are being forced to allow illegal aliens to receive in-state tuition discounts that are supposed to be reserved for residents of that state."[44]

To wit: In Texas, legislators have passed a law allowing illegal immigrants to pay lower in-state tuition rates when attending colleges or universities; a handful of other states do the same.[45] "Those who advocate the tuition breaks for illegals contend the policy encourages education among children of undocumented workers and ultimately could lead them to become natural-ized citizens," says an analysis by the National Center for Policy Analysis, a non-partisan public policy research organization. "But opponents argue that illegal immigrants have no right to be in the U.S. in the first place and shouldn't expect taxpayers to fund their college educations."[46]

The problem unfortunately feeds on itself, for the simple reason that you get more of what you subsidize—something former House Speaker Newt Gingrich told the American School Board Journal in 1996: "I think there's no question that offering free, tax-paid goods to illegals has increased the number of illegals."[47] Free education for illegals means more illegals showing up to collect.

As with everything else, the cost of jailing illegal immigrants is also on the rise. And at a time when states are feeling their own budget crunches, the federal government is dramatically reducing the amount of money it pays states to incarcerate illegal immigrants suspected of committing crimes, though Washington isn't doing much more to stem the flow of illegals. States say the federal government only covered about one-third of the $1.5 billion it costs to incarcerate illegal aliens in 2002.[48]

It gets worse: In fiscal year 2003, Congress approved President Bush's budget request of just $250 million for the State Criminal Alien Assistance Program (SCAAP), a Justice Department program begun in 1994 that reimburses states for the cost of jailing immigrants. The quarter of a bil-lion-dollar figure is down from $550 million the previous year. Worse, the White House's fiscal year 2004 budget, bloated with red ink already, included *no funding* at all for the program, leaving states to foot the entire cost of jailing illegals suspected of committing crimes. Bush administra-tion officials said the program is not directly related to fighting crime and "doesn't advance the core mission of the Justice Department."[49]

"I find that very ironic, because when he was governor of Texas he was screaming very loudly about SCAAP funds," said Stephen Green, assistant secretary of the California Youth and Adult Corrections Agency.[50] Indeed, said then-Governor Bush in 1995, "if the federal government cannot do its job of enforcing the borders . . . then it owes the states monies to pay for its failures."[51]

As usual, the border states will be hit the hardest by scrapping the reimbursement program. The reduction in funding is "going to hurt the border counties tremendously," said Dian Copelin, Washington representative for the U.S.-Mexican Border Counties Coalition.[52] "Looking at the big picture, Congress should realize that they are, in essence, penalizing the border states that have the largest illegal immigrant populations and cannot afford to house these inmates on local tax dollars," noted Roger Wade, a spokesman for the Travis County, Texas, sheriff's department.[53]

The administration's decision comes "at a terrible time for the states," added Kris Mayes, a spokeswoman for Arizona Gov. Janet Napolitano. In 1995, ten states sought funding under SCAAP; by 2002, that figure had climbed to forty.[54]

Whereas illegals may save the American people some money here and there, the costs of caring for, educating and incarcerating them are astronomical. For example, federal spending on border security in fiscal year 2003 was $10.7 billion, up from $8.6 billion the previous year, as funding for "homeland defense," which includes money to strengthen the borders, doubled from $19.5 billion in fiscal year 2002 to $37.7 billion the next year.[55]

Also, most illegal immigrants (and some legal immigrants) don't have driver's licenses and, hence, auto insurance. So when they get into accidents, the insured driver must bear the costs. There are a number of examples.

- Saul Diaz was a penniless, unemployed, uninsured illegal alien living in Georgia when he was severely injured in a car accident, racking up a $1 million bill during his yearlong hospital stay. He eventually died, leaving the hospital—and the auto insurance company—with the bill.[56]

- A Martin County, Florida, hospital spent nearly a million dollars caring for a Guatemalan illegal who appeared at the emergency room two years ago with a brain injury after an automobile accident (the patient had no job and no money, but apparently had the means to hire a lawyer, who prevented his deportation to Guatemala).[57]

- A pair of Tucson, Arizona, hospitals were stuck with the cost of treating a half-dozen illegal aliens who were injured when their car crashed at one hundred miles an hour.[58]

- San Diego hospitals had to face the burden of caring for thirty-one accident victims (not including the seven who were killed) from a van crash that was carrying illegals from Mexico and Brazil, while going the wrong way on an interstate at night with its headlights off.[59]

Indeed, "some aliens look upon an automobile accident as their entry ticket into the United States," writes syndicated columnist Phyllis Schlafly. They get treated at an American hospital and then may be released into no one's custody. No one has any figures on these numbers."[60]

"The world must realize that, while we gladly accept its tired, poor and huddled masses, we also have rules that govern their entrance," said Rep. Mark Foley (R-Florida) in a letter to U.S. Comptroller General David Walker of the General Accounting Office in July 2002.[61]

Then there is the cost to landowners, farmers and ranchers, who must pay to repeatedly fix fences, replace stolen items, buy cattle and livestock that have been stolen or poached and rebuild farming and ranching infrastructure. Illegal immigrants not only destroy private property by trampling and trashing it, they also "destroy" it, in a way, by reducing its value and making property hard (or impossible) to sell.

Finally, there is the cost of lost wages and jobs—a figure that may be difficult to calculate accurately. According to FAIR, "between 40 and 50 percent of wage-loss among low-skilled Americans is due to the immigration of low-skilled workers. Some native workers lose not just wages but their jobs through immigrant competition. An estimated 1,880,000 American workers are displaced from their jobs every year by immigration; the cost for providing welfare and assistance to these Americans is over $15 billion a year." Indeed, according to the Pew Hispanic Center in Washington DC, one of Mexico's largest revenue streams is money sent home every year by legal immigrants and illegal aliens working in the U.S.—a record $10 billion in 2002.

Tons of trash litter the U.S. southwest, left behind by millions of illegals. The cost to clean it up is staggering

According to the National Academy of Sciences, the net fiscal drain on American taxpayers, due to legal and illegal immigration, is between $166 and $226 a year per native household.[62] When taken in total, FAIR says the costs being incurred by taxpayers is out of hand: "Americans should demand that Congress reduce the immigrant flow and alter the criteria for admission to ameliorate the cost of immigration to our society. . . . Immigration creates an enormous fiscal burden on America and its citizens—a burden that Congress has levied upon us through short-sighted and haphazard immigration policy," the group says.[63]

In 2002, the Drug Enforcement Administration's budget was $65.2 million and the agency had a staff of 2,775 [1,470 were Special Agents]. By 2003 those figures had grown; the agency had a budget of more than $1.87 billion and employed 9,629 people [4,680 were Special Agents].[64] "The Southwest border has become the focal point of drug trafficking into the United States. The 2,000-mile Southwest border provides many opportunities for criminals to smuggle the majority of the cocaine, methamphetamine and marijuana into the United States, and facilitate crimes such as alien smuggling and other illegal activities," said Harold D. Wankel, then-chief of DEA operations, in testimony to the House Judiciary Committee July 31, 1996. He was arguing for an increase in the DEA's drug interdiction budget by asking the committee to authorize money to hire fifty-four more agents. "Today's well-financed and sophisticated international narcotics traffickers are a new breed of organized crime. Most Americans do not view drug traffickers as organized crime figures, because most Americans do not have an insight into the day-to-day operations of these ruthless drug organizations and do not see how wealthy, influential and well organized these organizations are."[65]

By 2001, not much had changed. Then–DEA administrator Donnie R. Marshall testified before the House Judiciary Committee's subcommittee on crime that the U.S. border with Mexico continues to be the preferred corridor for drug traffickers to smuggle cocaine, heroin, methamphetamines and marijuana into the United States. In his March 29 testimony, Marshall said the problem highlights the "vulnerability of the U.S.-Mexico border to Colombian- and Mexican-based trafficking organizations intent on introducing drugs into the U.S. market." He testified that the DEA had recently "approved the placement of fourteen supervisory Intelligence Analyst positions" in support of an anti-drug smuggling program along the U.S.-Mexico border.

How much cheaper would American tax rolls be—on the local, state and federal level—were they not footing the bill for hordes of undocumented migrants and cleaning up the drug-related messes created by massive Mexico-based smuggling? Yet in early February 2003, Federal Reserve

Chairman Alan Greenspan, in an economic report to Congress, advocated just the opposite approach in explaining how the administration can reduce its deficits: "Short of a major increase in immigration, economic growth cannot be safely counted upon to eliminate deficits and the difficult choices that will be required to restore fiscal discipline."[66]

Adding costs will *trim* deficits? Only in Washington is this called sound policy.

"*Nothing is ever enough,*" writes Vdare.com's Guzzardi, of illegal immigrants. "Illegal aliens and their advocates are always pushing; always demanding; always nagging; always editorializing; always whining; always hectoring; always cajoling. . . . American public officials always give in. And American taxpayers end up subsidizing their own dispossession."[67]

Said Paul Craig Roberts, economist and syndicated columnist, on February 14, 2003: "Recently, I asked if the United States would be a Third World country in 20 years. Many e-mails arrived from Americans saying that their communities had already been reduced to Third World status by the loss of jobs and the arrival of Third World refugees and immigrants. They said I was optimistic to believe that the United States had 20 years left as a superpower."[68]

"I live in Texas and the illegal alien problem is growing," one resident told me, in an e-mail following one of my WorldNetDaily.com op-ed columns on illegal immigration. "People are tired of the growing numbers in our state. Our government is ignoring the wishes of the majority of Americans. I don't have health insurance, but my tax dollars are giving free medical care to people who are breaking the law. So they get medical care and I don't."

"We are also sick of having such high school-taxes," says another border citizen. "We are spending a fortune teaching those who pay no taxes and are illegal and providing Spanish-speaking workers in the school system. The only difference between California and Texas is that in Texas they are quieter and more subtle in what they are doing."

Says one analysis by the International Union for the Scientific Study of Population: "Business interests however are short-term. Easy immediate access to labor will always be preferred to the costs of training and capital investment for the longer term. In the nature of economic cycles, yesterday's essential labor can often become, as the defunct factories and mills of Europe have shown, today's unemployed."[69]

The analysis goes on to say U.S. employers who required an ample supply of immigrant labor "are not held to account" for the end result of more domestic unemployed workers, nor are they required to cover the costs of their unemployed former employees. The analysis points out that workers migrating to the U.S. from another country are perpetually temporary, and it says if companies were made to tend the lifetime costs of their migrant labor force the way they must be responsible for the environmental costs of their products, they would likely demonstrate less enthusiasm for migrant labor and invest more in long-term employees.[70]

When it was passed by the U.S. Congress in 1994, the North American Free Trade Agreement (NAFTA), a trade pact between the United States, Canada and Mexico, was touted as the best way to lift Mexico from its centuries of poverty. But experts say when the math is done—and done correctly—NAFTA hasn't been the boon to workers in Mexico or the United States. In 1993, the year before NAFTA's passage, the U.S. ran a $1.7 billion trade surplus with Mexico; three years later, America had a trade *deficit* with its southern neighbor of $16 billion. By the first half of 2002, America's trade deficit with both Canada and Mexico soared to $83.2 billion.[71] Yet, American and Mexican politicians, media, and cultural elite, pushed for the passage of the agreement, promising huge economic growth on both sides of the Rio Grande.

One of the most famous of those predictions came from Gary Hufbauer of the Institute for International Economics, a free-trade think tank. Hufbauer boldly claimed that "NAFTA will generate a $7 billion to $9 billion surplus [for the U.S.] that would ensure the net creation of 170,000 jobs in the U.S. economy in the first year." On October

26, 1995, however, the *Wall Street Journal* reported that "Hufbauer . . . whose predictions of NAFTA job gains were embraced by the Clinton and Bush White Houses, now figures the surging trade deficit with Mexico has cost the U.S. 225,000 jobs."[72] The job loss has been especially hard along the border.

Says William R. Hawkins, a senior fellow at the U.S. Business and Industry Council in Washington and a former economics professor:

> Most of the debate about NAFTA has focused on the direct loss of American jobs as Mexican laborers earning less than $2 an hour replace American workers making five or six times as much, plus health and pension benefits. Though there are specific trade disputes with Canada, the United States' NAFTA partnership to the north does not receive the same kind of fundamental criticism. Income and living conditions are similar in Canada, which puts trade on a more level playing field.[73]

J. Zane Walley, a land-rights activist, also believes NAFTA has had a net negative effect on citizens of Mexico and the United States. "My view is that illegal immigration will unavoidably increase in following years unless international Agribusiness and the Mexican Government are made to be financially accountable for their actions," he told me in an interview. By that, he means, the Mexican government has forced a number of its own people off their land—land they were using to make their living— and hence displacing them from their homes. It makes sense; NAFTA, among other things, was supposed to bring enough prosperity to Mexico to make it economically feasible for Mexican nationals to stay there and earn a living, rather than trekking north to the United States. If anything, illegal immigration—and the problems associated with it—has only increased since 1994.

Walley says the Mexican government, not the American taxpayer, is responsible for providing its people with the tools and financial assistance to earn a living and become productive members of their own society. For one thing, he says, Mexico City could "use the massive profits of international agribusiness to fund a re-education system to the displaced so they are not forced across the border."

He told me, "I was in Yucatan and Chiapas (the Lacandon Jungle) in May 1994, during the je'rcito Zapatista de Liberacio'n Nacional revolution (Zapatista National Liberation Army) led by Subcomandante Marcos against the Mexican government, which was pushing the mestizo and indigenous peoples from their [homes] in the interest of corporate agribusiness. The government tried to paint the insurgents as Maoists or Trotskyites but I personally set around cooking fires with them and found them to be just simple farmers and ranchers trying to hold on to their tiny [piece of land]. They were unarmed masses with broad mobilizations attempting to create a crisis and get media attention focused on their plight. They were ignored or painted as some sort of communist guerillas by U.S. reporters who never set foot in one of their camps but rather did all their reporting from offices in Mexico City. Of course, all they did was cite government sources and use photos and footage provided by the Mexican army. The Zapatista only resorted to force of arms (and that was very small) after the Mexican army began rounding up and killing entire villages (such as Guadalupe Tepeyac) and burying them in mass graves. Additionally, the army was doing . . . things . . . to the men that made it very hard for them to reproduce. It got somewhat hairy with the Mexican authorities, so minus my camera, film and notes, I had to travel quietly to north of Mexico and come back into the U.S. at Ciudad Acuña, across the river from Del Rio, Texas. Since I was a witness to this, my personal view on immigration is much different than that of the average person who tries to deduce what is going on through very filtered media sources. These people are not coming to America because they want to . . . and they are not being stopped at the border (as any Border Patrolman will tell you), because of skewed politics, destructive treaties and deeply entrenched economic special interests."

Indeed, even Mexican nationals believe NAFTA has been bad for them and their country.

"Organized farmers [in Mexico City] are using every tactic they can think of—violent protests, hunger strikes and catcalls—to show Mexican President Vicente Fox that NAFTA is killing their way of life and driving many of them across the U.S.-Mexican border to earn a living," said Tessie Borden, a reporter for the *Arizona Republic*'s Mexico City Bureau.[74] "Mexican farmers, who make up 18 percent of the population but 30 percent of those in dire poverty, have been protesting since [December 2002]. They defied police and broke into congressional chambers Dec. 10, one of them on horseback and carrying a Mexican flag, breaking windows and causing lawmakers to run for cover. A threatened blockade of the border on Jan. 1 was averted only when Fox agreed to talks. . . . The farmers say they can't compete with cheap pork, corn, milk and other products from government-subsidized and highly mechanized U.S. farmers. More and more are being forced to rent or sell their land to corporations, then head to the United States, illegally crossing into Arizona, California and Texas in search of jobs. . . ."

The Chicago Tribune reported January 10, 2003: "All the Mexican countryside . . . worries have turned into threats of violence over the January 1 lifting of tariffs on the import of agricultural products between the United States and Mexico in the second phase of the nine-year-old North American Free Trade Agreement. . . . Farmers have threatened to block U.S.-Mexico border crossings; some stormed the chambers of Mexico's Congress on horseback last month. They are demanding that their government renegotiate the accord or provide compensation for what is expected to be a flood of U.S. pork, chicken and other farm products across the border. While Mexican officials say NAFTA has helped their country overall, rural Mexicans remained at a strict disadvantage. Mexico's admitted failure to make expected advances to level the playing field with the U.S. and Canada is part of the problem. . . ."[75]

On the surface, it would seem as though NAFTA has been worse for the United States; according to the federal government's 2002 trade figures, the U.S. ran a trade deficit with Mexico of $37.2 billion (America's other NAFTA partner, Canada, had a trade surplus with the U.S. of even more—$49.8 billion). With all the money pouring into Mexico, why, then, is illegal immigration to the U.S. at an all-time high?

Americans living abroad in Mexico also have some dire news for immigration reformists, ordinary Americans living on the border and—if they're listening—American politicians: Without major economic reform in Mexico, illegal immigration isn't going away. Ever.

"The US and Mexico sooner or later have to get a grip on a very awkward fact—Mexico does not have the educational and economic base to move into the 'first world,' and as long as it doesn't, immigration, legal, illegal, to the U.S. will be uncontrollable, and many of the migrants will want to import wonderful old Mexico into the U.S.," one American who visits often with friends living in ranches south of the border, told me in an e-mail interview.

"This is complicated by the element that thinks the whole Southwest U.S.A. *is* Mexico and that we stole it and should give it back," the source, who requested anonymity, said. He added:

> But deeply, structurally entrenched Mexican machismo will not allow the U.S. to help solve the problem—which would require large scale "Americanization" of Mexico by permitting Americans to own land and businesses without restrictions, which would bring in capital, create jobs, job training, boost Mexican income and educational levels, etc. . . . But they can't stomach anything that "loses face," or infringes on their sense of machismo, pride, since they insist on perceiving Mexican culture and history, for all its obvious problems, as the most glorious culture and history in the universe . . . while at the same time fleeing Mexico to find work.
>
> In order to sustain their mythic machismo, they will not permit the Americanization of Mexico, which would lift all the boats, surely, if not quickly; but they—at least a large political faction—will fight for the Mexicanization of America. . . . What has to happen—and what they can't face, at least not yet—is that there has to be a real quid pro quo. If the U.S. is going to accept millions and millions of Mexican immigrants,

Mexico is going to have to accept, eventually, millions of Americans and their dollars and investments and businesses, taking advantage of cheap land and cheap labor until the economic disparity is reduced, perhaps, in a century or two, eliminated, and Mexico moved into the "first world" economy. There has to be parity. There ain't no cheap and easy solutions here, and the problem is likely to get a lot worse before it gets a lot better.

He went on to observe that much about what truly defines the U.S. and Mexico is culture, not necessarily money:

At least in the parts of Mexico I'm familiar with, it isn't hard to find people living very simply at what we would consider a poverty level, near-subsistence standard, who appear to be happier, more content, than a lot of driven, neurotic, success obsessed Americans with six or seven figure incomes and six or seven figure mortgages. . . . Mexicans like money as much as anyone, but most see it as secondary to their family and cultural identity. . . . [T]hey want to provide a comfortable living for their family, certainly, but they tend to be far less defined by their jobs, their income, and their possessions, than many Americans are, and this is something a lot of Americans don't have an inkling of. . . . As long as America is more prosperous, Mexicans will come here, some to live, some to work and go home again, any way they can. But they will also be very jealous of the cultural integrity of Mexico, and they do not want it to turn into a wasteland of Wal-Marts and McDonalds. . . . [T]here is nothing simple about this equation . . . and I don't think anyone now living will live to see any kind of real resolution.

Besides the obvious monetary costs, there is also a quality of life cost, which cannot be measured. Citizens living along the border are being driven to vexation over the nation's unlimited immigration policies. Many communities complain of lower standards of living, higher crime, lower property values and a decrease in growth because they have been overrun by poor, uneducated migrants from a number of third world countries (mostly Mexico). That hurts some feelings, and these Americans who must endure this never-ending tide of humanity understand that. But, they say, that doesn't take away from the fact that uncontrolled immigration is strangling their lives, killing their towns, destroying their own hopes and dreams and—all too often—driving them away. Of course, there are those factors south of the border—in Mexico especially—that rejoice when Hispanics replace Whites in American communities close to the border.

"Immigration is a net drain on the economy; corporate interests reap the benefits of cheap labor, while taxpayers pay the infrastructural cost," says an analysis by the Colorado Alliance for Immigration Reform.[76]

If there is a reason why immigration—legal and otherwise—must be curbed, perhaps the economics of it will spur Americans to action. Endangering our nation's economy is every bit a threat as imminent and dangerous as all others. And if Mexicans are jealous of their culture and heritage, Americans are doubly jealous of their bank accounts.

ONE TOKE OVER THE LINE

You might not think much about seeing Mexican men carrying backpacks and walking along a well-traveled dirt road just over the border from Arizona. To the average person, it might seem like little more than an outing in the desert. A chance to get out and see the vast expanses of Mexican countryside. A time to "get away from it all" and enjoy the serenity of the great outdoors. If that's what you think, you're thinking like an American, and one from a state hundreds of miles from the U.S.-Mexico border. You don't simply "walk the desert" like it's some Midwestern nature trail. Also, this is Mexico we're talking about, not the United States. South of our border, few people have time for activities that are much more common in a society accustomed to leisure, like ours.

Besides being an arid, hot and notoriously dry climate, the desert in the American southwest and Mexican north-northeast is vast. One can look in all directions for miles and never see a house, a paved highway or a town. It's also a very hostile environment—certainly not one that invites casual adventurism or one that welcomes the power-walking sportsman. So when a pair of Mexican men carrying backpacks is spotted walking a desolate dirt road in the middle of a desert hell, it raises legitimate questions to the trained observer, especially when the backpack-carrying men are en route to a known drug- and human-smuggling jump-off site, and they are walking along a road that is literally just a few feet from the border.

Most Americans who don't live in such environments wouldn't know that drug smugglers south of the border routinely employ peasant "mules" to backpack their cargo into the United States. They don't know that in poverty-stricken countries run by men corrupted by drug money who are managing a bankrupt political system, a guy has to do *something* to make a living—and muling drugs is a decent living south of the border. They don't know that this is why drug trafficking all along the border is worsening, why it shows little sign of abating anytime soon and why it seems to be one of the most sought after jobs in a nation that is otherwise lacking other lucrative (and legal) employment opportunities.

While smuggling drugs is a lot more profitable than picking produce, working the fields or toiling away in a factory for $300 a month, it's also much more dangerous. If the desert doesn't get you, the drug cartels might; if they don't, rival drug gangs might; if not them, you might have renegade elements of the Mexican military to fend off. And if you make it across the border alive you'll have American federal law enforcement officials to contend with. Finally, more Americans living on the border are arming themselves and fighting back. Despite these odds, however, based on the statistics these are all risks increasing numbers of Mexicans are willing to take.

The Federation of American Immigration Reform (FAIR) estimates that 80 percent of the cocaine and 50 percent of the heroin smuggled into the

U.S. annually comes from Mexico. The *Washington Times* reports drug cartels spend a half-billion dollars per year bribing Mexico's corrupt generals and police officials, and armed confrontations between the Mexican army and U.S. Border Patrol agents are a real threat.[1] There have been 118 documented incursions by the Mexican military over the last five years [1997-2002].[2]

A pair of Mexican nationals tote backpacks along a border road in Mexico, just yards from the U.S. border. Mexican "mules" use the backpacks to smuggle drugs or carry supplies if they plan to sneak into the U.S.

Not every foot of border is a drug-smuggling alley. Certain sectors are more active for drug and human smuggling than others for a variety of reasons—proximity of resources in Mexico; absence of U.S. law enforcement and surveillance; remoteness; ease of entry into the U.S., to name a few. For instance, from January 1 to January 13, 2003, Tucson Sector Border Patrol agents detained smugglers with 22,498 pounds of marijuana; for the first thirteen days of 2002, the total amount was 12,035 pounds.[3] In the first half of January 2003, 7,951 pounds of marijuana were confiscated in Cochise County, Arizona, with agents from the Douglas Station seizing 6,146 pounds, Naco Station, 1,623 pounds and Willcox Station, 182 pounds, according to Border Patrol officials. Last year, the same thirteen-day period saw 1,192 pounds confiscated in the county.[4] By January 2003, the DEA said it had nabbed nearly 10,000 pounds of marijuana during weeks of operations in the area of the Big Bend National Park (BBNP), about 250 miles southeast of El Paso, along the Mexican border states of Chihuahua and Coahuila.[5]

Locals and law enforcement authorities alike, as well as members of the military assigned to interdict the flow of drugs across the border, know of the danger posed by the smuggling. In January 2003, drugs turned the border deadly again when four U.S. Marine Corps helicopter pilots flying a pair of AH-1W Super Cobras collided and crashed while engaged in an anti-drug trafficking operation with the U.S. Border Patrol in Falcon State Park in southern Texas, near the Rio Grande. "The helicopters were conducting a nighttime aviation reconnaissance counter-drug operation in support of the U.S. Border Patrol, Laredo Sector, at the time of the accident," said federal task force spokesman Armando Carrasco.[6]

On June 3, 1998, U.S. Border Patrol Agent Alexander Kirpnick was shot and killed by three drug smugglers along the Arizona-Mexico border; the shooter fled into Mexico but was eventually captured there. He was tried and convicted in the U.S. for the murder of a federal officer.[7]

In February 2001, during their first meeting, President Bush and Mexican President Vicente Fox—recognizing the threat to the health of citizens and the social fabric of both countries that illegal drug trade represents—pledged to aggressively and concertedly deal with it. The pair "resolved to strengthen law enforcement strategies and institutions as well as develop closer cooperation to reduce demand for illegal drugs and eliminate trafficking organizations," according to a statement released by the U.S. Embassy in Mexico. A year later, both signed a "22-point Agreement" to build a "smart border for the 21st century" that would, among other things, curtail drug smuggling. But some years later, not much progress has been made, except, perhaps, that U.S. officials are getting wise to many of the most heavily trafficked routes and, in response, have either stepped up surveillance of those areas or increased manned patrols.

Such techniques as using ground and motion sensors to detect foot and vehicle traffic when manpower is in short supply have helped reduce the flow of drugs in some areas. But usually it only forces the smugglers to take other, more creative measures to get their "product" into the U.S. market. And in many cases, stepped up enforcement has also led to an increase in smuggling, as south-of-the-border drug cartels employ more resources to get the same amount of product to "market."

"Haul it away, Jim." Hundreds of pounds of marijuana seized by U.S. authorities near Organ Pipe National Monument in Arizona.

One of the most creative methods today could remind some Vietnam veterans of their tours of duty. U.S. and Mexican officials have found numerous tunnels along the border in recent years, leading from jump-off points in Mexico to locations sometimes hundreds of yards inside the United States. Officials in both countries believe the tunnels are used to transport illegal immigrants as well as drugs; Mexican soldiers have been discovered in a known drug-smuggling tunnel near Nogales, Arizna. U.S. officials also worry the tunnels have been used to smuggle terrorists and their weapons inside the country.

In February 2002, federal authorities found a 1,200-foot tunnel on a ranch some seventy miles east of San Diego.[8] The tunnel's opening in Mexico was about two hundred feet from the border. "The tunnels can be used for contraband as well as drugs," said then-Drug Enforcement Administration chief Asa Hutchison in January 2003. Later that same month, Mexican agents patrolling near the border city of Nogales found an additional four tunnels.[9] The agents entered a drainage canal as part of their patrol and found a door at the border that led to four separate tunnels, each about one yard in diameter. Agents also found chisels and picks used to carve out the tunnels, but no drugs or suspects—only some old clothing. Since 1992, U.S. and Mexican authorities have discovered seventeen tunnels along the border, seven since December 2002, leading officials to speculate that tighter security has driven smugglers underground.[10]

One of the worst areas for drug smuggling is Organ Pipe Cactus National Monument, in Arizona—site of Kris Eggle's murder. There, opposite the Mexican state of Sonora, U.S. Park Service agents must wear camouflage, carry assault rifles and spend much of their day pursuing drug runners, because their smuggling counterparts also have two-way radios, night-vision gear, body armor and automatic weapons. And in many of the five parks and national monuments along the border, shootouts with suspected drug and illegal alien smugglers are becoming more frequent. For park rangers—the most assaulted federal law enforcement agents—that is an exceptionally high risk.[11] Critics say rangers are poorly trained to meet this kind of threat. And they say the ranger force is grossly under-staffed and under-equipped for the task. Further, drug runners are beginning to carry automatic weapons and, say local authorities and federal agents, they are often escorted with their cargo into the U.S. by bought-off Mexican army units, who are also heavily armed. With the additional firepower, the smugglers can be more than a match for lightly armed U.S. law enforcement agents and, especially, park rangers.

Since at least the mid-1990s, federal law enforcement officials—as well as local ranchers, homeowners and others—have suspected that some elements of the Mexican military have been complicit in the cross-border smuggling of drugs, migrants or both. Bureaucrats in Washington say they believe rogue units of Mexican police may be involved but largely for political reasons have either downplayed or ignored the Mexican military's involvement, despite the fact that a number of high-ranking Mexican military commanders and generals have been arrested in recent years for their involvement in drug smuggling.

"Mexican drug lords, backed by corrupt Mexican military officers and police officials, will move tons of marijuana, cocaine and heroin this year over rugged desert trails to accomplices in Phoenix and Tucson for shipment to willing buyers throughout the United States," the *Washington Times* has reported.[12] And in July 2002, *Human Events* magazine reported that American law enforcement officials "are convinced that Mexican military units are crossing the Arizona-Mexico border to aid smugglers in carrying drugs into the United States."[13] "In one incident," said the magazine, quoting senior U.S. law enforcement sources, "a major in the Mexican army was caught at the U.S. port of entry at Naco, Arizona, carrying a detailed drug-smuggling map among his papers."

"The Mexican officer," one official said, "was 'coming into the United States and they found the drug-smuggling maps on him that showed all the drop points and trails' that local smugglers used for bringing narcotics into the United States."[14]

In Arizona, squads of Mexican troops riding in Humvee military vehicles and jeeps are spotted almost daily on a rural route that runs parallel to the border and leading to a remote ranch on the Mexico side locals and Border Patrol agents call "the Compound" (I witnessed them personally; see the next chapter for details). Easily visible from the U.S., the Compound looks like a simple ranch; there is a main house, along with a few outbuildings and a corral. Some livestock and farm equipment are in evidence, and ranch hands are seen from time to time on the property. There is only one road which bypasses the Compound, and it leads out of Naco, Arizona, running for several miles along the border—in some places only a few feet from a poorly kept border fence consisting of a few rusty, broken strands of barbed wire (where it isn't cut completely or missing altogether). On the Mexican side, the road is obviously well maintained; it is in much better shape than the rutted, rough and washed out road on the U.S. side. In some places, both roads are ten feet apart or less.

Leading from the Compound into the U.S. are several visible trails, many strewn with trash, clothing and personal items, as well as backpacks and plastic shopping bags. As stated, the border fence is dilapidated and torn in many places. In others, entire sections measuring from a few inches to several feet are missing. Regardless of the fact that Border Patrol agents, local cops and ranchers have seen, on many occasions, suspected drug smugglers and illegal aliens traversing into the U.S. via this remote site, it is still obvious even to the most casual of observers that the area is being overrun by foot traffic.

While there are innumerable points along the vast border where illegals can and do sneak into the U.S., the frequent presence of Mexican troops at the Compound and other known smuggling sites make it particularly worrisome to officials because it alleges that the Mexican government is, at least in a semi-official capacity, involved in—and profiting from—the smuggling activities. But it's not just at the Compound where federal agents, local immigration reform activists, ranchers and land owners have spotted units of the Mexican military showing up regularly near suspected smuggling routes. U.S. law enforcement officials all along the border report such occurrences. In California, Border Patrol agents told me they have conducted successful "joint anti-drug operations" with the Mexican military before, only to watch helplessly from the U.S. side as the drugs were "stolen" by Mexican troops.[15]

In one instance, a group of Border Patrol agents conducting "line-watch" (watching the border) operations spotted smugglers just inside the Mexican border at night using a high-powered night vision scope. The suspects were carrying backpacks—common drug-smuggling gear—and were spotted by agents as they made their way north into the United States. The suspected smugglers were far enough away from the U.S. side they could be intercepted by Mexican officials before crossing, so American agents contacted a nearby Mexican military unit by radio, which responded in time to catch the half-dozen or so smugglers. In radio traffic monitored by the American agents, Mexican troops—which are commonly used in anti-drug operations, ironically—initially reported to superiors that they had discovered cocaine. But mysteriously, a few seconds later, the soldiers reversed themselves and reported instead that no drugs had been found. Yet Border Patrol observers, viewing the entire bust through the night vision scope, watched Mexican soldiers disperse the smugglers after confiscating and making off with their backpacks.

While that's not "proof" drugs were involved, agents told me that everything about the suspected smugglers fit the "profile" of hundreds of other such incidents, when other Mexican suspects were caught red-handed smuggling drugs into the U.S. Besides, agents said, if there were nothing of value in the backpacks, the Mexican troops would have left them behind, a detail that rings true, considering the inordinate number of backpacks used and carelessly discarded by illegal aliens sneaking into the U.S. In fact, federal agents tell me, some units of Mexican anti-drug military and police are so corrupt that U.S. agents have refused to work or cooperate with them.

One battalion-sized unit of Mexican soldiers was found to be so corrupted by the drug cartels that Mexican officials admitted that they considered disbanding it. In October 2002, Defense Minister Gen. Gerardo Vega Garcia ordered a six-hundred-man unit of soldiers back to their garrison in Guamuchil—in the Pacific coast state of Sinaloa about 680 miles northwest of Mexico City—after officials were tipped that many of the unit's soldiers had ties to drug cartels. Nearly fifty of the soldiers came under investigation; forty failed drug tests. The unit, the 65th Infantry Battalion, had been assigned to locate and destroy drug plots in the Sinaloa Mountains.[16]

As enforcement efforts increase and become more sophisticated in the U.S., Mexican drug smugglers are also getting more complex and exotic. Detective Sgt. David Cray, who heads the anti-drug unit of the Tohono O'odham Indian Nation Police Department in Arizona—where much drug activity takes place—says smugglers "put people on the hills to act as lookouts and use portable solar panels to power their communications equipment. . . . They have powerful four-wheel-drive vehicles and are under orders not to stop — to shoot their way through if they have to." He adds: "They keep us running like you can't believe. They have two-way radios, night-vision gear, body armor and carry automatic weapons."[17]

In some cities, Border Patrol officials report that drug cartels employ migrant workers or even U.S. citizens as counter-surveillance personnel whose job it is to monitor American law enforcement agencies and warn Mexican drug runners when there is danger. In Nogales, Arizona, an undercover Border Patrol officer, working with local police, discovered that a drug-smuggling ring had placed agents posing as gardeners on the city streets, *Human Events* magazine reported. "They witnessed an individual," he said, "who poses as a landscaper who watches Border Patrol agents and other law-enforcement vehicles driving down the roads and then gets on his radio and calls and says, 'Hold up on your load. A Border Patrol agent just drove down. He is coming through your area.'" Another law-enforcement officer referred to a site in Coronado National Monument as "smugglers' ridge," the magazine said. The monument sits right on the border, with the top of the ridge in U.S. territory and the south side of the mountain in Mexico. On that ridge, law-enforcement authorities have "identified twenty-seven different counter-surveillance locations in which people working for the smugglers will spend days observing everything that goes on in the park," the officer says.[18]

"There isn't a soul down there on that border, either the Tohono O'odham police or the Border Patrol, who do not believe [smuggling] is exactly what the Mexican military is doing," says U.S. Rep. Tom Tancredo. "U.S. law-enforcement personnel actually have watched the Mexican military unload drugs from their Humvees to awaiting vehicles for transport into the United States." Tancredo said the amount of drug trafficking is intensifying and is always connected to incursions into the U.S., as well as shooting incidents between elements of the Mexican military and U.S. law enforcement.[19]

Washington officially doubts it, but border enforcement personnel—many of whom are ex-military types—know better. They've seen it. They live with it every day. They've monitored elements of the Mexican army involved in drug- and human-smuggling operations. They know many of the enlisted men—most of whom are draftees—may not be voluntarily involved but instead are merely following the orders of corrupt officers above them. However, individual soldiers as well as some Mexican naval units have reportedly been paid off to ignore what they see; in the case of Mexican coastal patrols, often they are paid by the drug cartels to ignore shipments via the U.S. coastline, such as the open border regions near San Diego.

Regardless, experienced border field personnel can recognize military units when they see them. The Mexican soldiers they have watched in action along the border smuggling routes wear combat fatigues, wear load-bearing gear and equipment, carry G-3 or M-16 assault rifles and drive military vehicles—all equipment widely used by the Mexican military. When observed in field operations, the Mexican personnel behave like trained soldiers and not drug smugglers, say border agents.

"Things out [here] are a mess," one Border Patrol agent told me. "[We have border] drive-throughs every night, drugs . . . saw what myself and a couple of partners believed to be Mexican military attempting to drive through in a remote area. It was a convoy of vehicles with 'blackout' lights, which is usually a tactic employed by military personnel."[20]

In the 1990s cases of drug-related corruption in the Mexican military began to surface more and more often, especially as Mexico City increased the military's anti-drug and anti-drug cartel role. In 1997 for instance, Reuters reported that the Mexican Defense Ministry said thirty-four military or ex-military personnel had been arrested that year "for their presumed responsibility in drug trafficking or for collaborating with it." That report followed a similar one in the Mexican news weekly *Proceso* naming generals and other top military officers who, in the previous six years, had been given cars, farm machinery and other gifts by drug lords.[21]

Instead of denouncing the corruption outright, some Mexican politicians have even attempted to justify or, at a minimum, soft-peddle military drug corruption by claiming that the military should never have been used as an anti-drug force in the first place. "It's not right that the Mexican army is involved in actions against drug trafficking, because it runs the risk of ending up co-opted and perverted by the [drug] mafias," said Cuauhtemoc Sandoval, a high-ranking Party of the Democratic Revolution member of the Defense Committee.[22]

Analysts agreed. "I never thought the military should be involved in the drugs war. This just illustrates that it opens up the institution to even more corruption than already existed," said Roderic Camp, professor of political science at Tulane University in New Orleans, an expert on the Mexican armed forces.[23]

Yet despite this widespread corruption by drug lords of Mexico's government and military officials, the White House has repeatedly certified Mexico as an "important ally in the war on drugs"—this in spite of advice from outside critics and experts not to do so. Thomas Constantine, former head of the DEA, said in testimony before Congress in February 1999 that corruption within Mexican law enforcement institutions was "the worst he has seen in his thirty-nine-year law enforcement career." He added, "Continuing reports of corruption and the rapidly growing power and influence of the major organized criminal groups in Mexico cause us great concern about the long-term prospects for success."[24]

Benjamin Nelson, director of international relations and trade issues for the General Accounting Office, Congress's non-partisan research arm, reported that, "Corruption remains widespread within Mexican government institutions, including the criminal justice system." He said that Mexican drug cartels spend "over $6 billion annually to bribe Mexican government officials 'at all levels.'"[25] Yet the Clinton administration ignored those warnings and certified Mexico in 1999 and 2000; the Bush administration certified Mexico again in 2001, but has supported congressional efforts to do away with the certification process, in place since the Reagan administration began it in 1986. In 2003, Bush named Mexico as one of twenty-three "major drug-transit or major illicit drug producing countries."[26]

Keeping up with drug smugglers is tough because they are always finding creative new ways to slip their cargo into the U.S. In early 2003, for instance, U.S. officials discovered nearly a ton of marijuana inside two stolen sport utility vehicles doctored to look like U.S. Border Patrol vehicles.[27] Smugglers had stowed 1,879 pounds of marijuana in a 2000 Dodge Durango and a 2001 Ford Expedition that had emergency lights and were painted with the Border Patrol logo and striping and had government license plates.

"We've never seen any vehicles with simulated markings of the U.S. Border Patrol like this," said Lee Morgan, Customs resident agent in charge in Douglas. "There has been nothing of this caliber."[28]

Drugs are also smuggled into the U.S. from Mexico aboard tractor-trailer rigs and other trucks that, because of NAFTA, are given special quick-check status at the border. Because there are so many trucks coming into the U.S. on any given business day—more than 57,000, according to the Department of Homeland Security—it is impossible, especially given current resources, for inspectors to personally examine each one.

Besides buying off Mexican military and police officials, the drug cartels south of the border have reportedly hired ex-U.S. special forces soldiers and counter-intelligence personnel.[29] Special forces soldiers are highly trained in escape and evasion tactics—useful to smugglers—as well as all types of weapons. In 1997, one report said the soldiers were being paid upwards of a half-million dollars to work for the cartels. U.S. Rep. Silvestre Reyes, Texas Democrat and a former U.S. Border Patrol official, says the highly trained personnel have been used to scout potential smuggling routes monitored by electronic sensor equipment. He said part of their job for the cartels would be not only to scout the areas but also to jam the sensors.[30]

Americans who have difficulty believing that Mexican military and police elements could be involved in drug smuggling need only realize how prevalent drugs are to certain portions of the country, especially the northern half of Mexico: "The narcotics economy has become part of everyday life in northern, not southern Mexico," says one assessment. "The underground economy built on decades of smuggling contraband, people and drugs to the United States, has become so intertwined with the region's legitimate wealth that the two are nearly indistinguishable. The extent and depth of corruption can be understood since drugs funnel as much as $30 billion per year[31] into the Mexican economy, more than the country's top two legitimate exports (including oil) combined. Drug-based corruption is so institutionalized that normal government channels are simply not able to clean it up. There is too much money at stake. An average policeman in Mexico might be paid the equivalent of $335 per month by the government. A drug operative can pay the equivalent of $1,000 dollars a week, or $4,000 a month, for protection."[32]

Also, the *New York Times* reported in 1997 that one reason why institutionalized drug-related corruption reaches the highest levels in Mexico is because the Mexican drug traffickers' political patrons are seldom targets of law enforcement in either the U.S. or Mexico, even though they play an important role in trafficking. That high-level corruption includes, quite obviously, the Mexican military.

Students of Mexico and its armed forces, like author Tom Barry, have said that for a number of years senior officers were allowed to enrich themselves with a variety of often illegal activities, including drug trafficking.[33] This corruption assists in the military personnel remaining subservient to the politicians. Further, Mexico experts say unwritten agreements between the government and the military assures the military officers will not be prosecuted by civilian authorities for their illegal or "extra-official" activities.[34]

A journalist in the Mexican state of Oaxaca said in 1996 that land owned by the Mexican military was commonly used to grow drugs, including marijuana. The journalist said this phenomenon was "common knowledge" among locals. The army grew and sold so much, in fact, that it is often able to finance much of its own operation from the proceeds.[35] Eventually the DEA officially acknowledged drug trade cooperation between Mexican drug traffickers and elements of the military—mostly among senior army officers. Richard Fiano, the DEA's chief of operations, told Congress in September 1999 "continuing reports of corruption and the rapidly growing power and influence of the major organized criminal groups in Mexico cause us great concern about the long-term prospects for success."[36]

These burlap packs contain nearly a quarter of a ton of marijuana.

Photo: James Tourtellotte/U.S. Customs & Border Protection.

What may be the most compelling issue regarding cross-border drug smuggling is the U.S. government's indifference to it. Newspapers have quoted anonymous U.S. officials as saying Washington consistently gives trade and other economic and political interests more weight than forcing Mexico to stop the flow of drugs. One top DEA official even admitted in 1997 that drugs were never the number one issue in relation to Mexico. The drug issue "ranks somewhere below the North American Free Trade

Agreement, economic bailout and other bilateral trade and commerce issues," Robert Nieves, former DEA chief of international operations, has said. [37]

As expected, there are dangers associated with drug smuggling. One problem U.S. authorities have discovered is that profits from illicit drug sales are going to purchase powerful and often exotic weapons, which are then smuggled into Mexico to drug cartels by their American suppliers. "The growing number of assault rifles and semiautomatic weapons showing up in shootouts and assassinations has bolstered the arms caches of Mexico's drug cartels," the *New York Times* reported.[38] The smuggling of weapons feeds "one of the highest rates of gun homicide anywhere in the world."[39] A $125 handgun bought in San Diego sells for perhaps three times that amount eighteen miles south in Tijuana, Mexico, as firearms are strictly prohibited south of the border.

One report said that in 1997, U.S. Customs inspectors opened a pair of crates in the "left cargo" area of the Otay Mesa Port of Entry near San Diego, California, after they had been sitting unclaimed for two months.[40] Inside inspectors found, at the time, the largest illegal weapons shipment ever intercepted in the U.S. headed for Mexico—thousands of grenade launchers and parts for M-2 automatic rifles.[41] In short order, Mexico City quickly turned the focus away from its own internal drug corruption and blamed the United States for creating a climate of ready access to firearms—even though all of the weapons discovered were (and remain) illegal to own by private citizens in America.[42]

In a sign that drug smuggling could be reaching a new level of danger and maturity, some reports have indicated that a number of Mexican drug cartels may be attempting to form a huge alliance. Drug lords and their bodyguards, along with various associates and their contacts in government, showed up at Apadaco, Mexico, in April 2001 for a three-day summit meeting with the aim of joining forces.

"A participant in the three-day meeting, as well as associates of the smugglers, government officials and others familiar with the drug trade, gave independent accounts of the summit, speaking on condition of anonymity. Their descriptions differed slightly in detail but agreed on the central purpose of the meeting: to join forces after twelve years of bloody turf wars and form a new cartel that would unite operations and cut costs," the Associated Press reported.[43] "The alliance has been in the works for three years, but was made urgent by a tough line from Mexico's new president, Vicente Fox; by a court decision making it easier to extradite drug smugglers to the United States; and by a proposed U.S.-Mexico crackdown on money laundering, according to government insiders as well as associates of the smugglers." U.S. officials estimate that about half of the $65-70 billion of drugs bought by Americans annually comes through Mexico.[44]

AP reported that the list of attendees at the April 2001 Apodaco meeting read like a "who's who" list of drug world figures. The meeting included Juan Esparragosa Moreno, who has been identified by Mexican authorities as the drug boss known as El Azul, for his dark, near-blue-toned skin. Also attending was Amado Carrillo Fuentes, aka the Lord of the Skies, and "El Metro"—a former policeman named Ramon Alcides Magana. Authorities say the latter saved the life of Carrillo Fuentes's son and became a close confidant. These figures represented the Juarez smuggling operation, which ran things along Mexico's Caribbean coastline, central Mexico and a region along the west Texas border.[45]

Also attending, AP reported, was Humberto Garcia Abrego. Mexican authorities say he ran the Gulf [of Mexico's] drug cartel started by his brother Juan, who is in prison in the U.S. serving eleven consecutive life sentences for smuggling drugs.

AP reported Ignatio "Nacho" Coronel, the purported leader of the Colima gang that operates in the Pacific coastal state of Colima and the far eastern Texas border, was also in attendance, along with other drug cartel operatives, Ismael "El Mayo" Zambada and representatives of Joaquin "El Chapo" Guzman, the latter of whom escaped recently from a Mexican maximum security prison.[46] Others included "Gilberto Valdes, a businessman who sources said represents smugglers in the southern state of Chiapas," and "two men in military uniforms with generals' stars, to whom the others referred as 'representatives of the attorney general's office,'" as well as a "group of Colombians acting as consultants," reported AP.[47]

The report said the new, larger cartel would encompass a number of smaller drug gangs. "The only major group to decline the invitation to the meeting was that of the Tijuana-based Arellano Felix brothers, who run the bloodiest organization," said the AP.[48] [Shortly after this event, Benjamin Arellano Felix was arrested by Mexican authorities[49]; his brother Ramon, Benjamin's "enforcer," was killed a month later, in April 2002[50]]. The formation of a huge alliance of drug barons in Mexico is, most likely, at least partially the result of enhanced enforcement efforts, if not rival gang bloodletting. "The last major drug cartel in Mexico collapsed in 1989 when its longtime boss, Miguel Angel Felix Gallardo, was arrested. The new alliance would end the war of succession that has killed hundreds of people. It would mean a major shift in the drug trade in the Western Hemisphere, creating a syndicate better equipped to evade law enforcement," AP reported.[51]

The conclusion of many is that as long as demand is so high in the United States, it will be nearly impossible to stop the drug trade completely.[52] That, and the fact that there are huge profits to be made as long as drugs remain under legal prohibition. The amount of money involved in the drug trade, escalated in price because of its black market value due to legal prohibition, makes systemic corruption inevitable.[53] And in poverty stricken Mexico, drug trafficking tops the other leading industries of oil production, manufacturing and tourism in terms of revenue earned.

"Trying to stop drugs at the border or at the source makes no economic sense, so long as drugs remain illegal in the United States," says L. Jacobo Rodríguez, the assistant director of the Project on Global Economic Liberty at the Cato Institute, a libertarian think tank in Washington DC[54] "In the illicit drug industry, most of the value of those drugs (as much as 90 percent) is added after they enter the United States. That merely reflects the fact that the risk premium of selling drugs increases as the drugs approach the point of retail sale."[55]

Whether legalization of drugs is or is not sound public policy, the fact is that, in the meantime, drug smuggling from Mexico is fraught with bloodshed, danger and violence for all parties involved, including law enforcement and civilians on both sides of the border. To allay the violence, even Mexican President Fox has suggested legalizing drugs.[56] The Mexican president said legalization was the only way to eliminate the profits caused by illegal trafficking.[57]

Steven C. McCraw, Deputy Assistant Director of the Investigative Services Division at the FBI, testified before the House Judiciary Committee's subcommittee on crime on December 13, 2000, and described some of the drug-related violence:

> Drug trafficking organizations engage in other criminal activities to support their operations. Similarly, organized crime groups, street gangs and some terrorist organizations are involved in drug-related activities. For example, drug trafficking organizations are engaged in the corruption of U.S. law enforcement officials, kidnappings, tortures and murder to further their drug trafficking operations. Mexican drug trafficking organizations use street gangs to murder rivals and to distribute drugs throughout the United States. . . . El Paso, Texas, which is contiguous with Juarez, Mexico, has long been a gateway for drugs controlled by the Carrillo Fuentes Drug Trafficking Organization (CFO) and illustrates how violence is an integral part of drug trafficking. During the past few years, there have been approximately 300 drug-related disappearances in Juarez, Mexico, including 27 U.S. citizens. In El Paso, there have been 120 drug-related homicides and 73 drug-related disappearances.[58]

Meantime, drug cartels remain well-financed and heavily armed. And increasingly, drug smugglers working for them are "criminals who have proven they will resort to violence to protect their business interests," reported Fox News in July 2000.[59]

Such affinity for violence may be one reason why drug-related corruption is so widespread. According to a special op-ed for the *Los Angeles Times*, drug cartels often offer their allies and enemies alike "plata o plomo"—silver or lead; the bribe or the bullet.[60]

"The graves now being exhumed on the Mexican-U.S. border near Juarez are thought to contain the remains of anti-drug agents, informers and rival gangsters who refused the silver offered by the Juarez drug cartel and their allies to join up or shut up during the last half decade," say Eva Bertram and Kenneth Sharpe, authors of *Drug War Politics: The Price of Denial.* "Hundreds of families of victims of violent crime in the area are now coming forward to see if the graves might contain their loved ones."[61] So extensive was the brutality that President Bill Clinton declared it "reinforces the imperative" to "work with the Mexican authorities to try to combat these cartels."[62]

Bertram and Sharpe say the sheer magnitude of the drug-related deaths around Juarez "cries out for action" from Mexican authorities. But it also should fuel calls from drug warriors in Washington DC for more money to wage the drug war, as well as more resources to beef up Mexico's efforts to fight the battle as a U.S. proxy. Trouble is, say the authors, many so-called allies south of the border have already chosen payola. They say the "lead" America provides is, very often, being used against authorities on either side of the border who seek to disrupt the drug flow. The problem, they add, is especially bad along the border, "where the flow of drugs meets the lucrative U.S. market ."[63]

For its part, Mexico appears to be making an effort to crack down on its own inherent drug-related crime and corruption. Mexican troops raided and closed the offices of a federal anti-drug force in a crackdown on agents who work for and protect drug lords.[64] The raids, ordered by Mexican Attorney General Rafael Macedo, shut down the two-hundred-agent unit, and Macedo said personnel would be investigated. "We have to admit there are people who have not understood that this [tolerance of corruption] is over, and we are going to finish with them," he said. "We have to clean up our house. We will not rest until we have totally cleaned up these federal police forces, and we will insist that every police force at the state and local level is also in the same shape."[65]

And in 2001, Mexican government officials arrested Brigadier General Ricardo Martinez Perea and a pair of junior officers for allegedly having ties to the Gulf Cartel; as of 2003, Martinez Perea was the *fourth* general arrested in the past decade on charges he protected the nation's drug traffickers.[66] Also, mid-level military officers have been arrested; several captains and majors serving as anti-narcotics agents in the Mexican attorney general's office have been busted on drug trafficking charges. Even Mexico's one-time anti-drug czar, General Jose de Jesus Gutierrez Rebollo, was arrested in 1997 and convicted of supporting one trafficker while battling another. Gutierrez was, in fact, the model for a corrupt character in the 2000 movie, *Traffic*.

The administration of President Vicente Fox has repeatedly stated it is committed to cracking down on such drug-related police and military corruption. Since he took office in December 2000, his government has captured or killed several leading traffickers, including Benjamin and Ramon Arellano Felix, two brothers who led the country's most ruthless drug gang. But despite stepped-up enforcement efforts, money so often speaks much louder. Drug cartels, say U.S. border officials, stay one step ahead of the government by bribing army officials, judicial officials and police. Indeed, the raids on the federal anti-drug offices in eleven Mexican states came a week after seven agents were arrested in the northern border city of Tijuana for allegedly offering to free two captured drug smugglers and give them back their drugs in return for a massive bribe.[67]

Along the border, violence trumps congressional hearings, public policy statements and, in many ways, increased law enforcement efforts. So often, expanded drug-related law enforcement efforts come with a price— often a heavy one. In the summer of 2001, Mexican state police officer Jaime Yanez Cantu and his assistant, Gerardo Gascon, were executed in broad daylight only blocks from state police headquarters in Matamoros. Their bodies were found in their car; each had been shot several times in the head only days after they had received death threats following their arrest of three members of the Gulf drug cartel. The assassinations followed more than two dozen other drug-related homicides in the Laredo, Texas-Nuevo Laredo, Mexico, border area.

"The victims include a young Laredo couple whose bodies were found buried in the back yard of a suspected drug dealer in Nuevo Laredo on June 20. Two more bodies were found July 5 at a nearby ranch owned by the family of a man suspected of carrying out drug-related killings," said one report.[68]

In March 2002, three men were found dead from execution-style wounds in Tijuana, sparking fears that a bloody gangland war was in play for the lucrative drug-smuggling corridor leading into San Diego and much of the U.S. west coast. "The victims had apparently been tortured," The *Los Angeles Times* reported.[69] "At least one was found with a plastic bag over his head, and the men's arms and legs were bound with gray duct tape. One of the dead had two bullet wounds, and the other two had apparently been beaten to death," Tijuana law enforcement sources said.[70]

Also, Mexican authorities reported in November 2002 that in the preceding two months, at least fifty murders in and around Nuevo Laredo were likely related to the drug trade; among the victims were eight police officers. And the Department of Justice's National Drug Intelligence Center has reported that drug-related violence occurs "often" along the Mexico-New Mexico border and elsewhere. U.S. officials say Border Patrol agents have been fired upon many times by drug smugglers (eighty-six agents have been killed in the line of duty; seventeen have been killed since 1995).[71]

The violence created by drug running is an integral part of the U.S. southwest border at virtually all its points. And with tens of billions of dollars at stake, relief is not yet in sight. An Arizona University Press review of the book, *Lives on the Line: Dispatches from the U.S.-Mexico Border* by author Miriam Davidson, sums it up succinctly:

> Straddling an international border, the twin cities of Nogales, Arizona, and Nogales, Sonora, are in many ways one community. For years the border was less distinct, with Mexicans crossing one way to visit family

and friends and tourists crossing the other to roam the curio shops. But as times change, so do places like Nogales. The maquiladora industry has brought jobs, population growth, and environmental degradation to the Mexican side. A crackdown against undocumented immigrants has brought hundreds of Border Patrol agents and a 14-foot-tall steel wall to the U.S. side. Drug smuggling has brought violence to both sides. Neither Nogales will ever be the same.[72]

The evident conclusion is that as long as the border remains a sieve for humanity, it will also remain a sieve for drugs and other contraband.

And Washington hasn't helped much.

In 1996, the Clinton administration set free nearly one thousand drug smugglers who were caught along the Southwest border, even though they were arrested with substantial quantities of narcotics.[73] Citing U.S. Customs Service records, Border Patrol records and interviews with law enforcement officials, the *Los Angeles Times* reported in 1996 that about 2,300 suspected drug traffickers were taken into custody in the past year, but more than 25 percent were released and sent home to Mexico. Officials at the U.S. Attorney's office in San Diego said they adopted a program a few years earlier in which first-time drug smugglers were given the choice of prosecution or being disallowed from emigrating legally to the U.S. Assistant U.S. Attorney John Kramer said in an interview that immigration exclusion "is, in our opinion, a powerful prosecutorial tool." Officials said if the smugglers are arrested for another drug-related offense in five years, the original charges are reinstated and the offender is prosecuted for both crimes. But the paper said some smugglers had been apprehended multiple times—even in the same week—and never jailed.

The controversy prompted then-California Governor Pete Wilson to call on GOP leaders in Washington to conduct congressional hearings. Sen. Bob Dole (R-Kansas) asked Attorney General Janet Reno to explain whether the Clinton administration supports the policy. In a May 16, 1996 statement, Reno defended the exclusion program contending that evidence in all one thousand cases was insufficient to support prosecution.

INCURSION!

The simple truth is that we've lost control of our own borders, and no nation can do that and survive.

—President Ronald Reagan

No one in our Jeep noticed the Mexican army Humvee until it was right on us. Everyone had been focusing on the road ahead, partly because the dirt trail was bumpy and rough, having been washed out in a few places by rare desert rain, but also because we were busy scanning the miles of horizon ahead for any sign of border crossers. As our driver made his was carefully, yet expeditiously, along the trail road, bumping along less than five feet away from the oft-non-existent barbed wire fence separating the U.S. and Mexico, no one had thought to look behind us. It could have been a deadly mistake; the Humvee was full of Mexican soldiers with automatic weapons, and they had gained on us quite rapidly. Since they, too, were on a dirt track less than five feet from the border fence, we were well within range of their G-3 and M-16 assault rifles.

"Oh, sh—!" said John Petrello, also known as "JP," my local guide who, in an earlier chapter, demonstrated he had much experience with border issues involving illegal aliens and the terrain in which we were deployed. He had agreed to show me and another guy—a volunteer with Ranch Rescue, a property and border rights group—what was really happening on the border.

"Where'd *they* come from?" he asked.

"I don't know," I said naively. "What's the big deal?"

"Do they have weapons? Can you see any rifles?" JP asked excitedly, as he slowed his Jeep to allow the Mexican soldiers to pass us by. I noticed the soldiers were trying their best to ignore us.

"Yeah, I saw some rifles," I said. The Ranch Rescue volunteer said he saw them too. "Can you drive a little faster so we can get some pictures?"

JP looked back at me for an instant, incredulous. "Do you *want* us to get shot?" he asked sarcastically. "They've shot at Americans over the border before, you know."

I didn't know that *per se*, but I guess I had heard as much. Nevertheless, with armed Mexican soldiers less than ten feet away, his statement got me to thinking about our safety. In the end, however, I dismissed such concerns ever so briefly. I really needed the photo. While politicians and pundits go back and forth about deploying troops along our border, few people know that the Mexican military patrols its side, and it's hard to argue with a picture.

A squad of Mexican army soldiers patrol just feet from the Mexico-U.S. border in Arizona. Border Patrol agents, other federal officers and local law enforcement agents say "foreign" (i.e. Mexican military) incursions occur frequently along the border.

"Let's risk it," I said. "I'll be quick." The Ranch Rescue volunteer said he'd like one too, so JP, shaking his head and smiling nervously, agreed to speed up.

The problem with that was that the road on our side of the border was abysmal; it was rutted, washed out, and full of holes and crevices. On the Mexican side, however, the dirt road had obviously been improved. It was smooth and well-maintained; in fact, it looked as if it had been graded recently. We were at a distinct disadvantage because of the poor quality of our road. I had seen Border Patrol vehicles using our road, and I wondered to myself why they hadn't requested the road be better maintained, so their patrols would go much easier and much more quickly. I found out later agents in the area *had* requested the road be made smoother.

With that in mind, I knew it was going to take a little while to catch up to the Mexicans, who had already passed us and were speeding along ahead of us at a good pace. I could tell they were still close because of the cloud of dust they left behind.

"They're probably heading to 'The Compound,'" JP said as we bumped and banged our way down the road. "I was hoping we'd see them today, but I didn't really think we'd be chasing them."

"What's the compound?" I asked.

"It's a place coyotes and smugglers use as a jump-off point to smuggle drugs and illegals into the country," he said. "It's nothing more than a small ranch, but it's just up the road. The Border Patrol knows all about it."

It suddenly occurred to me why the Mexican road was in much better shape than ours; they have a "higher purpose" for their road. On "our" side of the fence, the road is simply used to get from one point to another (and Border Patrol uses it to patrol). But it seemed as though some Mexicans, including the Mexican army, used their road for "business."

"So these guys are out here all the time, eh?" I asked JP.

"Yeah. I mean, I don't know about *these* guys in particular, but yeah," he said, "I see soldiers out here all the time. I've told people about them, but no one is ever with me when I see them." Getting more excited he said, "It's about time I saw them with witnesses."

"What're they doing here?" I asked. "Patrolling?"

"I think they're helping the smugglers and coyotes," said JP.

"They're here to help them smuggle drugs and illegal aliens?" I asked, incredulously.

It was obvious from JP's expression he was taking pleasure at my innocence. "Yeah, man. That's what they do down here. And they don't just stay on *their* side of the border, either," he said.

That sent chills down my spine. After all, we had been just yards from armed Mexican troops. I had been in the service and could handle a weapon; but between the three of us, we had a pistol and one rifle—hardly a match for a squad of trained soldiers with automatic weapons.

And though JP's daunting statement about elements of the Mexican military sounded far-fetched, looking further there was some corroboration. It seems that one of the earliest incidents occurred in 1985, involving southern California property owner Robert Maupin and his daughter.

According to one published account, Maupin and his daughter may be the only American citizens to have been disarmed and detained at gunpoint by Mexican troops—all while on American soil. In 1985, Maupin told a friend, he smelled ether on his property near Tierra del Sol, California, he recalled to a friend. He told his friend he used to be a narcotics agent and that's why he recognized the smell; ether, he explained, is an ingredient in the manufacture of methamphetamines. Maupin said the only nearby structure was a building about a half-mile from the U.S.-Mexico border. He said usually it was empty but at times someone would occupy it and hoist a Mexican flag for display. At those times, he said, there was activity inside the building. During these times, the building would be guarded by, he said, plainclothes men carrying military weapons. After giving him the details, Maupin's friend said he would pass the information onto drug enforcement officials in Mexico, yet, Maupin commented later, "I'm pretty sure that's where my problems began."[1] A few days later, Maupin and his daughter, Denise, went out on the property for some target shooting. While shooting, Maupin said he saw what looked like kids wearing toy helmets near their line of fire. But when they went to investigate, Maupin said he and Denise were quickly surrounded by Mexican troops carrying .308 NATO-caliber FN/FAL automatic rifles.

The sergeant in charge of the squad told Maupin, in what he described as "fairly good English," that they were looking for illegal guns and drugs. He also said that they were looking for "Señor Maupin" by name, which, according to Maupin, "made it pretty clear to me that I had made somebody in the Mexican government angry by sticking my nose into their drug business." Maupin then went on to tell the sergeant, "We're in the U.S.A. The guns that I and my daughter are carrying are legal, but yours aren't."[2]

Maupin's warning had no effect. He said the sergeant told his men to disarm the two Americans. When one of the soldiers reached over to take Denise's holstered .357 Magnum pistol, "she backhanded him and just about knocked him flat," Maupin said.[3] That got the other Mexican soldiers to "working the bolts" on their rifles, ostensibly loading a round into the chamber and readying for a firefight. Maupin said that action got him to empty his rifle and hand it over, since he and his daughter were severely outnumbered and outgunned. He told the Mexican army sergeant he had the proper paperwork for his weapons back at his house, then led the Mexican squad to his home. As he led them away from the border, Maupin said he told his daughter he would stall the soldiers at his corral long enough for her to call Border Patrol agents. Maupin later recounted it was lucky for him this particular squad of Mexican troopers weren't particularly professional. "They didn't notice Denise was gone until they heard the door closing," he said.[4] "But when they realized she had gone into the house, they dropped the bipods on their rifles and aimed them at the house," he added.[5] But by then Denise had contacted the U.S. Border Patrol, which set up a roadblock while sending three agents to the Maupin house. The Mexican troopers calmed somewhat, and Maupin got some of them ice water while amusing them with broken Spanish.

Shortly thereafter, Maupin told the soldiers he had called for an "official interpreter" to come help him out. "The guy in charge got an 'uh-oh' expression on his face, and ordered one of his men to scribble out a receipt for our guns," Maupin said.[6] "He got really agitated and yelled at his men

to move out. When they got to our fence line they took off." Shortly thereafter, the Mexican squad was captured and disarmed by U.S. Border Patrol
agents, who also retrieved the Maupins' weapons.

Robert Maupin was planning to pursue legal remedies but federal
officials told him he would have to be in court for three to four months
straight, upon which time he decided to let the matter drop. "When we
grabbed those guys [involved in the border incursion], they were decked
out in full combat gear, carrying fully automatic rifles, and they claimed
that they had gotten lost," former Border Patrol agent Bob Stille recalled.[7]
But Stille and his Border Patrol colleagues weren't buying the story: "Even
back then we had dealt with border incursions of this sort, which were
usually connected in some way to drug smuggling."[8]

While Maupin's incident seems extreme, U.S. Border Patrol agents report
that on several occasions they have encountered, then arrested, Mexican
army personnel on U.S. soil. "The vast majority of the American people
are totally oblivious that armed forces of a foreign nation routinely violate
the sovereignty of the U.S. Our government is aware of these incidents,
but refuses to take any steps to stop these flagrant violations," a Border
Patrol agent told Rob Krott, senior foreign correspondent for *Soldier of
Fortune* magazine, in the March 2003 issue.

Federal agents have said that in 2001, for instance, the U.S. government officially recorded twelve separate incidents in which Mexican military personnel crossed over the border into Arizona alone. "Without a
doubt" Mexican military have made incursions into Arizona, said one
Border Patrol official. "We have actually made arrests of both military and
police. And as far as I know in all events the people were released to
Mexican custody within twelve hours, as well as returning them with the
weapons that they made the incursion with."[9] Local law enforcement officials also have recorded multiple incidents. One Texas sheriff even published a warning that said unidentified armed men dressed in military

fatigues had been spotted on numerous occasions in his county near the border with Mexico. WorldNetDaily covered the story:

> For the "country's safety," Sheriff Erasmo Alarcon Jr., of Jim Hogg County, published a letter in a local newspaper to alert citizens of reports he has received for some years from ranchers who have spotted the unknown troops, equipped with "professional backpacks" and walking together in a military cadence. . . . The county's deputy sheriff, Guadalupe Rodriguez, said he believes the armed men were foreign and were not drug smugglers. "They are not your regular traffickers that you get," he told WND. "But we don't want to draw conclusions at this point and get everybody worked up." Alarcon said in his letter that "these military-type individuals have been sighted in very remote locations of our county," which "stretches 50 or 60 miles from end to end." We have reported this information to higher-up law enforcement agencies, but no one really knows who these individuals are, not even the military," he said in his letter. . . . The sheriff said that reports of sightings most often were received the next day, meaning that there was little that could have been done. On one occasion, a report was received within several hours of the sighting. "That particular time, we formed an immediate multi-agency task force between the surrounding counties, but we were met with little success," Alarcon said. "We even brought in air support." [He] said he is bringing "this information to light because of the security crisis our nation faces."[10]

I later visited the county and the area Sheriff Alarcon described; there is ample opportunity for such men to cross. The terrain is largely rural and barren, save for some desert scrub. If they were spotted, it is highly unlikely authorities could be summoned in time to intercept them.

There is also a sinister aspect to the incursions. Though U.S. government officials have publicly denied knowledge of such incidents—most likely in an attempt to keep up relations with Mexico City—U.S. agents in the southwest have discovered that Mexican drug lords have put price tags on their heads. As confirmed by Border Patrol officials, the Juarez cartel placed a bounty of $200,000 on U.S. lawmen. The "rewards," federal agents say, are intended to warn off any U.S. law enforcement agents whose job it is to stem illegal smuggling activity along the border.[11]

Also, the threat of bounties was made public at least once. A former Mexican oil worker-turned-immigration activist, Carlos Ibarra Perez, offered a $10,000 bounty for the killing of Border Patrol agents in the spring of 2000, though upon investigation by authorities on both sides of the border, Perez—a spokesman for an advocacy group called the Citizen Defense Committee—told prosecutors he was misquoted by the press. "I showed him the various newspapers and the various articles," said Jesus Trevino, a prosecutor in Reynosa, Mexico. "I asked him if he made these statements. He said that at no time did he make those statements or offer a bounty." But on the steps of Reynosa's city hall in early June 2000, Perez, sixty, said he was making the offer because too many illegal immigrants were being slain by federal agents and private landowners while making their way into the United States.[12]

The border is fraught with all kinds of unique problems, issues and occurrences. For example, there have been a series of incursions into the U.S. by Mexican soldiers and police since the mid-1990s, which have left U.S. border residents, immigration reform advocates and Border Patrol agents convinced that they are not accidental.

According to U.S. border officials, on March 14, 2000, shortly after 10 P.M. local time, two Mexican army Humvees carrying about sixteen armed soldiers drove across the international boundary and into the United States near Santa Teresa, New Mexico. There the vehicles pursued a Border Patrol vehicle, which was outfitted with decals and emergency lights (that were activated for much of the pursuit) over a mile into the United States. The lead Mexican army vehicle, said National Border Patrol Council officials, contained nine soldiers "armed with seven automatic assault rifles, one submachine gun, and two .45 caliber pistols,"[13] and was eventually apprehended by other Border Patrol units. The second Humvee, however, "pursued a Border Patrol agent on horseback and fired a shot at him. The soldiers then disembarked their vehicle, fired upon one more Border Patrol agent and chased another agent before fleeing [back] to Mexico in their vehicle."

That incident was the most serious to date, and "is but one of hundreds of incursions that have been reported over the past several years," the union said, adding that it led them to call on Congress and, at the time, the Clinton administration, to deal with it. Neither did, but Mariela Melero, the regional spokesperson for INS, based in Dallas, said high-level contacts with the Mexican government regarding the incident were in the works but the INS official declined to offer specifics.

The El Paso, Texas, Border Patrol office told me, "in both instances, Mexican soldiers apparently were not aware they had crossed into U.S. territory." The El Paso office acknowledged that two shots had been fired by the Mexican soldiers, but said that after "Border Patrol agents identified themselves and explained" that the Mexicans were on U.S. soil, one of the Humvees carrying the soldiers "retreated" south while the occupants of the second vehicle "surrendered to the Border Patrol agents."[14]

The Mexican soldiers were debriefed and allowed to go back to Mexico. Paul M. Berg, chief of the Border Patrol Agent's Association, said that U.S. border officers had been caught armed in Mexico before as well, but U.S. officials had been able to negotiate their release "with their weapons over the outcry of the Mexican people, who wanted the agents prosecuted."[15]

Following the March 2000 incursion and shooting incident, Mexican army soldiers crossed into the United States and fired upon U.S. Border Patrol agents again, leaving Border Patrol union members furious and demanding federal intervention. According to L. Keith Weeks, vice president of the National Border Patrol Union Local 1613 in San Diego, California, two border patrolmen who had just disembarked from a "clearly marked Border Patrol helicopter" immediately came under fire from a 10-man unit of what appeared to be soldiers with the Mexican army. In a statement, Weeks said the incident occurred October 24, 2000 in Copper Canyon, about eight miles east of the Otay Mesa Port of Entry near San Diego. "It happened," said Weeks in an interview. "These agents departed their helicopter and were immediately fired upon."[16] A number of agents told me Mexican police and military regularly are found within the borders of the U.S.; often, shots are exchanged, they say, and never reported in the media.

In this instance, Weeks said, about eight shots were fired. The Mexican unit was dressed in military-style uniforms with tactical vests and carried "high-powered military rifles with bayonets." As the agents began to receive fire, they took cover in thick brush nearby. Weeks said they shouted in Spanish that they were U.S. Border Patrol agents, but "were nonetheless pursued by some of the soldiers," who crossed into the United States by entering through the barbed-wire fence marking the international boundary. Border officials said the soldiers deployed in military fashion against the agents; they said as Mexican troops pursued agents, others set up sniper and over-watch positions, so they could cover their own men from being outflanked by U.S. agents. Still under cover, the U.S. agents were ordered by the Mexican soldiers, in Spanish, to get out of the brush, but they refused. Instead, the agents re-identified themselves and ordered the soldiers to return to Mexico. "Once other Border Patrol agents neared the scene," Weeks said, "the soldiers retreated to Mexico and drove off in a minivan."[17]

And remember the incident discussed earlier when a Border Patrol agent near San Diego encountered a group of four Mexican soldiers, who were armed with three submachine guns and one M-16 rifle. The agent was following footsteps left by the Mexican patrol and encountered them just as they crossed the border near Tecate, Mexico. One of the Mexican soldiers had his sidearm unholstered. As the agent told superiors, the Mexican troopers then realized they were inside the U.S. and did cooperate with the Border Patrol agent. But as Border Patrol spokesman James Jacques said, "This could easily have escalated into a real tragedy. Thankfully, cooler heads prevailed."[18]

About a dozen Mexican troops were caught again by Border Patrol agents inside the U.S. near Tecate in January 2003. According to published reports, the soldiers were wearing black ski masks and carrying automatic rifles; the troop commander said he and his men were part of an anti-drug unit and were unaware they had crossed into the United States.[19] "The Mexicans were first encountered about dusk Thursday . . . in an area known to be frequented by drug traffickers," said a *San Diego Union Tribune* newspaper report. A border patrol agent "had become suspicious of potential illegal activity when he spotted boot tracks some 30 feet into U.S. territory near a barbed-wire fence marking the border. . . ."[20]

The Mexican border is not the only place where the U.S. border is porous, or U.S. border enforcement personnel are undermanned, under-equipped and overrun. There are other places as well, such as U.S. borders which meet oceans.

"So how good is U.S. homeland security if four uniformed Cuban agents can climb out of a vessel and trundle down a Key West street before detection?" said the *Miami Herald*, in a February 10, 2003 article.[21] "Or if a boatload of 235 Haitian migrants can run aground off the Rickenbacker Causeway? Questions about U.S. preparedness to intercept terrorists arise after such blunders—and spark concern." The *Herald* story went on to point out that just nine days before, Homeland Security Secretary Tom Ridge warned the nation only "one slip, one gap, one vengeful person, can threaten the lives of our citizens at any time." Though the Cuban border agents who arrived in Miami—one carrying a Chinese-made handgun—didn't mean to harm anyone, the breach of U.S. territory laid bare the complexity of securing the U.S. homeland. Coast Guard and Border Patrol resources are stretched thin. Couple that with America's long perimeter, and you have severe risk factors affecting homeland security. Worse, there are any number of points where terrorists could breach U.S. borders undetected, with a selection of weapons [of mass destruction?] at their disposal.[22]

Despite these incidents, it is often difficult for Border Patrol, U.S. Customs and other immigration agents to get adequate protection, armament and equipment to do their jobs. Even before many of the aforementioned incidents, Border Patrol union officials were pressing Clinton administration officials for such necessities as body armor. The National Border Patrol Council made an appeal to the Department of Justice for more body armor for Border Patrol agents, thousands of whom, the union says, are currently on the job without adequate protection.[23]

The plea, made in a letter to then–Attorney General Janet Reno June 1, 2000, came just days before Border Patrol agents were put on alert and told to don bulletproof vests because of bounties having been placed on their heads. According to Daryl Schermerhorn, the Border Patrol Council's vice president, "the U.S. Border Patrol has failed to continue the purchase of body armor for its agents," leaving "over four thousand agents working (in the field) without proper body armor." He said officials of the old INS claimed "body armor is too costly" and that "the expense is not justifiable." "After hearing you state at the recent law enforcement memorial service that providing police officers with body armor is a high priority for you, I can only believe that you are unaware that the Border Patrol is not outfitting its agents with proper body armor," Schermerhorn said in his letter to Reno. "Failure to act promptly in this matter could cost an agent his or her life," he added.[24]

Border Patrol spokeswoman Nicole Chulik said agents are issued body armor when they take up field assignments, but that because of complaints by agents that Border Patrol-issued body armor was cumbersome, the INS adopted the "pick your own" program so agents "could get body armor that they were comfortable with."[25]

A popular excuse used by Mexican officials is that army and police units don't know when they've crossed into the United States. And though the border fence is in disrepair in many places, it is still easily recognizable as an international boundary—and the fence is in addition to concrete international boundary markers placed every half-mile or so along the border.

Mexican officials also publicly deny that their army and police units cross into the United States. They say such reports are either fabricated by local authorities and border control groups or, at a minimum, overblown. If any cross-border incursions are occurring, it is not with Mexico City's approval, they say, adding that sometimes overzealous Mexican authorities may "mistakenly" cross into the U.S. in pursuit of drug or illegal alien smugglers.

But occasionally even Mexican government officials acknowledge border incursions into the U.S. by their military and police, even if by accident. *Human Events* magazine reported that one Mexican Embassy official in Washington DC, who asked not to be named, said Mexican military and law enforcement personnel crossed into the U.S. some twenty-three times in 2001. The official was confirming the claim of Rep. Tom Tancredo (R-Colorado), chairman of the Congressional Immigration Reform Caucus, who said in a May 1, 2002 press release there had been twenty-three incursions by Mexican authorities. But the official backed off somewhat after the embassy was contacted by the U.S. State Department. "This happened, I believe, twenty-three times in the last sixteen months," he said. "We have had no documented cases [in 2002]. We don't like the word 'incursions' because that is a military term for taking up a position. . . . In some cases, it was civilian [law enforcement], and some cases it was military." The State Department later said its figures were closer to a "half-dozen" incursions, not anywhere near Tancredo's or the Mexican Embassy's twenty-three.[26]

In another sign that Mexico at least tacitly acknowledges the incursions, Mexico City in June 2000 announced it was drafting a directive to the army on how to handle any future accidental crossings into the United States, such as the March 14, 2000, incursion that precipitated an armed standoff on the Texas side of the border. Jose A. Polo Oteyza, an official with Mexico's Foreign Ministry, said the proposed directive provides detailed instructions on what to do if Mexican army soldiers inadvertently cross to the U.S. side, and U.S. Consul Edward Vazquez said that the directive "looked good to us. . . . [W]e're going to give them our [views]. . . . It's meant to prevent confrontation when these things occur."[27]

But it's not uncommon for many U.S. and Mexican officials to either deny or downplay these incursions, usually for political reasons. For Mexico to admit readily to them would mean it could be sanctioning an invasion of its powerful northern neighbor, analysts and experts say; for the U.S. to admit to them would mean harsh scrutiny from the electorate and a hue and cry for action that would be politically impossible for either major party to ignore. So both sides deny what countless others along the border—law enforcement, federal agents, civilians and a few politicians— have often witnessed.

Because of the near blackout here, for Tancredo, getting acknowledgement of these incidents as well as some official action to prevent them is a crusade. "I cannot in good conscience stand by and watch another incursion along our border take place," he says. "Unless we open our eyes and recognize that what's happening along the U.S.-Mexico border is real, one of our guys is going to get killed. Everyone keeps claiming that these 'incursions' don't take place, that people are just getting lost, and the whole idea of incursions is erroneous. Unless the U.S. and Mexican governments admit these incursions exist and take action to stop them, then an international incident, in my opinion, is foreseeable."[28]

It is difficult if not impossible to believe Mexico's official excuse that its soldiers and *federales* can't tell when they have entered the United States. Besides being a stretch, such excuses don't explain why some Mexican military and police units have fired upon American law enforcement personnel and civilians. One Border Patrol official said he thought the incursions were often, but not always, drug-related.[29] Dan Bauer, an official with the U.S. Forest Service who accompanied Tancredo on an Arizona fact-finding trip in 2002, has said that in addition to officially documented incursions, there have been others involving people "who appear to be Mexican military or paramilitary."[30]

There is also concern that Islamic terrorist groups could be using the poorly enforced U.S. southwest border as a staging point for incursions into America. According to Joseph Farah, editor-in-chief of WorldNetDaily.com, the Mexican government has said that Islamic groups could be working in conjunction with Mexican guerillas:

Mexico's National Security Adviser Adolfo Aguilar Zinser made the sensational announcement that Islamic terrorist organizations have a presence along the U.S. border and may be making contacts with Mexican guerrilla groups. "We have evidence that organizations or people linked to Islamic organizations could have a presence here or be passing through," Aguilar told a local [San Diego] radio program. Though declining to identify the specific groups, he also said the groups could have indigenous guerrilla ties. The announcement was not intended to alarm U.S. authorities, but rather to quell fears in Mexico about the possibility of guerrilla attacks. "Our duty is to find them and send [them] away from the country so they don't put roots down here or try to use our territory as a haven," he explained.[31]

The threat of incursions by Mexican military was made worse, locals say, when President Vicente Fox announced he would deploy some eighteen thousand Mexican troops to the border as the U.S. launched its war against Iraq, supposedly to crack down on border jumping, drug smuggling and terrorist infiltration north. That deployment seemed never to materialize, but even with the threat of placing more Mexican military on the border, American residents just across the line were nervous, not reassured.

One thing is certain: The continued incursions increase the risk of armed exchanges between U.S. law enforcement agencies and Mexican troops and police, especially at a time when Americans are on heightened alert for possible terrorist attacks. Another thing is certain; many Border Patrol agents are fed up with the incursions and the U.S. government's lack of concern over them.

"They violated the laws of our country, and nothing was done about their violating the laws," says Charles Newcomer, president of the local USBP union in southern Arizona. "It's almost like saying they have carte blanche, a get-out-of-jail free card."[32]

Interestingly, and despite regular incursions by Mexican police and military into the U.S., Mexican officials have complained about Americans taking up their arms to protect their homes and property—though these citizens don't cross into Mexico to do it. In May 2000, Mexican Foreign Minister Rosario Green complained to Secretary of State Madeleine Albright and other U.S. officials in Washington about the treatment reportedly received by some illegal immigrants traversing private land.[33] She alleged that the detention of illegals by private U.S. ranchers—mostly in Arizona—had resulted in two deaths and seven injuries since January 1999. "The issue of the Mexicans and the Arizona ranchers is seen, without a doubt, as a red alert that could generate a relatively tense situation," Green said in Mexico City.[34] She also accused the ranchers of violating numerous state laws, including illegal detention of immigrants and aggravated assault, adding that she wanted a U.N. special envoy for immigration issues to visit the U.S.-Mexico border and look into the accusations. At the same time, Mexican officials have reportedly been contacting attorneys in the United States in preparation of civil action against the ranchers.

U.S. officials countered Green's complaints by saying Mexican officials were doing little to stop the incursions of both troops and immigrants. But some are sympathetic to the immigrants. "[Ranchers] must understand that people entering the United States illegally have universal rights that we must respect," said Border Patrol spokesman David Gonzalez.[35] American ranchers and property owners along the border say they wonder when that same respect will be afforded them, and why it has become unfashionable to protect their own land from what many describe as wanton destruction.

In January 2003, Homeland Security Director Tom Ridge pledged to merge four agencies responsible for border security into one, allegedly to plug gaps in a border-security system whose weaknesses were laid bare by the 9-11 attacks. "Instead of four faces at the border, America will have one," Ridge said during a speech in Miami. "The focus here is to help legitimate goods and people enter our country swiftly and keep dangerous people and their weapons out."[36]

In phasing out the old INS, the new Homeland Security department created the Bureau of Customs and Border Protection, which will deal with people before they enter the country, and the Bureau of Immigration and Customs Enforcement, which will track down potential violators once they have entered the country. "The sheer depth and breadth of this nation, the magnitude of what occurs here from sea to shining sea, means simply that one slip, one gap, one vengeful person can threaten the lives of our citizens at any time, in any number of ways," Ridge said. "We will organize to mobilize. It will lead to outcomes that better protect our country."[37]

But T.J. Bonner, head of the National Border Patrol Council, poured water on Ridge's aspirations. He said if anyone had bothered to consult agents, they might have come up with a different, more effective plan. "Not a single person from Border Patrol was consulted when they dreamed this thing up and launched it," Bonner said, noting that the restructuring plan will do little to improve security. How, for instance, will combining agencies keep out Mexican troops and *federales*, when Washington defers to Hispanics politically?

And how, agents wonder, can Ridge's new agencies keep out armed Mexican military units when some personnel cannot even spot fraudulent identification at regular border crossing checkpoints? In the months preceding the formation of the new agencies, the General Accounting Office—Congress's independent investigative arm—tested INS and Customs inspectors at selected border checkpoints. GAO investigators reported having little trouble entering the country with fraudulent identification or carrying undeclared cash. "Bouncers at college bars could spot the kind of fake IDs that were used by investigators," said Sen. Charles Grassley (R-Iowa) of the GAO's dismal findings.[38]

"For several years now, Mexican troops seem to have waltzed into U.S. territory pretty much whenever and wherever they felt like it," says columnist Samuel Francis. "Some of these incursions may indeed be accidents or the results of enforcement operations in uncertain territories. Then again, the fact is that Mexico really doesn't much care whether it's U.S. territory or not, since a great many Mexicans think the area belongs to them anyway.

Meanwhile, Mexican cops and troops can act as though the border doesn't really exist by crossing it whenever they feel like it and doing whatever they please, including firing on American government agents. What should be done, now that the Border Patrol itself has confirmed that armed Mexican police and soldiers seem unable to stay out of a country that isn't theirs and where they have no business, is to deploy the U.S. Army to round up the illegal aliens and drug smugglers on our side of the border and to keep the Mexican army and police on theirs."[39]

Not likely, given the current political trends, and in the meantime, the border insanity continues.

MISSION: ILLEGALS

7

"If there's a need in this country for people for agriculture, then let's set up a guest worker program so we can keep track of the people coming into our country and control this thing."

—GENE DAVIS, FORMER BORDER PATROL AGENT

SOUTHEAST ARIZONA—From the road, the wash looked like any other. It was empty of water, as is usually the case in the desert, but its base of craggy rocks and sandy dirt, both endemic to the region, formed the skeleton of the river it becomes during the rainy season. Since the desert soil cannot absorb the torrential downpours that come, such washes are created as tens of thousands of gallons of run-off cut huge swathes several feet into the earth, searching for somewhere to pool and gather, or empty. The power of such acts of nature is awe-striking.

An avenue of run-off at times, the empty wash was being used of late as a natural trail for illegal aliens and their coyotes. Bifurcated by a road with a small bridge, the wash, with its low-profile appearance and ability to conceal, was perfect for smuggling; drivers could easily pull off the road, quickly relieve the coyotes of their human cargo, then speed away in moments virtually undetected. A few houses were scattered here and there in the area—sources of water and maybe some clothing that was left out on a line to dry.

Local John Petrello Jr., or JP, had been gracious enough to spend several weeks explaining the smuggling problems to me and taking me around to the most heavily trafficked spots. On several occasions he agreed to accompany me to see if we could spot any illegals who were using the wash as an avenue into the country.

"Jim" as he wanted to be known, a friend of JP's, was a white-haired retiree who had begun to devote more of his time to learning about the illegal immigration problem and help stop some of the smuggling; he was waiting for us in a small SUV as we pulled into a clearing near a bridge by the wash. After exchanging greetings and introductions, Jim explained that he'd let us walk the wash while he drove a little further up the road to check out a spot where he thought he saw some fresh tracks in dirt that had been hit pretty heavy with rain the night before. It was another spot, he said, where locals reported seeing an increasing number of illegals—probably some of the same groups that were using the wash in recent weeks.

It made sense, Jim said, because the wash—as a main thoroughfare—could also be used as a primary trail that branched off into a number of other smaller trails, making ingress into the country easier while making detection more difficult. The more trails there were, the harder it would be for Border Patrol (and us) to guess which one was being used on any given day.

What also made spotting illegals difficult was the terrain. The surrounding desert scrub made it hard to see much farther than twenty feet in front of you. Even large groups of people could—and did—hide from view as they assembled in predetermined areas before embarking on the last several hundred yards to their pick-up points. The aerial reconnaissance helicopters used by the Border Patrol made spotting larger groups of people a bit easier, but that was mostly if pilots first spotted a few in open desert.

After a few minutes of discussing strategy, JP and Jim tested each other's radios, then Jim drove away, heading down the road about two miles to watch a suspected trail. JP and I got out of his Jeep and "geared up" for our jaunt into the wash; we put on extra clothes to ward off the crisp air of the desert; we tested our radios; we strapped on our sidearms. It was already late afternoon, so we knew we'd have to hurry if we were going to catch anyone; the groups, if they were coming, would likely be there shortly. The coyotes liked to use the darkness as a means of extra cover to hide their groups.

As evening approached, the weather got worse. There were clouds and drizzle in the area and lots of wind, along with falling temperatures—not much different than the weather we'd been experiencing for the past several days. On-again, off-again rain had soaked much of the area for the past forty-eight hours, and while that wasn't good for anyone traveling in the elements, it was good for anyone looking for illegal alien traffic. The rain meant any tracks we would find would be fresh. The locals said the immigrant traffic slowed somewhat during bad weather but never stopped completely. That made sense, considering where we were standing was about five miles from the border, and that in order to get where they needed to go, border jumpers would not likely be willing to spend much more time outside than they had to. Also, I imagined that the coyotes would not have much patience to wait for long, and would want to keep moving at all costs so they could dump their cargo and get another group; time was money to them.

Before we left, JP made sure he had one more thing: his SKS rifle. Nothing like having something to put a little distance between us and any hostile coyote who figured to take a shot at a couple of "gringos." In the face of a threat—especially when you're alone in the middle of nowhere—self-defense is no longer an option, it's a requirement. Given the history of escalating violence along the border—a local Border Patrol agent had just been assaulted days before, within a few miles of where we were standing—I welcomed a little more protection than our sidearms could offer. Nevertheless, I breathed a little easier when I pulled back the slide on my pistol and put a .40 caliber round in the pipe. Clicking on the safety and returning my pistol to my open-carry holster, JP did the same for both his weapons. We were ready.

As we headed out, both of us were scanning either side of the wash for any signs of motion or evidence that people had come through recently. Before we were a hundred yards from our vehicle, we began to see evidence that illegals had been through: trash, discarded items, water bottles. As JP led the way, the wind picked up again, as did the rainy drizzle, forcing me to zip up my jacket some more, to guard against the elements. It was a tough break because the wind and rain would mask the sounds of voices and the noise that large groups of people make as they find their own way through the wash, en route to some pick-up point and then another destination, perhaps Phoenix or Los Angeles, or even further north and northeast, to Missouri, to New York City and New Jersey, or to North Carolina.

Because of the worsening weather—and decreasing daylight—JP and I knew we'd have to be extra watchful for the sights and sounds of anyone moving through the wash ahead of us or the brush on either side. These were ominous circumstances that could put us at a distinct disadvantage, especially if we ran into any armed coyotes or drug smugglers. I reached down and readjusted my pistol and thought again how glad I was JP had brought his rifle.

The locals said the numbers of illegal border crossers had been increasing steadily for the past few weeks, so JP and I were confident we'd find evidence that some had been through recently. Right after Christmas, in January, a few were coming through here and there, said the locals, but nothing like what had begun to show up recently. Immigrant traffic generally increased at certain times of the year in certain regions because of a few things: Border Patrol checkpoints changed; members of a civilian border group showed up in old areas; smugglers changed routes to throw off law enforcement; a route had been found that offered better cover and concealment and took less time to travel. It was impossible to say which reason led smugglers to choose this particular wash at this particular time, but one thing was certain, judging by the history of illegal alien traffic, if not this route, then another route. The border was a sieve, pure and simple. Like any leaky dike, if you plugged the hole in one place, the water would break through somewhere else.

We began to see trash, like these discarded clothes, very shortly after entering the wash. The light-colored piece of cloth in the tree branch is a pair of pink panties.

As we made our way around a corner, we spied a small collection of multi-colored backpacks spread over a small area on the ground. The packs were new, which was not uncommon; it is almost as if the illegals buy backpacks just for the trip north, knowing they will eventually discard them when they meet their pick-up contact. After spending some time in the desert you can tell when items are new and when they've been on the ground for a while; the harsh climate is not kind and items left discarded only for a short time become weathered. Also, we knew it had been raining for a few days; the packs should have been soaking wet but they weren't. Rather, they only had some small droplets of drizzle on them from the day's light rain, and that could only have meant they had been left there just hours earlier, JP said. The packs themselves were empty, but alongside them were several "migrant raincoats"—black trash bags rolled up tightly and secured with a bread tie. Illegals made them into raincoats by cutting a small hole in the sealed end and slipping them over their heads, thus keeping themselves relatively dry and protected from the elements. We also found a few pieces of clothing—jeans and shirts—a couple of water bottles, a toothbrush and a couple of empty food cans.

The writing was in Spanish but I could tell a few of the cans were refried beans, some had contained tuna, and others had fruit cocktail. Judging from the size of the trash pile, it looked as if only a small group of border crossers had stopped there to change clothes, get a bite to eat and refresh themselves before moving on. But it was equally obvious that, as JP and Jim had been told, the wash was now "active" and was being used to smuggle illegals into the country. JP picked up the "raincoats" and stuffed them in his jacket pocket. Other locals working to turn something negative—unlimited illegal immigration—into something good had begun to pick up the better-looking clothing, too, and would then take it home and wash it before donating it to local shelters and charities who were in need of such items. Many of the clothing items were new or nearly new (especially the backpacks). It was a great idea; the people who had begun collecting the better backpacks and clothing figured Americans in need may as well get some use out of them; otherwise, the stuff was just going to rot out in the desert.

After a few minutes of gathering things, taking pictures and looking around to make sure nobody was hiding nearby, we moved out again into the wash. We hadn't walked very far when we began to see more water bottles—a few here, a few there—indicating that we definitely were on the right track. Some of the water bottles even had some liquid left in them—a rarity, since migrants generally drain them before tossing them away in the wilderness. Confident now that that people were moving through the area—and recently—my anticipation as well as anxiety were heightened.

The bulk of illegals heading north were mild-mannered people who would never hurt or threaten anyone, but, I was told, you couldn't necessarily tell the good from the bad simply by looking at them. The most innocent-looking, bedraggled migrant standing eyes-down in front of you one moment would be the guy picking up a large rock and driving it into your head the next, if you turned your attention away from him for an instant. To be fair, it wasn't just the men; the women, in their own right, could be just as dangerous. The point was, if you ran into illegals, you never took your eyes off of them. Otherwise, you just might become the next head-bashing victim on the border. And if you were packing a pistol and it was stolen from you, chances were that even it could be used on you. Desperate people in desperate situations sometimes do desperate things—things they would never ordinarily do under otherwise normal circumstances. And if the people who were walking miles and miles for days on end after paying someone to sneak them into the country weren't desperate, then who was?

A half-hour passed as we continued to make our way along the wash, occasionally detouring to one side or the other, either because we found more trash or because JP thought he had seen something moving. As the wind blew, the slow, steady drizzle continued to fall and it got even darker as we moved slowly, quietly, carefully, continuing to watch our surroundings. Then the amount of trash began to increase, and we noticed there were greater numbers of empty water bottles and other items tossed around a larger area.

I was straining to hear any sounds besides the whistling of the wind. I heard nothing, and there were no indications that anyone was moving toward us. The road and bridge where we had started were now several hundred yards to our rear, and JP said something about going only a little further before heading back while we could still see. I began to think that maybe the weather would keep any illegals holed up for the night, but I quickly dismissed that notion, remembering that we had already found some makeshift raincoats—that, and the fact that some illegals may use the inclement weather to mask their movement. The fact that many migrants had probably been walking for as much as a week already led me to believe they were, by now, well accustomed to the elements and were anxious to reach their destinations.

Suddenly, as we rounded a small bend in the wash, JP stopped for a moment and held up his hand, staring intently at . . . *there!* Perhaps a hundred feet ahead was just a glimpse of a man wearing a tan-colored jacket, blue jeans and a dark-colored ball cap. We made eye contact simultaneously, for just an instant, then with a quick, instinctive turn, the man disappeared into the maze of desert brush and scrub.

"*Alto!* (Stop!)" JP yelled, but the man didn't stop—nor did I seriously think he would. JP ran up ahead to see if he could catch up to the fleeing man, as I followed at a slower pace, eyes sweeping both sides of the wash, making sure we weren't running blindly into something worse. Within seconds, though, JP—perhaps realizing the same thing—quickly broke off his chase, and as he caught his breath he tossed a glance behind him, making sure I was on my way. When I reached him moments later, he had already scouted out the area ahead of him. Neither of us saw the man again, nor did we see or hear signs of others.

For several more minutes we searched an ever-widening area around the spot where we'd seen the man, but came up empty. JP thought maybe the guy was a scout or something for a larger group, but that since he ran into us, now the group would either go to ground or, more likely, backtrack the way they came and pick another route to the highway—perhaps the trail where Jim sat. The man could have also been a drug mule, though, and may have been traveling alone or, at a minimum, in a small group. Either way, it wasn't likely we were going to see him again, which was probably a good thing, considering that by now we had only a half-hour or less of daylight left. It would take us nearly that long to walk back to our vehicle. And as time went on, the weather was getting worse. Heavier clouds were rolling in past a nearby mountain range, darkening the sky even further, promising much more than just the few drizzly rain drops that had been falling all evening. We would have to take up the search again the next day, and hope that the weather would be at least a little better.

———————

And it was. We got back to the wash around 10 o'clock the next morning. The drizzle had stopped and the sun was making a decent appearance, though clouds still took up much of the sky. Temperatures continued around forty-five degrees and the wind blew steadily, but there was definitely a touch of spring warmth in the air—a welcome respite, especially for JP, who had shivered most of the previous day. The sighting of the tan-clad man the day before had emboldened us, and we decided to walk further into the wash to see if we could find others or, at a minimum, get a feel for the number of illegals heading north. We had told Jim of our sighting and asked him if he had seen anyone come by, but the man's group—if there was one—had either laid low or gone another way. Out in the desert there were literally thousands of runs leading away from the border, and the coyotes knew most all of them. They would have taken one that would have provided them the best chance of getting away.

Jim couldn't join us on our second trip to the wash, but it was a moot point, since we were on our own the day before. Besides, JP would bring his rifle again, both of us would pack sidearms, and we had much better light to work with.

We quickly walked to where we'd seen the tan-clad man. As expected, the heavy clouds from the previous evening had dumped a lot of rain on the area, and many of the fresh tracks we'd found were gone. But there were new tracks—lots of them—in the same area, and that meant either the man we saw had gone ahead and led his group through the area after we left, or an entirely different group—or several groups—had come through instead. The thought of the tan-clad man leading a group through after we left was a bit disturbing, because if that were the case, it could have meant they were watching us. And if they were armed, it meant we could've been hurt—or killed.

Some Border Patrol agents told me that, in certain sectors of the border, up to half of the illegals coming through were criminals in their home countries. That reality struck home.

Also, just across the border in Mexico, major gun battles between drug smugglers and Mexican federal police and troops had been occurring more frequently. Some battles took place in the streets of Mexican towns; some involved the use of heavy weapons, including bazookas and rocket-propelled grenades. And while JP had lots of experience dealing with and tracking illegals, unlike me he had no military experience. I vowed to use more of my training and to be more careful. In the desert, sometimes you only got one chance to be careless.

Judging from the direction of the footprints, it looked as if the crowds were coming from further down the wash. With that in mind, we continued to walk further into the desert, away from the road where we parked—but towards a few of the scattered homes in the area. Most homeowners, I noticed, had erected barbed-wire and other types of fences not simply to mark their property, but to protect it and their homes from "uninvited guests." On more than one occasion, JP and I found tracks which led from these parcels of private property and headed into the wash, indicating that some fences weren't keeping intruders out.

We still had not found what JP was looking for—and knew was "out there"—a major rally point or place where the illegals were gathering. But almost as quickly as that thought struck us, we happened on one.

It was huge, and it was recent. The area of trash spread out over a couple hundred yards, and it was inundated with fresh footprints. We found dozens of new backpacks and bottles of water, many unopened. There were also scores of food cans—most empty but some were still unopened and fresh—along with dozens of loaves of bread, remnants of lunch meat, apple cores and bottles of hot sauce. Clothing was everywhere, including what we believe had to be a sort of ladies' changing area, because it was filled with new panties as well as unopened feminine products, underarm deodorant, make-up, shave cream, razors and perfume. Some of the backpacks also contained items: walkman-type tape players with headphones and cassette tapes (containing Latino music with labels in Spanish), more food, changes of clothing, diapers, toothpaste and toothbrushes and personal care items. And, of course, there were several piles of excrement all around, along with half-used roles of toilet paper.

JP and I donned rubber medical gloves—you didn't want to touch anything with your bare hands because of the possibility of contamination—and we began going through the items and the packs. Many of them were obviously new; a couple of them even had store tags (in Spanish) still attached to them. There were so many packs it took us several minutes to search them all, but ultimately we didn't find anything of importance, though someone had recently found a backpack nearby with a diary containing Arabic writing.

Where's the maid? Glimpse of desert rally point near the wash.

The *Sierra Vista Herald-Review* reported in February 2003 that while it was not uncommon to find backpacks near their home, one local couple happened to find one that contained a diary of sorts . . . with writing in *Arabic*.[1] Harold Kolbe, while chasing Javelinas away from his home, found the backpack containing the diary and brought it home. He and his wife went away for the weekend, but when they returned, Harold's wife was curious and decided to look into the pack. That's when she found the diary. Oddly enough, a local Border Patrol station spokesman, Rob Daniels, told reporters he wasn't allowed to discuss the number of non-Mexicans the agency encountered in their sector.[2]

The amount of debris was staggering, and what struck me was none of it was visible from the road, which was several hundred yards away by now and long obstructed from my view by the ground cover and scrub trees. It was that way all over the desert—trash piles, sometimes a couple feet deep, lying just out of view of homeowner and driver alike. Some areas that were filled with debris were just feet from major highways, yet totally obstructed from view, save for the occasional empty water bottle blown onto the highways by the high winds.

By now we were sure that not only was the wash being used as a major smuggling route, but it had been used very, very recently and, most likely, within the past twenty-four hours. Foods such as bread don't last long in the desert, even if the weather's cool and rainy. Yet it was clear that the loaves we found were still very fresh, and the half-eaten apples we saw lying about had only hints of the brown coloring that occurs after exposure. Many of the clothing items were bone dry and had no traces of dirt or sand on them. If anything, judging by the excess water and food, the area was going to be used again, and soon, by other groups being smuggled in.

JP and I walked the perimeter of the site to make sure no one was around, then spent an hour examining everything. Though there was plenty to indicate recent use, we never saw anyone. By now I had seen many smuggling routes, many places where illegals gather to eat, sleep and refresh before moving onto final destinations, but never had I seen one that had been used so recently.

It was mind-boggling, really, to consider the amount of time and effort it would take for a property owner to clean up this one mess, in just this one spot, after just one stopover by a group of illegal aliens. I could only imagine what the area would look like in another week, a month or a year. I had seen a great deal of destruction visited upon many private and public lands along other areas of the border, but I knew I had seen only a fraction of what was out there. When I considered, for a moment, how long it would take to round up the debris from this site, I realized that it would be next to impossible to clean up the tens of thousands of acres of similar trash sites in each of the southwestern U.S. states—if they could all even be found. I had heard some people estimate that one-fourth to one-third of Arizona's land closest to the border had been tainted, if not ruined outright, by illegal immigration. Yet, to hear some politicians and immigration supporters tell it, all illegal aliens, including the group we had narrowly missed, somehow had a "right" to visit such destruction upon American soil.

SAN DIEGO, California—The "undocumented migrant" emerged slowly from the concrete water pipe he had just crawled through tugging at his britches and looking around intently, no doubt checking to see if anyone had seen him. The pipe, located just inside the United States, was only yards from a massive border fence separating the U.S. and Mexico. It was an odd scene, not so much because it is truly "odd" in the sense that it is uncommon; illegal aliens sneaking into the United States are hardly that. Rather, it was odd because it wasn't taking place in some remote locale in Arizona, New Mexico or Texas—it happened in urban California, in one of the best-patrolled sectors of border in the country. In fact, less than thirty feet away, one of the Border Patrol's finest was watching everything, a slight smile forming on his lips.

Is this Tijuana? Illegal alien emerges from a drain pipe on the U.S. side, near San Diego. He was being watched ten feet away by a Border Patrol agent.

Based on some reports, the casual observer might expect Border Patrol agents to rush the illegal, slam him to the ground while shouting obscenities, shackle him in chains and drag him away to some dark, dank dungeon, where he would be questioned and tortured for hours before finally being released back into Mexico. But this is the U.S. not Mexico; the lone agent watching the scene unfold before him calmly confronted the illegal, muttered a few words of Spanish to him, then pointed towards a small one-way gate about fifty feet away leading out of the U.S. and back into Tijuana, Mexico. The illegal brushed himself off, smiled at the USBP agent, and walked the few feet back to Mexico—probably already planning a new way to sneak into America.

I had just hooked up with a Border Patrol agent—call him "Steve"—who had agreed to show me around his USBP sector on his off-time, because, he kept telling me, "people need to know what's going on down here, so I want you to see it first-hand." So did I.

One thing I noticed right away was that the sectors closest to San Diego were much better protected and patrolled than many wilderness areas of Arizona, New Mexico and Texas. For one thing, the southwestern California sectors had a *real* fence—actually, a couple of real fences, an outer and inner fence. The outer fence, comprised of matting used by the military to construct makeshift runways, was built right along the U.S.-Mexico border over time by National Guard units from around the country. At about fifteen to twenty feet high it seemed formidable, but as is the case everywhere along the border, looks are often deceiving. The second fence is located about a hundred feet inland, and the grounds between the fences are largely leveled and cleared of brush or anything else that could hide illegal border jumpers. It too is about fifteen feet high, the final couple of feet angled outward (towards Mexico) to make it more difficult to penetrate. But it has also been breached—often—by illegals using homemade iron "ladders" with hooks fashioned on the end of them; there are spots all along the top of this inner fence where "dips" in the mesh wiring indicate a laddered crossing point. Steve said increased USBP patrols and the presence of two large fences didn't thwart all of the border jumping—as the drainpipe crawler proved—but "it sure cuts it down."

After talking to his fellow agent for a few minutes, Steve and I got back into his truck and started driving along a well-maintained road that runs between the two fences. Also positioned strategically between the inner and outer fences is a series of light poles, so agents can illuminate the area at night. The road, built specifically for use by USBP agents on patrol, is at times close to the outer fence. Steve said it's often that USBP vehicles, when they are in those areas, are pelted with rocks thrown by Mexican nationals from their side of the border. Even if the rock attacks get severe—and at times they are—agents risk job loss and prosecution if they fire at citizens inside Mexico. Gunplay from across the border is a different matter, supposedly, but Steve and many other USBP agents have seen bureaucracy and political correctness swallow the careers of too many good agents to trust what will happen if they ever have to defend themselves with deadly force.

Tijuana is easily visible. Its appearance is depressingly poor and is the diametric opposite of urban, bustling, beautiful San Diego. Looking at the run-down homes, dirt roads and garbage, you can begin to develop an appreciation for why so many Mexicans want to flee. People openly burn trash, even along the community's streets, and as I scanned the squalor while we drove along the U.S.-maintained border road, I spied a young boy urinating in public, right outside the front door to his home. At one location a huge drain pipe juts from a culvert and points straight into the U.S.; Steve says the pipe carries sewage and filthy run-off water into America. I asked why the U.S. government had not insisted the pipe be rerouted back towards Mexico; he just shrugged, and to me, that said everything.

We drove on for several more minutes and I quickly noticed that the number of agents along this urban stretch of border far outnumbered those in other, more rural areas of the southwestern border states. While it seemed to make sense given the greatly increased population on both sides of the border here—the proximity of an urban Mexican community, and the congestion of people and traffic traversing nearby San Ysidro and Otay Mesa ports of entry—it puzzled me that there would be such a dramatic difference in the numbers of USBP agents given the overall better security afforded by fences, lighting and other technologies. I wondered why more agents weren't being stationed in the rural regions of the southwestern frontier, but then it hit me—the number of agents that would be needed to man the entire border, as it was being manned here, would likely be staggering. It would take an army—something the politicians weren't eager to deploy.

About an hour later, we were visiting the outlying regions of Steve's patrol sector, where USBP vehicles patrolled dusty dirt roads parallel to the border all the way to the Pacific Ocean. Along these routes, as in other border states, trash left behind by invading illegals was in evidence all around. We drove by one area that floods often during the spring rains and, when it does, fills with so much filth that agents patrolling that sector have actually gotten sick after being there for a length of time. Even when the area is dry, Steve said it was still dangerous because it remained contaminated. He warned me not to get out of the truck and go wading into the middle of it, but I told him I had to at least get a look at it. He said as long as I didn't stay too long I'd probably be okay. *Probably.* I took his advice; I got my photos and we left.

The area reeked. Another piece of America made unusable by hordes of illegal invaders.

USBP vehicles were also fairly evident in these outer regions closest to the ocean. As we drove, I snapped pictures of the rolling southern California hills that stretched into Mexico, appreciating the fact that much of the landscape could remain green, especially in the dead of winter. At one point we encountered a USBP vehicle that appeared to be abandoned, but Steve said the agent it belonged to was likely out on foot, patrolling the nearby border fence. As we passed the vehicle, I noticed its passenger window had a series of cracks; Steve said the vehicle had been hit with rocks thrown by Mexicans and the window hadn't been replaced yet. No one was hurt, he assured me. Not this time, anyway.

Raw sewage and other contaminants flow from Mexico into the U.S. The fence in the foreground is the border.

Later still, we went to see the ports of entry at Otay Mesa and San Ysidro. I was amazed at the sheer numbers of people trying to get into the U.S. The lines seemed to go on forever, as dozens of Immigration Inspectors worked diligently to screen visitors and process them as fast as possible. Steve said at times the Immigration Inspector supervisors—who have been instructed to shuffle "visitors" through quickly by their bosses—order line inspectors to "open the gates" essentially, and begin admitting people willy nilly, without adequately checking their identification or screening them in any meaningful way. Once the lines clear, the supervisors order inspectors to implement "normal" screening procedures—until the lines back up again. "It's a joke," Steve said.

Some of the Mexican nationals trying to gain entry appear nervous when they are in line with inspectors. Many don't speak much English, if any at all, but inspectors generally speak fluent Spanish. Those trying to enter illegally, however, are taught to respond a certain way to specific questions being asked by the inspectors. They rehearse their answers before arriving at the port of entry. So sometimes, to flush out migrants who may be guilty of a crime or are not who they claim to be, agents will ask off-the-wall questions and use unconventional likes of query. It works, Steve says, but agents here complain that supervisors often order them not to stray from the standard lines of questioning out of "respect for the visitor."

Outside of the ports of entry the sea of humanity is just as thick, but they are crammed into cars instead. The smell of exhaust is stifling and, during the summer months, must be nearly unbearable; it's a smell that belies the otherwise green serenity of San Diego, with its sand and beaches, palm trees, bikinis and tanned bodies. Lanes of inspectors perform duties similar to those of their counterparts inside, but these inspectors must check back seats, truck beds and trunks, as well as any on-board luggage and shopping bags. Inspectors in auto lanes must endure "busy" times of the day—morning and late afternoon, before and after work and on Saturdays—and they must open and close lanes to accommodate the heavy traffic. The ports never close completely, as there is always north-south traffic. These inspectors have discovered illegal aliens being smuggled into the U.S. inside of automobile seats, dashboards, and special hidden compartments inside a trunk, to name a few. If there is a creative way to smuggle someone inside a vehicle, it's been tried at the U.S.-Mexico ports of entry.

In other ports of entry, tractor-trailer rigs by the thousands cross from Mexico everyday, and that traffic is particularly heavy near San Diego. While USBP, Customs and Immigration agents all do their best to screen them, all trucks are not thoroughly inspected. There's no doubt that a thorough inspection of each truck would slow traffic to a trickle through the ports, but I saw some trucks—perhaps those driven by drivers very familiar to port inspectors—waved through without so much as even asking the driver a question. A smile and a wave between an inspector and a recognizable driver is all it would take to get a terrorist weapon into the U.S.

Yet everywhere in evidence along the San Diego sectors is the Border Patrol. As the forward deployed force against the 9-11 terrorist threat, these agents, however, are demonized and abused by politicians and bureaucrats on a local, state and national level—especially in California, where the "new majority" of state residents, legal and otherwise, consists of Hispanics. Democrats and Republicans alike use them as political pawns in a never-ending game of one-upsmanship and vote-buying. So often, however, Americans are led to believe by these same politicians that they are serious about securing our border. They claim they are doing everything in their power to assist the Border Patrol and the Immigration inspectors along the ports of entry in doing their duty. A few conversations with seasoned agents who work the thin green line everyday, however, will change your mind about believing these politicians.

Worse, as Steve pointed out, it seems as though whenever and wherever agents make progress, there is some group or some bureaucracy or some corporation or some politician standing in their way. In San Diego alone, for instance, he said USBP agents—who are permitted by law to enforce immigration statutes everywhere, not just on the borders—used to board city mass transit buses in an effort to find illegals. But when the effort became too successful, local city officials, bowing to a vocal Hispanic activist leadership, complained to USBP and INS managers, who then ordered field agents to cease and desist. The same is true of so-called "pursuit" policies; USBP agents are often criticized, especially by state leaders, for chasing vehicles full of illegal immigrants. The criticism is worse if, unfortunately, drivers of vehicles carrying illegals crash and kill or injure their charges. Rather than blaming the illegal immigrant or immigrant smuggler, the USBP takes the heat for doing its job (or local police take the heat). Consequently, in an effort to avoid such criticism or incidents that could spell disaster for an agent's career, more of them are opting to back away from controversial situations altogether. As bad as that sounds, it is not as much of a problem in rural New Mexico, where illegal immigrant traffic is far less. It is, however, a major problem in places like San Diego, where there is ample illegal immigrant traffic and a dense U.S. population that presents, perhaps, a more lucrative target for terrorists.

And as always, Steve reminds me, bureaucracy is a major problem. Near ports of entry around San Diego, for example, Border Patrol agents, immigration inspectors and U.S. Customs agents cannot even access one another's radio frequencies, even though officers from all three agencies have overlapping job descriptions and responsibilities and must, on many occasions, contact each other for assistance.

San Diego is noted for its moderate weather, but sometimes the weather turns sour. And on days when it's raining or foggy, the USBP will close a number of its roadway checkpoints. The smugglers, Steve says, know this and use that to their advantage. They have "spotters" who monitor the checkpoints and when they close will notify smugglers the coast is clear, usually by cell phone. Such spotters also monitor USBP and local police radio traffic, via a scanner. Steve told me he has suggested to Border Patrol hierarchy that they only *appear* to close the checkpoints, then station USBP agents nearby to intercept suspected smugglers when they come through. Nobody wants to do that, he says—too "underhanded" and "unfair" to the illegals.

By late afternoon we had toured the San Ysidro port thoroughly. We had walked the catwalk across the highway overlooking the lanes and lanes of northbound traffic. We had seen the Mexican children who had spent the day in American schools walking back home to Mexico. We had seen perhaps a hundred people Steve readily identified as "suspected" TONCs (pronounced "tonks;" the acronym, he said, stands for "temporarily out of naturalized country"). Near the port's entrance was a small pocket of shops and eateries, and from there we watched the Mexican "gypsy cabs" in operation—Hispanic drivers who approached "suspected" illegal aliens, and offered to take them north to Los Angeles and other cities for cash. As Anglos, we stuck out in this Hispanic enclave—though we were solidly on U.S. soil—and Steve suspected most people there knew he was an agent of some sort. Maybe they thought the same of me, but it didn't matter; gypsy cabbies continued to approach luggage-bearing Hispanics waiting on street corners within a few feet of us, and the alleged illegals continued to hand the cabbies cash. It was so blatant it was almost surreal.

San Ysidro Port of Entry leading to Mexico.

We stayed out all day and into the early evening. Steve had brought along his duty radio, so we were able to listen to the chatter between agents as night fell. There is always an increase in border jumping at night; aliens use the cover of darkness to mask their entry. But in this sector, as in others, USBP agents station vehicle-mounted infrared cameras at over-watch positions all along their sectors, and the night to illegals becomes daytime to patrol agents. Border jumpers are aware of USBP capabilities. They know the I-red camera is out there. They also know that, despite the number of patrol agents here, there are still more of them than there are agents. So while some get caught, others don't. Often they rely on numbers rather than skill to get inside the U.S. And the "game," so to speak, lasts well into the night; on the USBP frequencies, you can hear agents spotting and reporting illegals into the wee hours.

One issue that weighs on the minds of USBP agents here and elsewhere is that the U.S. government will eventually strike another amnesty agreement with Mexico. If that happens, Steve says, it will make a mockery of enforcement efforts. He told me—as I watched scores of Mexican nationals streaming into and out of the country—that "any amnesty would be granted not only to the TONC's but also their families, immediate and extended. So the TONC gets in but so do two, three, maybe six others as well. The amnesty grows from eight million to thirty-two million, instantly. And that's *if* the 'extended family' is really the TONC's 'extended family.' Maybe they'll just claim to be, and who's going to check another twenty- to twenty-four million illegals to see if they are really related to TONC's already here?"

Remembering how I saw immigration inspection supervisors order officers to "clear the lines," I knew he was right. God knows who would get in under such general amnesties. And they'd become automatic citizens to boot.

The more time I spent along the border, the more I realized what an exercise in futility our current immigration policies have become. Having actually been down to the border several times and seen its vastness, the thousands of foot trails worn into the earth by tens of thousands of feet, the tons of trash and filth created by so much human traffic, it was evident America is losing control of its borders. When you see so much destruction to private property, hear the frustration and anger in the voices of Americans who endure the invasion daily, you start to realize that our policies are protecting—nay, *rewarding*—the wrong people. The more I saw illegal immigrants as they tried to sneak in or as they prepared to sneak in, the more I believed we have already lost the fight to control our borders. Somewhere, in the scrub of the desert, lies the ruins of our sovereignty.

In March 2003, a U.S. representative from Missouri, Republican Sam Graves, introduced a plan to temporarily halt immigration to the United States. He said his proposed legislation was a matter of national security. Naturally, he was roundly criticized as a "demagogue" by immigration rights groups and fellow legislators. But holding his ground, Graves said, "No one ever fixes a leaky faucet while the water is running. We must temporarily suspend immigration until we can properly identify everyone who comes into this country."[3]

I agree. Call me kooky.

WAY UP NORTH

While none of the September 11 hijackers entered via Canada, several unsuc-cessful plots to attack American targets have been planned by foreign terror-ists operating out of Canada. Moreover, Canadian intelligence officials estimate that some fifty known terrorist organizations have cells in Canada. But before September 11, U.S. border agencies were focused almost exclu-sively on stopping drugs and illegal migrants from crossing the Mexican bor-der. Both the INS and the Customs Service had shifted staff from the Canadian border to the Mexican border, despite a 90 percent increase in the volume of U.S.-Canada trade since 1990.

—COUNCIL ON FOREIGN RELATIONS ON WHETHER
TERRORISTS HAVE ENTERED THE U.S. FROM CANADA

Many of the people in charge today are responsible for [an INS] that won't allow line agents to do their jobs. That's why the immigration serv-ice is having so many problems. That's why there are so many screw-ups. And no one is held to account." That's what a retired Border Patrol sector chief, who finished his tour of duty with the USBP supervising a district along the U.S. border with Canada, told me during a tour of the Blaine, Washington, Border Patrol sector and port of entry.

No volume describing life on the U.S. border would be complete without providing at least a glance of life along *both* borders, though gen-erally speaking, America's border with Canada garners a lot less national attention than does its border with Mexico. One of the most glaring differences between America's northern and southern borders is the length; the Canadian border is much longer. At about five thousand miles, it is more than twice the stretch we share with Mexico.[1] Theoretically, then, that should mean the U.S.-Canada border is twice as likely to have a smuggling and illegal immigration problem. But that's not the case. First, Canadians experience a similar lifestyle as Americans, so there is no mass exodus of poverty stricken souls streaming south into America. Also, the Canadian government provides much more infrastructure support for its people than does Mexico (a higher standard of living up north means Ottawa collects more in taxes to support infrastructure costs). Finally, in terms of drugs, marijuana is one of the most smuggled, and though the trade is in high-grade, lucrative weed, Canada's climate allows for a much shorter growing season than does Mexico's.

––––––––––––

Though the governments of Mexico and Canada are both friendly to the U.S., because of the social and economic differences between our two neighboring nations, there are few areas up north where a fence separates the U.S. and Canada. Also, most of the Border Patrol's 10,500-plus agents are stationed along the boundary with Mexico; only about four hundred or so are stationed along Canada's border, as of late 2002.[2] That's about one agent every sixteen miles, according to Justice Department statistics (agents assigned to the Mexican border could be stationed every 1,100 feet, by comparison).[3]

"It's hugely disproportionate in terms of the exposure," says Rep. George Nethercutt (R-Washington), co-chairman of the Northern Border Caucus. "Terrorists aren't stupid. They're going to go where we are vulnerable, where we have gaps."[4] The administration, in 2002, pledged more money—$150 million over two years—to bolster the ranks of the Border Patrol. The White House sought to hire some 570 new agents each year, with about 245 going to the northern border and 285 going to the south.[5]

But despite these pledges, and as is the case with Mexico, political con-

Customs Service fast boats and Blackhawk helicopters patrol northern and southern sectors of the U.S. border, including our border with Canada.

cerns will probably factor heavily in any U.S. effort to strengthen its own security along its northern border. Indeed, since 9-11, even modest efforts by Washington to beef up northern border security have been met with disdain and hostility by Ottawa. But there is reason for concern among Americans wanting a more secure border—the problems along America's border with Mexico duplicate themselves up north, along the Canadian border, even if they occur much less frequently. There are some differences, too. With Mexico, U.S. officials worry about rampant illegal immigration; with Canada, they mostly worry about terrorism.

"Irony is often a partner to tragedy, a collection of coincidences, consequences, and random circumstances that can make the kind of grief we experienced on September 11 even harder to process," says a U.S. Customs statement, announcing American and Canadian border cooperation. "One of the clearer ironies tied to the attacks on New York and Washington DC is that the decades of good will and cooperation that made the U.S.-Canadian border the 'longest open border in the world' eventually made it a target for terrorists as well."[6]

As in the southwest, the northern border also has vast areas of isolated terrain, which makes it hard to guard but easy to sneak across. For example in Blaine, Washington, a quiet, serene community situated in the northwestern most corner of the continental United States, there are few people and even fewer obstacles standing in the way of illegal aliens, drug smugglers and potential terrorists. In much of that border sector, there is only a small ditch separating the two countries, and in many places a four-wheel drive SUV would have no trouble crossing. There are video and infrared cameras in place up and down the sector, but local retired agents say they don't work properly, despite the government having spent several million dollars erecting them.

A place called "Peace Arch Park," a public area near the northwestern edge of town, is wide open. Half of the land is administered by the U.S. Park Service, the other half by the Canadian government, and is said by locals to be a place where Canadians and Americans can meet, talk and interact without fences, borders or impediments. They aren't kidding; near the park is a concrete walkway that leads from the U.S. directly into Canada. Though there is a port of entry located there, the surrounding area isn't heavily manned by border personnel from either country, and that, say U.S. agents, has led to security problems.

In March 2003, Border Patrol agents near Blaine intercepted nearly 140 pounds of cocaine that a Canadian citizen was attempting to smuggle into the country. Officials said the drugs were contained in 45 packages; the bust was the third major arrest in the area that year. In February, the Royal Canadian Mounted Police arrested three men sneaking into Canada with forty-one guns, more than two dozen diamonds and wads of U.S. currency in what was likely a guns-for-drugs deal, authorities said.[7] A month earlier, Bellingham, Washington police and U.S. Customs Service agents arrested brothers Brandon and Jay Reyna and seized sixty pounds of "B.C. Bud" marijuana, less than half an ounce of cocaine and $153,000 in cash from their Ontario Street home. Officials said the Reynas were smuggling thirty to fifty pounds of marijuana from British Columbia each week for the past year, worth an estimated total of $6.5 million.[8] All these problems occurred in one small community in one small corner of the border, in a sixty-day window. Imagine what it is like elsewhere along the northern border.

Besides having to deal with a massive open-land border, agents say they are also concerned about the wide open expanses of Pacific Ocean in and around northern border towns. Most coastal and inland communities have a number of docks where boats can pull ashore unchallenged; from such docks, criminal aliens, smugglers or terrorists could have an easy time gaining ready access to the United States. In December 2002, U.S. immigration officials arrested seven Chinese nationals attempting to make their way from a safe house in Toronto across the treacherous St. Clair River into the United States. Royal Canadian Mounted Police task forces busted a similar Chinese smuggling ring the same month. Toronto is considered a traditional staging base used by Chinese smugglers, who often pay "snakeheads" $90,000 each to be smuggled into the U.S. from China, a trip that takes them through seven countries.[9]

Also, veteran agents say, the northwest corridor provides a direct link with the southwestern U.S., via Interstate 5. "What does the northernmost tip of I-5 have in common with the southernmost tip of I-5?" one agent asked rhetorically. "On the northernmost end there is a foreign country—there's 'BC,' or British Columbia, Canada—and on the southernmost tip, there's 'BC,' or Baja California, Mexico. There's a straight shot up and down." Along the way there are major urban centers: Seattle, Washington, Portland, Oregon, San Francisco, Los Angeles and San Diego. That's important, agents say, because the threats to this country don't hang around the border areas. And with no interior enforcement, "illegal aliens, terrorists and other foreign criminals can go anywhere in this country," said the one former BP agent.

––––––––––––

Indeed there is ample evidence that terrorists are taking advantage of the United States' lax northern border with Canada. USBP agents and officials say Vancouver, British Columbia, is a haven for a number of terror groups.

Worse, they say Canadian officials are aware of that fact but have done little about it, mostly because they—like some elites in the U.S.—are politically afraid of being seen as hostile to Arabs and Muslims. But such politically correct concern could eventually cost more lives, both in Canada and the United States; in fact, a pair of incidents almost did. Some of the nation's most serious pre-September 11 terrorist incidents occurred along the U.S.-Canada border, near the Blaine sector.

The first event occurred in 1996, when Border Patrol and INS agents arrested Abu Mezer, a twenty-three-year-old Palestinian, as he tried to sneak into the U.S. from British Columbia. Though he had no identification and had a criminal past, he was allowed to return to Canada and was never charged in the U.S. But former and current Border Patrol agents say Mezer was eventually caught and released two more times—the last time in 1997. He was finally arrested and detained later that year when he was caught in New York City planning to bomb the subway. Gene Davis, a former Border Patrol agent who was working the Blaine sector when Mezer was arrested and shipped to a jail cell in Seattle, told me another illegal alien bonded him out six months later. "They were going after bombs they'd already put together," Davis said. "They were going to be suicide bombers in the New York subway . . . right here along [the northern] border, he just walked across."

Davis said a Border Patrol agent working the Bellingham, Washington, area was checking a passenger bus when he found Mezer for the third time: "The agent was so convinced that he was up to no good that he called the Bellingham FBI office and left a phone message for them, then went over and slipped a copy of the arrest report under their door, saying, 'I think you need to talk to this guy.'" In Seattle, Mezer tried to claim asylum in the U.S. by telling authorities he was a member of the Mideast terror group Hamas, which "wasn't a big deal back then," Davis said. "The judge lowered the bond to $5,000, and they didn't even check the guy who bailed him out. He was in the country illegally on an overstay, a student visa. The money for Mezer's bond, we found out, came from a third party in Saudi Arabia."

In the second major incident, border officials caught Ahmed Ressam in December 1999. With U.S. intelligence agencies and the nation already on alert for potential Y2K attacks, American officials arrested Ressam with explosives in his rented car after he crossed the border on a ferry to Port Angeles, Washington. Ressam trained in camps in Afghanistan funded by Osama bin Laden. He later confessed he was on his way to bomb Los Angeles International Airport, and Davis said Ressam nearly got away with it.

"The U.S. Customs Service did an outstanding job catching the guy. He came through [the Blaine Port of Entry] all sweaty and nervous. The Customs agent had him open the trunk to his car and open a wheel-well of his vehicle [after which] he split off running. They chased him down and brought him back," Davis said.

Davis explained Ressam was tested for drugs but tested negative.[10] However, agents checked his vehicle and discovered electronic timers. At that point, Customs officials notified the agent in charge, who in turn notified the federal Bureau of Alcohol, Tobacco, Firearms and Explosives. Ressam was transported to Bellingham where a Border Patrol agent who had been working there since 1997, when Mezer was captured, was waiting. Davis said the BP agent was told by other federal officials he wasn't needed.

"Nevertheless," Davis continued, "later that night the special agent and the ATF called the U.S. attorney's office and they said, 'We got this guy, we think it could be explosives,' etc. The U.S. attorney's office asked, 'Did he test positive for drugs?' They said, 'no.' The U.S. attorney asked, 'Did you find a detonator?' 'No.' So the U.S. attorney said, 'Let him go.' At that point, they called our guy back—by this time it was around 2 o'clock in the morning—and they said, 'Get down here; the U.S. attorney's office said we have to cut this guy loose.'"

Then, he said, the BP agent placed a "Border Patrol 'hold'" on Ressam, arresting him and informing the other agencies he wasn't going to be released until the BP found out for sure who he was. "If our guy hadn't been called to come down there, he would have walked," Davis said. "What was really remarkable about this is that [several] months ago I was watching the congressional hearings into intelligence failures that led to 9-11.

[CIA Director] George Tenet was asked what the single most important intelligence failure was that led to the attacks and he said, basically, that [Ressam] was because we [the U.S.] didn't realize who he was."

Davis said Ressam was a guy who attended the same terrorist training camp as suspected 20th 9/11 hijacker Zacarias Moussoui. But other federal agencies were about to cut Ressam loose.

Davis and other agents told me that CSIS, or Canadian Special Investigations Service—Ottawa's equivalent to the American FBI—even knew about Ressam and eventually called their FBI counterparts and told them to make sure they didn't let him go.

Nevertheless, even U.S. Customs hierarchy knew Ressam was trying to get into the U.S. with weapons of mass destruction. "When Ahmed Ressam was intercepted by U.S. Customs inspectors at the Canadian border last December 14 in a car loaded with explosives, it changed the way Americans viewed our nation's borders, U.S. Customs Commissioner Raymond Kelly," said in a Customs press release.[11]

Despite an obvious Canadian-based threat, agents say they weren't supposed to mention the "T" word—terrorism—to their supervisors. Washington also didn't want to hear it.

"They would say, 'You guys see terrorists behind every tree, don't you?'" one agent complained to me. "Quite simply, we weren't supposed to talk about it. I was told, 'Blaine's time will come.' Well, it didn't come until we caught a guy trying to come across with explosives. Then [our] people began to take us seriously."

Other officers said intelligence agents of the Border Patrol and other agencies had identified some fifty-five separate terrorist organizations that had cells operating in British Columbia, yet superiors in Washington didn't want to hear about them. Ressam himself, one USBP agent said, had been caught three times. "When I mentioned this to [former INS Commissioner Doris Meisner], she said, 'well, at least you caught him,'" the agent said, incredulous.

As is the case along the border with Mexico, immigration agents up north praise the agencies' "forward deployment" strategy—stationing agents along the border in greater numbers—but complain that an internal enforcement strategy is also needed, especially along the northern border, where the impediments to gaining illegal entry in the United States are few. (In some spots paved Canadian highways are less than ten feet from paved U.S. roads, separated only by a shallow ditch.) That means agencies charged with border security should also be given permission (they already have the authority) to patrol deep within the U.S., in areas known to attract illegal immigrants, to round up and deport those who manage to get past the forward deployed agents. "What we're doing is sending a message to aliens," a former BP agent told me, "that if you get past the guy up here on the line, then you don't have to worry about a thing."

Many may have eventually gotten past agents, but only after they had been apprehended at least once. Worried about Islamic terrorist after 9-11, a sector supervisor in Washington state had his personnel cross-check the list of people who had been caught trying to sneak across from Canada with Arabic-sounding names. The suspects were let go, agents said, because there was either too little jail space available to detain them or because there were no funds available to pay for their detention. "We got about thirty pages of names," the sector supervisor told me, "that we had caught that we had to release because we didn't have the money to keep them. Now, we don't know where these people are. These are people who are potential terrorists. All of these red flags we tried to bring to management's attention; they didn't want to hear it." Added another USBP agent: "We saw 9/11 coming long before it did, but no one [managing the northern border sectors] wanted to hear about it."

———————

Bush administration Department of Homeland Security chief Tom Ridge and Canadian Deputy Prime Minister John Manley, in December 2001, signed a document called the "Smart Border Declaration and Associated 30-Point Action Plan to Enhance the Security of Our Shared Border

While Facilitating the Legitimate Flow of People and Goods."[12] This high-sounding, high-minded agreement set forth "four pillars:" (1) the secure flow of people, (2) the secure flow of goods, (3) secure infrastructure, and (4) information sharing and coordination in the enforcement of these objectives.

A year after 9-11, in September 2002, President Bush and Canadian Prime Minister Jean Chrétien met to discuss the progress of the program. Among the program's highlights:

- "The United States and Canada have agreed to develop common standards for the biometrics that we use and have also agreed to adopt interoperable and compatible technology to read these biometrics," says a White House press release. "In the interest of having cards that could be used across different modes of travel, we have agreed to use cards that are capable of storing multiple biometrics."[13]

- Canada, since June 28, 2002, required all new immigrants arriving there to accept and carry a near-fraud-proof Permanent Resident Card.

- Both nations agreed to more readily share immigrant information.

- Both nations agreed to provide safe third-country havens so their governments can "manage the flow of individuals seeking to access their respective asylum systems."

- Both nations have agreed to enhance cooperation between their respective embassies overseas, regarding immigration issues and visa policy coordination.

- Ottawa and Washington "have agreed to a co-location of Customs and Immigration officers in Joint Passenger Analysis Units to more intensively cooperate in identifying potentially high-risk travelers."

- Both have agreed to move toward development of "parallel immigration databases to facilitate regular information exchange."

There are other measures to be taken, but these are the main points of the agreement. Perhaps they are even necessary, but when standing alone in the tree- and valley-filled expanse of border separating both countries, they seem overly bureaucratic and wholly ineffective. In fact, say northern agents, they probably will be.

Like their southwestern brothers and sisters, northern agents want more bodies on the border because a wider law enforcement presence is what deters illegal immigrants and dope smugglers, not exalted agreements containing flowery diplomatic language. As it is, considering the pure openness of the northern border, it is ludicrous to assume that most illegal alien traffic is being intercepted, and the same for contraband. One analysis suggested agents were only intercepting 10 percent of the drugs headed out of Canada to the U.S. market.[14] Federal border agents say it's easy for smugglers to take advantage of the lax approach to U.S.-Canadian border security and simply cross in a rural, obscure location instead.

"Although concern is mounting over the rising level of Canadian-grown marijuana entering the U.S., the main cause of congressional preoccupation with the northern border centers on the threat posed by international terrorism," said a July 1998 analysis by the Council on Hemispheric Affairs.[15] "Recent arrests have highlighted the ease with which terrorists establish themselves in Canada and move south to infiltrate the U.S. For example, a Palestinian from Israel won refugee status in Canada despite two criminal convictions there. The twenty-four-year-old man was arrested three times by the border patrol while trying to sneak into the U.S. via the major crossing point at Blaine, Washington. However, he was released by an immigration judge pending a deportation hearing. He is now on trial in New York, after being arrested there, along with another Palestinian, on charges of building a bomb allegedly intended to explode a local subway station [Author's note: this is not Mezer or Ressam]."

Bill Miller, a *Washington Post* reporter, also sums up the northern border, post 9/11:

A shallow ditch is all that separates Boundary Road, which winds through the fields and farmhouses of this dairy community, from 0 Avenue, a similar rural highway that parallels it just 12 feet away—in Canada. If not for a small stone marker with "United States" on one side and "Canada" on the other, the border between the two nations here would be impossible to discern. Where Boundary Road ends, rows of raspberry plants run right to the border, offering cover to illegal immigrants and smugglers toting backpacks filled with marijuana. . . . Before September 11, 57 Border Patrol agents were responsible for this 120-mile stretch of border in Washington state. . . . Since then, the U.S.-Canadian border has received the kind of attention that authorities have long spent on the boundary with Mexico, where efforts to halt the flow of drugs and illegal immigrants demanded it. Although the teeming points of entry present their own kinds of problems, halting terrorists who might try to cross these vast open stretches has become the focus of increasing concern among homeland security authorities.[16]

But the problem goes both ways. One U.S. Border Patrol agent, who helps guard the border along the St. Lawrence River and the St. Lawrence Seaway in Upper New York State, and who spoke on condition of anonymity, told the American Free Press that Canada has a "Who cares?" attitude about border security, and that Canada regularly allows aliens to enter "totally without identification papers." Ottawa then releases them into Canadian society without follow-ups or surveillance. "This posture by the Canadians," he said, "allows dangerous terrorist types from throughout the world and particularly the Middle East to enter Canada and then simply slip across its unguarded border into the United States."[17]

In terms of numbers alone, some 260,000 people a day—or an annual total of ninety-six million people—entered the United States from Canada by land in 2000. Ninety-four percent of these border-crossers came in personal vehicles, according to a report from the U.S. Department of Transportation's Bureau of Transportation Statistics. That's a far cry from U.S.-Mexico border crossing figures. The same year about 800,000 people per day crossed the border from Mexico, around 290 million a year. That's about the same as the 2003 population of the United States, though many are likely repeat crossers.[18] In terms of economic figures, however, Canada is America's largest trading partner, followed closely by Mexico; some $1.6 billion in merchandise trade crosses U.S. borders daily.[19] Cross-border trade and merchandise sales dropped 30 percent along America's southwest border with Mexico following the 9-11 attacks because visitors to the U.S. didn't want to wait in long lines.

And now it seems as though commerce is again trumping security. The trend among some Canadian groups—business leaders especially—is not to beef up security at the borders. "Members of the Canadian Council of Chief Executives . . . envision a border reduced to a 'checkpoint' managed jointly by Canadian and American police officers," said a report in Canada's *National Post*. "Tom D'Aquino, president of the CEO council . . . said the council wants to divert the vast majority of border security resources away from the 49th parallel, to focus on the continent's air and seaports, to relieve increasing delays at the Canada-U.S. border." There is also an Orwellian aspect to D'Aquino's plan: He advocates "a voluntary North American identity card" to make border crossings quicker. "According to the council, everything should be up for debate except for a shared currency, shared political institutions, a shared military and uniform immigration and refugee policies," the *Post* said.[20]

But some U.S. lawmakers want more, not less, border security with Canada. "We must improve our threat assessments, control our borders and ports and establish an intelligence infrastructure that attacks and exposes terrorist threats," said U.S. Rep. Lamar Smith (R-Texas), whose district includes San Antonio. Smith, the former chairman of the House Judiciary subcommittee on immigration, was selected in February 2003 by House Speaker Dennis Hastert (R-Illinois) to serve on a panel that will oversee the newly created Department of Homeland Security. He wants to tighten northern and southern U.S. borders. "You never know where individuals with suspicious backgrounds are going to enter," Smith said. "I think we need to spend more money on the borders. We have to have more to secure our borders, clearly."[21]

Perhaps ironically, U.S. policies implemented since 9-11 have driven some asylum seekers to Canada—even those who were legal U.S. residents but feared new rules requiring registration (especially men from key Middle Eastern countries) would lead to eventual deportation. "There's been an increase at some points of entry . . . mostly from the U.S. parts bordering Quebec and Ontario," said Rene Mercier, an Immigration Canada spokesman in Ottawa.[22] Canadian officials and some human rights groups are complaining, saying the new U.S. policies and laws unfairly target certain ethnic groups. But U.S. officials counter that most who seek asylum way up north are doing so because they have to for other reasons, not because they are being forced to by the American government. "The individuals who are rushing toward Canada are doing so because they realize what their situation is, that they don't have any legal basis to remain in the United States," said Bill Strassberger, a spokesman for U.S. Immigration and Customs Enforcement in Washington. "They made a personal choice when they overstayed a visa. They're making a personal choice to not register and to go to Canada."[23]

"You just can't pick and choose who to keep, who to let go," one northern Border Patrol agent told me. "There will never be any homeland security if you do. A country that cannot control its borders cannot control its destiny."

With so much at stake in terms of national security in an age of terrorism, the agent is right; just one illegal with bad intentions, just one mistake, could lead to the death of thousands.

BAD APPLES

"Among the number of applications . . . cannot we find an American capable and worthy of the trust? . . . Why should we take the bread out of the mouths of our own children and give it to strangers?"

—PRESIDENT JOHN ADAMS IN AN 1800 LETTER
TO SECRETARY OF STATE JOHN MARSHALL,
LAMENTING OVER APPLICANTS FOR PUBLIC OFFICE

No federal agency is completely bereft of so-called "bad apples"—rank-and-file personnel, field supervisors, mid-level managers and top bureaucrats who are less than capable of doing their jobs, corrupt or perhaps a little of both. There have been times when border and immigration agents have abused their positions. In March 2003, for instance, a former USBP agent was sentenced to more than two years in federal prison for kicking and punching a Mexican man who illegally crossed the U.S-Mexico border into Texas. After catching up with a group of ten illegal aliens in January 2001, Gary Mark Brugman, began kicking and punching one of the men, according to the U.S. Attorney's office; a pair of agents witnessed the assault.[1]

But at the same time, America's border agencies are at the forefront not only of the conflict to secure our boundaries, but they are waging a public relations battle as well. That is making a tough job even tougher, because one is exclusive of the other. You can't enforce *any* laws (especially laws that seem to target particular ethnic groups with populations in this country) and not step on a few toes or hurt a few feelings. But border agencies seem to generate an undue number of charges of racism, racial profiling or similar ugly, if not incorrect, claims. Hispanic rights groups make such claims especially often, which is ironic considering that many federal USBP, Customs and Immigration agents are themselves Hispanic. But now, especially after 9-11 and the adoption of tougher visa regulations, persons of Middle Eastern descent are also crying foul and are making arguments that the federal government is trying to treat them as it treated Japanese-Americans after Pearl Harbor.

There have also been complaints—usually among federal agency rank and file personnel but also from lawmakers and outside analysts and experts—that the bureaucracies of the immigration agencies perform poorly. Field personnel believe that the performance of overly bureaucratic and top-heavy agencies won't change just because Congress and the Bush administration created a huge new multi-agency Department of Homeland Security. In fact, field agents predict that mid- and upper-level managers, civil servants and bureaucrats who were corrupt, lazy or incompetent before the March 1, 2003, merger will remain unchanged in their performance—but harder to spot now that new layers of bureaucracy are going to be added to old ones that were already shielding them from scrutiny.

———————————

Border agencies are supposed to enforce immigration laws, but perhaps one of the biggest complaints agents have about top immigration and border patrol managers is that few, if any, are enforcement-minded. Agents believe their top managers are more politically motivated in doing their jobs (since they are appointed by, and serve at the pleasure of, the elected administration) than they are in seeing that immigration laws are enforced.

I spoke to current and former Border Patrol agents while researching this book and rely here on their candid opinions about the politics of immigration policies and enforcement. Worried about official reprisals, many were willing only to speak if quoted anonymously.

In describing Clinton administration INS Director Doris Meissner's approach to running her agency, one retired Border Patrol sector chief told me: "[She] was not enforcement-minded at all. . . . And if an officer or an agent was accused of something, whether it was correct or incorrect, she automatically assumed, from the beginning, that the officer was guilty of misconduct. The special interest [pro-immigration] groups have tremendous influence [on the agency]. And rather than fight them and stand up for law enforcement, [she] would immediately roll over and give no support to the officers. . . ." The former sector chief told me that the agency's Washington bureaucrats would micromanage field supervisors: "If an accusation or something was made, instead of allowing me to handle it, it would be immediately handled from headquarters (or higher) level. Then, instead of solving the problem or fixing it, more restrictions would be imposed [on the agents], making it harder for them to do their job. So what's the use of having [field] managers if you're not going to listen to them or allow them to do their job?"[2]

Others have said Bush administration Homeland Security Director Tom Ridge is equally motivated by politics, not enforcement. In fact, Colorado Republican Congressman Tom Tancredo says when he implored Ridge and the White House to put American troops on the border to beef up federal personnel and enhance security, he was told by Ridge that "cultural and historical" reasons prevented the U.S. government from being able to do that.[3] Most immigration reform observers saw that as a nod to Mexico as a historic U.S. ally, as did Tancredo, and faulted the Homeland Security chief for sacrificing American safety for political correctness.

He may not have had a choice, however. President Bush also reportedly opposed long-term U.S. troop deployment along the borders as a deterrent to illegal immigration, drug smuggling and even terrorist infiltration. Agents were upset by the decision. "For forty-five years I've been a constant observer of America's immigration problem and I'm deeply concerned that Congress and the last several administrations have consistently ignored the negative impact on this country caused by illegal immigration," said Bill King, a retired chief U.S. Border Patrol agent, at a June 18, 2002, news conference in Washington DC, held by Tancredo to highlight the problem of continued illegal immigration. "I'm here today to relay the concern of most retired border patrol managers, as well as current border patrol agents who are fighting this fight, in my opinion, all on their own."[4]

Veteran agents say a "bureaucracy knows best" mentality is rife throughout the border agencies. "[INS] began to increase its staff at the regional and then headquarters level," a BP officer told me, "[but] that doesn't streamline operations or make them better or more efficient. What it does is put more layers of bureaucracy in there that you have to go through before you get to someone who can make a decision . . . or help you with a problem that you have."[5]

Rep. Jim Kolbe (R-Arizona) has criticized USBP bureaucracy. He said he thinks the agency "is not well managed. It's very lacking in supervision and leadership. It has poor morale." He says the answer "is more resources for the Border Patrol, better use of technology and intelligence," but he also supports "a guest worker program that controls and legalizes the flow of people coming across the border so then the Border Patrol can concentrate on those who are the bad guys, the drug smugglers, the coyotes who are smuggling people, and perhaps terrorists who might be coming in."[6]

Many agents complain that the entire immigration system has been set up to fail by policymakers. They say the government spends millions of dollars annually training new officers, teaching them to do their jobs and drilling into them that they are doing something productive for their country. But then, when they finish the academy and are put into the field to work, they realize that politics often dictates policies—even policies that are counterproductive to the agents' sworn duty. "And they wonder why morale is so low and why the government can't keep them," one agent says. "You're supposed to train us, empower us to do our job, then stand behind us. But [they] don't do that."[7]

One former chief Border Patrol agent told me he was once instructed by superiors to participate in a conference call with then-INS Commissioner Meissner: "I was returning from a station in Oregon, and I got the call to participate in the conference call. So I had to find a place to stop so I could dial in to the call. You know what it was for? It was because the Tucson [Border Patrol] sector had gone out and worked with the Phoenix Police Department and arrested some people. Well, the agency got a bunch of complaints, so immediately that was wrong. . . . 'You don't go out and do that. . . . You don't work with these other agencies.' But these were things we had historically done for years. None of the arrested subjects were abused or anything, but instead of coming out and defending its agents, the BP came out and told us, 'You can't do that.' Those are things that make it difficult for agents to do their jobs. Many of them say, 'If I don't do anything, then I can't get into trouble.'"[8]

Some of these relationships of cooperation with local police agencies took years to build, USBP officers said. And many of the local departments had even been led by police chiefs and supervisors who were reluctant to participate in immigration enforcement. But it took just one bureaucrat's decision thousands of miles away to wreck those relationships overnight and in the process put the nation and the American people at greater risk. All because officials beholden to special interests took a little heat.

Other agents say the old INS used to enforce a "catch and release" policy, whereby they would ask illegal immigrants caught in one part of the country to voluntarily notify immigration officials when they arrived at their final destinations. "You had no address for many of them," said one former BP agent, "but you gave them a piece of paper and told them, 'Now when you get to [where you're going], you notify INS that you're there and show up for an [immigration] hearing.' How many of those people do you think showed up? This was a common practice, and they did it for years." Agents say it is impossible to tell how many serious criminals—including terrorists—abused such lax enforcement procedures to get into the United States and disappear. Though the new Homeland Security Department's immigration division no longer enforces this policy, veteran and retired agents say they're certain some of the nation's worst enemies who got into the country back when it was being used are still here and are working behind the scenes to plan more mayhem.

Though the bureaucrats in Washington like to anguish over how best to stem the tide of illegal immigration coming from Mexico and the poor Central and South American countries, most line agents have a good grasp of what needs to be done. "Shut off the flow of jobs," says one, reflecting a point of view heard often among agents. "That would do it."[9] In fact, some agents point out that there has even been an extensive study proving such a measure would cut immigration to the U.S. dramatically.

In 1990, Congress established the U.S. Commission on Immigration Reform, via the Immigration Act of that year. The first commission chair was the late Barbara Jordan, a law professor and former U.S. representative from Texas. Jordan died before the commission completed its work; in her place, President Clinton named another law professor. Shirley Hufstedler, who was the first U.S. secretary of education and a former federal judge on the Ninth Circuit Court of Appeals, to replace her. The panel issued a series of reports and recommendations from September 1994 until its final report in September 1997.

According to an assessment by the Federation for American Immigration Reform, an advocacy group seeking immigration limits, a number of the commission's recommendations to shore up border controls and prevent asylum abuse were enacted. But, FAIR said, key in deterring illegal immigration is to make sure those entering improperly or overstaying visas don't have viable employment opportunities. "Although big business likes to claim that our present high level of immigration is necessary for its survival and the robustness of our economy, many Americans find the idea that American know-how and ingenuity must be imported from abroad absurd," said FAIR.[10] One way the commission recommended limiting employment only to American citizens and legal immigrants was to use a computerized registry, then require employers to check every employee and prospective employee's name and Social

Security number with the government, to ensure an illegal immigrant wasn't using a phony name and/or number to obtain a job.[11]

The Jordan Commission, in published statements released in 1994, made dire, if not accurate, statements regarding U.S. immigration reform—statements very familiar to most first-year Border Patrol agents: "[N]othing will take away from the fact that we remain a country of immigration. But at the same time, while we are so hospitable . . . our patience grows a little thin when people . . . try to manipulate our laws and overwhelm the American people by actions that ignore and circumvent the law. The U.S. can reclaim control of our borders without sacrificing our most cherished principles. . . . [Efforts to control immigration are not anti-immigrant.] Rather, it is both a right and a responsibility of a democratic society to manage immigration so that it serves the national interest."[12]

———————

Agents also complain that the hierarchy rarely has anything positive to say about their efforts—unless it's in public in front of a television camera. But behind the scenes, agents who are accused by illegal immigrants of violating their rights are presumed guilty until proven innocent. And, the government system of managing border agents is tilted against officers and for criminals, say veteran agents.

A case in point involved a pair of Border Patrol agents employed in the Chula Vista sector near San Diego. Patrol Agents John R. Wallace and Robert Curtin were dragged into federal court for allegedly "violating the civil rights" of Erik Mendoza-Rubio, who falsely claimed Wallace and Curtin beat him while in custody. Following is what really happened, as eventually proven in a court of law and as described by the National Border Patrol Council Local 1613 (which represents San Diego BP agents):

> On August 30, 2001, San Diego Police officers arrested Mendoza, who was in the possession of a stolen vehicle. Officers later discovered three

illegal aliens in the trunk of the stolen car and one of them was a seven-and-a-half month pregnant female who required immediate medical treatment. Unable to identify Mendoza, police transported him to the Chula Vista Border Patrol Station. At the station, Mendoza was identified as a previously deported criminal alien with convictions for drug smuggling and false claims to United States citizenship. Mendoza also had several previous arrests for alien smuggling. During the course of an interview, Mendoza lashed out at Agents Wallace and Curtin. A forty-four second struggle ensued *and was caught on videotape*. Mendoza filed a complaint of abuse with the United States Department of Justice Office of Inspector General. The Federal Bureau of Investigation's Civil Rights Division later joined the investigation. A year later, Assistant United States Attorney (AUSA) Christopher Tenorio, of the San Diego office's Civil Rights Division, announced the indictments of the two agents. Tenorio's only supporting evidence was the videotape, which contained no evidence of the alleged assault, and the testimony of Mendoza, an illegal alien and career criminal. During cross-examination of Mendoza, *he admitted that he misled investigators and was prone to lying when it was to his personal benefit.* Consequently, his testimony resulted in laughter from the audience several times. . . . [emphasis added][13]

The agents were found not guilty of Mendoza's charges on November 25, 2002—more than a year after Mendoza's arrest by San Diego police.

The NBPC Local 1613 reflected the attitude of many agents when it criticized the conduct of the U.S. attorney's office: "Local 1613 . . . is dismayed by the conduct of the Civil Rights Divisions of the U.S. Attorney Office and the FBI" for pursuing the charges despite a lack of evidence and only the testimony of a known illegal alien criminal. The union said it "attributed this conduct to a few special interest groups in San Diego that influence the investigations of the U.S. Attorney's Civil Rights Division. . . . Local 1613 asserts that the indictment should have been filed against Mendoza for filing this frivolous allegation and lying to federal investigators. However, the U.S.

Attorney's Office does not pursue individuals who file frivolous suits against Border Patrol agents, thereby creating an environment for frivolous allegations to increase, shielding criminals like Mendoza, and ultimately diminishing the safety of the American public."[14] During the period of their investigation and indictment, the agents were confined to station duties and forbidden to perform field operations, limiting the capability of the Chula Vista sector.

––––––––––––––

Political concerns means agents are required, more or less, to be selective in their enforcement of immigration laws. And not all border sectors are alike, despite the uniformity of regulations from Washington and laws passed by Congress; some Border Patrol, U.S. Customs and Immigration Inspector sector chiefs run their divisions like little fiefdoms, often demanding that agents in their charge give special consideration to immigrants—legal and otherwise—who are of similar ethnic backgrounds. "I've seen lots of Hispanic supervisors giving breaks to Hispanic illegals," one agent told me, echoing complaints heard by many others. "They don't want us coming down too hard on their brethren."[15]

Immigrations inspectors at various ports of entry say supervisory kinship with—and concern for—fellow Hispanics attempting entry into the country means they are often asked to look the other way when they encounter violations. Inspectors provided some examples:

- One Immigration Inspector says he was told by a Hispanic supervisor and native of Douglas, Arizona—a border community—that he couldn't cancel the visa of a visiting Mexican woman after he found American food stamps in her purse during an inspection. At the time of the occurrence, inspectors had a right to cancel travel visas if Mexican citizens were discovered to be on U.S. welfare rolls.[16]

- Another inspector says he had an Equal Employment Opportunity complaint of racism filed against him because he had not issued enough permits for visiting the United States—a charge that was later found unsubstantiated by superiors.[17]

- A white male inspector says some Hispanic inspectors were given answers to post academy tests prior to taking them by Hispanic supervisors.[18]

- One inspector said supervisory agents released a three-time convicted child molester who was a Mexican national before he got an answer from higher INS authorities regarding the criminal's status.[19]

- Inspectors have denied entry to Mexican national relatives of Immigration inspector supervisors because they did not meet entry requirements, only to have those denials overturned by those same supervisors.[20]

- Hispanic supervisors, said one inspector, have told line agents not to provide Arizona gang task force authorities with information on suspected Mexican nationals who were allegedly members of gangs and were operating in the U.S.[21]

- Some Immigration inspectors have been caught trying to get dates with young Mexican females in exchange for letting them come into the country improperly.[22]

- Another inspector told me, "A Hispanic supervisor was standing behind me when I asked three Mexican women, 'If none of you work or don't earn enough to bring comprobantes (proof of residence and economic solvency or school attendance), how can you afford to go to Phoenix?' The supervisor immediately interrupted and yelled, 'You can't ask that! That's none of your business!'"

Such "favoritism," if that's what it can be called, is also being noticed by the public. "Our borders will never become secure so long as we have Hispanic Border Patrol agents more interested in protecting their people than doing their jobs," says one Caucasian border resident. "There are also too many Hispanic politicians meddling in this process and protecting the illegals too."[23]

Experienced field officers also decry formal agreements between Mexico and Canada designed as "anti-drug efforts" or "efforts to reduce illegal alien smuggling." In 1999, the Honorable Lawrence Macauley, Canada's solicitor general, convened the third annual "Canada/U.S. Cross Border Crime Forum." Touting cooperation between Canada's Royal Canadian Mounted Police (RCMP) and other territorial police agencies and their American counterparts, he bragged that "RCMP and Customs officers have seized over $4.2 billion worth of contraband products" since both nations began an anti-drug initiative. But agents say while such initiatives may work (to some extent) at ports of entry and formal border crossing checkpoints, such paper initiatives are not effective outside of those parameters; in the wilderness, which amounts to 99 percent of the rest of the northern and southern borders, it's anything goes.

Still, there are instances where agents themselves have abused the trust of the public they were hired to serve:

- Agent Dennis Johnson, a former supervisor, faced felony counts of kidnapping and sexual assault in connection with a September 28, 2000, incident. Johnson allegedly sexually assaulted a twenty-three-year-old El Salvadoran woman who was in custody, naked and hand-cuffed. He has since resigned from the Border Patrol.[24]

- Agent Charles Brown, a twenty-three-year veteran, was arrested in November 2001 for allegedly selling classified information to a drug cartel. Brown worked in the agency's intelligence unit. He was suspended indefinitely without pay by the USBP pending his trial.[25]

- Agent Jack Cockerel was arrested for allegedly assaulting a Douglas, Arizona, man in an off-duty fight in July 2001. The alleged victim, twenty-four, told police the agents said "no one could do anything to them, not even the Douglas Police Department, because they were Border Patrol agents." The case was dismissed without prejudice.

Cockerel was removed from contact with the public after his arrest but returned to the field after the charges were dismissed.[26]

· Agent Matthew Hemmer was arrested in August 2000 on Arizona state charges of kidnapping, sexual assault, and sexual abuse. A criminal complaint said Hemmer took an undocumented woman, then twenty-one, to a remote location and sexually assaulted her before allowing her to return to Mexico. In May 2001, he pleaded guilty to aggravated assault for transporting the woman in a Border Patrol vehicle without telling her where they were going. Upon Hemmer's successful completion of thirty-six months' probation, his crime will be recorded as a misdemeanor. The victim in the case retained a lawyer for a civil lawsuit.[27]

Isabel Garcia, a Tucson lawyer and immigrant activist, claims a double standard exists in the handling. "If the kinds of allegations were made against police or sheriff's departments across the country that are made against the Border Patrol, it would be a scandal," she said. "They get away with anything. Even murder."[28] But agents dismiss such criticism as unwarranted, insisting that any bad apples are quickly and properly dealt with, and that the actions of a few should not reflect poorly on the actions of the many agents who are trying to work hard under less-than-ideal conditions.

And those conditions—which sometimes foment bad behavior—aren't likely to improve anytime soon. That's because, agents say repeatedly, neither they nor the American public can get any traction with either major political party in Washington, in an effort to clean up the corruption and dereliction of duty within agencies, as well as getting politics out of the business of border enforcement. Individual complaints vary, but essentially, most agents want to be left alone to do their jobs. They want the government to employ the available technology—satellite imaging, ground sensors, thermal and heat-seeking eavesdropping devices—as well as commit the necessary manpower to the effort. They feel they can accomplish so much more and provide much better security for the nation if they are provided the tools and equipment, and are given the political support, necessary. The American people, by and large, support such tough measures. But many of our politicians—and the supervisors they place in charge of border security—do not.

In early March 2003, Senate Minority Leader Tom Daschle (D-South Dakota), said: "It's a dangerous approach to governance . . . We get weaker, not stronger, by limiting the scope of government."[29] While he was talking about President Bush intentionally leaving money out of the federal budget in order to limit the budget deficit for 2004, Daschle's comments are an interesting take on American government. And there is no reason to believe he, and many other politicians and career bureaucrats, don't feel the same way about border security, based on the available evidence and their past documented performances.

If you subscribe to Daschle's rules of government—bigger is better— then the absorption of the INS, with all its border control components, into the massive fold of the new Department of Homeland Security should mean our borders will become impregnable. Will they? Not likely. In fact, the larger the old INS became over the years, the more inefficient it became at securing the American people against the scourges of illegal immigration, drug smuggling and the importation of terrorist elements. Indeed, little has actually changed along the border since 9-11. True, politicians and bureaucrats in Washington have claimed advances in security, but line agents and border-patrol elements sitting on "X's" in the desert and along our northern border with Canada know better.

As one example of the adage, "the more things change, the more they stay the same," former Border Patrol officials say a multi-million dollar camera system erected near in the Blaine, Washington border sector since the attacks on Washington and New York City has turned into an expensive boondoggle that doesn't work.

And agents say supervisors, sector chiefs and other mid– to upper-level managers in the border-control agencies have a history of downplaying threats and warnings of threats for political reasons. Many, if not most, of these people will remain in their posts as part of the process of merging some twenty-two agencies under Homeland Security. Based on the government's history of empire-building, a history shared among federal bureaucrats, there is absolutely no reason to doubt this will happen. In the end—even though this new super-agency will cost tens of billions more to operate, will employ some 170,000 people, and generate reams of new regulations—border security may still be as abysmal as it always has been, because the dual impetus driving Washington to look the other way—cheap labor and new votes—will continue to take precedence.

Some immigration experts say they believe enforcement efforts should be aimed not so much at borders but at the U.S. interior. Other law enforcement agencies also decry immigration bureaucracy.

The New York Police Department, for example, complains that INS red tape makes it nearly impossible for the NYPD to report illegal aliens for deportation when they commit crimes. Mayor Michael Bloomberg's criminal-justice coordinator, John Feinblatt, said immigration bureaucrats are difficult to reach and have reams of regulations and red tape for dealing with alien criminals. "In law enforcement, we have to make split-second decisions . . . and this is not a split-second process," Feinblatt told a congressional hearing.[30] The city's complaints were prompted by the brutal gang rape of a woman in a shantytown near Shea Stadium in December 2002. Four of the five men accused of the rape are illegal immigrants; three of those four have long rap sheets. The *New York Post* reported that "the rap sheets showed that time and time again the men had missed court appearances, had been arrested while on probation and had been allowed to plead guilty on reduced charges before committing crimes again."[31] Feinblatt also said the NYPD requires cops to put a referral request in writing and have it signed by a commander before it can be forwarded to the INS, a process that can literally take weeks. He added that immigration service red tape—not the city's official policy, which includes an Ed Koch-era rule extending city services to illegal immigrants—prevents police officers from telling the INS about crimes. "I am not sure if today New York citizens are any better off . . . than they were on December 18, 2002, when that woman was horribly assaulted," said

Rep. John Hostettler (R-Indiana), chairman of the House subcommittee on immigration.[32]

———————

If some conscientious agents want to do their jobs and speak out against internal malfeasance and incompetence—as they are supposed to be able to do under federal whistleblower statutes—they are often targeted for retribution. In one case, a pair of INS agents—Steve Letares and Mathew Markiewicz, both assigned to the Law Enforcement Support Center (LESC) in South Burlington, Vermont—were accused of releasing "unauthorized official/sensitive information to the press" when they told the Williston, Vermont, *Whistle* in November they were confined to desk jobs instead of investigating criminal aliens and would-be terrorists.[33] Both said they were targeted for an internal probe after telling the newspaper they and other criminal investigators at a critical INS center that tracks illegal aliens, including potential terrorists, were not allowed to do their jobs. Internal INS documents said the agency accused Letares and Markiewicz of releasing information used to identify foreign-born visitors at U.S. ports of entry—a charge they denied. Also, there was no mention of any intelligence data in the newspaper article. The agents said the only comments they made to the newspaper were about employee grievances, including their concerns that mismanagement and a lack of aggressive investigations at LESC threatened national security, one report said.[34]

The case caught the attention of Sen. Charles Grassley (R-Iowa), who complained to Attorney General John Ashcroft in an August 2002 letter that LESC criminal investigators were paid to do investigative work and while LESC claimed that investigations constituted 90 to 95 percent of the work being done by the agents, that was not the case. "The agents do none of the criminal investigative work that supposedly entails 90 to 95 percent of their work," he said, adding that they currently compare information from police agencies nationwide with LESC information on file and then advise local INS agents of a positive or negative match. "Such administrative work could easily be handled by the dozens of law-enforcement technicians on staff," Grassley wrote.[35]

A February 13, 2003, editorial in Florida's *Palm Beach Post* called U.S. immigration policy "so chronically disjointed that even when a good idea comes along, it is likely to get lost in the bureaucratic and political shuffles." The editorial provided an example. In the mid-1990s, the Palm Beach County Jail conducted an experiment to illustrate the problem. Washington had recognized a need for the INS to "identify and deport illegal immigrant offenders at the front lines of the criminal justice system." The *Post* said lawmakers ordered the INS to station agents in county jails while passing a law "authorizing expedited deportation methods" for illegal aliens. The *Post* said prosecutors who were working at the jail liked the changes because INS agents on-site were able to resolve questions quickly about the immigration status of foreign-born criminals and then send them home. "This sounds sort of cliché," said Assistant State Attorney Robert Shepard at the time, "but we were actually making a difference here." Nevertheless, the experiment ended in 2001 when an understaffed and overworked INS pulled its agents out of the jail, assigning them to other duties. That left just the U.S. Border Patrol—historically also understaffed and overworked manning the nation's borders—to review jail bookings and, if they were discovered, hold illegal aliens for deportation hearings.

"A *Cox Newspapers-Palm Beach Post* study found that illegal immigrants the government should have deported were allowed to become chronic repeat offenders: 140 jail inmates in Palm Beach County between 1999 and 2001 had been arrested at least three times; one man had at least 10 arrests," the paper said. In one of the worst examples, the *Post* editorial said, Romeo Sifuentes managed to avoid deportation to Mexico on two separate occasions after being arrested each time for drunk driving, actually killing another driver in one accident while driving the wrong way on a highway.

"Based on experience, it is clear that putting INS agents at county jails improves the efficiency of dealing with immigrant offenders and plugs a hole in the system," the *Post* said.

"Deportation is proper for foreigners, especially illegal immigrants, who break the law. Ideas about immigration enforcement that work are too valuable to let fade away. The INS must make screening offenders at county jails a priority."

In another case, one INS manager had a "creative" way of getting rid of mail that was piling up. "Tens of thousands of pieces of mail come into the huge Immigration and Naturalization Service data processing center in Laguna Niguel, California, every day, and as at so many government agencies, it tends to pile up. One manager there had a system to get rid of the vexing backlog, federal officials say. This week the manager was charged with illegally shredding as many as 90,000 documents," said a report in *The New York Times*. "Among the destroyed papers, federal officials charged, were American and foreign passports, applications for asylum, birth certificates and other documents supporting applications for citizenship, visas and work permits. . . . The manager, Dawn Randall, 24, was indicted late Wednesday by a federal grand jury, along with a supervisor working under her, Leonel Salazar, 34. They are accused of ordering low-level workers to destroy thousands of documents from last February to April to reduce a growing backlog of unprocessed paperwork."[36]

There are many "priorities" for the newly created Bureau of Citizenship and Immigration Services [BCIS], but according to agents, bureaucrats, politicians and outside experts, bigger government may be better for empire-builders in D.C., but based on its track record, bigger hasn't been better along the border. In fact, it may be a hindrance. On March 1, 2003, the day the old INS and its agencies became the new BCIS in the Homeland Security department, border protection may have gotten a great deal worse.

VIGILANTE JUSTICE

If police can't—or won't—do the job, then . . . residents living in fear should take back their neighborhood. In some circles, that is called vigilante justice. I call it self-defense.

—ALBERTA PHILLIPS, COLUMNIST FOR
THE *AUSTIN STATESMAN*

The term "vigilante" is a Spanish word originating around 1865 and derived from the root word "vigilant," meaning "watchman or guard." Merriam-Webster's defines it as "a member of a volunteer committee organized to suppress and punish crime summarily (as when the processes of law appear inadequate); *broadly* : a self-appointed doer of justice."

Throughout American history, so-called "vigilante justice" has been applied by ordinary people facing often extraordinary circumstances that threatened their health and welfare, or their communities, or their homes, or a combination of each, whenever traditional law enforcement was unavailable or unwilling to step in. Some groups of Americans have also become vigilantes despite a readily available and willing law enforcement apparatus, simply because they were either too impatient to wait for the wheels of justice to turn, or because they knew they would not be satisfied with the type of punishment allowable under the law for a given crime.

It is in this latter context that a number of groups formed to help control the unending flow of illegal aliens, drugs and contraband from Mexico have been labeled, mostly by pro-immigration organizations and many members of the mainstream media, as vigilantes.

———————

Without question there is a certain vigilantism associated with these self-styled border groups, but only insofar as they are defined by formal parameters.

None of the groups researched for this project, however, fit the "we're out to punish immigrant lawbreakers our own way" label; in fact, few of the groups actually detain immigrants and one doesn't even permit its members to carry firearms despite the fact that the law allows it. But these groups definitely were formed because the entity most responsible for security along our borders—the federal government—has been derelict in its duty. And much of that is Washington's fault; the federal government has claimed it has the exclusive right to enforce immigration laws, so when they go unenforced (or are poorly enforced) the federal government rightly gets the blame. Yet lawmakers and policymakers in Washington DC are the first to criticize the citizen border groups trying to stem the sieve that is the southwest border. In fact, some lawmakers have even called for special investigations against the civilian groups.

Shortly after his election to Congress in 2002, newly minted U.S. Rep. Raúl Grijalva (D-Arizona) began calling on legislators to authorize hearings into the activities of the civilian border groups. In a January 2003 letter to the U.S. Attorney's Office in Phoenix urging action against the groups, Grijalva complained that "an atmosphere of fear exists in southern Arizona that threatens to ignite in a flashpoint of violence."

"The words and actions of these groups are ample evidence of an armed racist movement intent on taking the law into their own hands," Grijalva warned. "We cannot allow the complex issues involved in U.S.-Mexican border policy to be hijacked by individuals who have chosen to break faith with our government and take matters into their own hands. . . . I think this rhetoric you're hearing from some of the leaders of these groups is very dangerous to the overall security of the region. The potential for violence is escalating and I think the whole situation has to be investigated."[1]

Patrick Schneider, a spokesman for Grijalva's Phoenix office, said U.S. attorneys would look into his complaint. But as this book went to print, these groups were still in operation and were still working on a volunteer and invited basis to protect private property from illegal immigrants.

Preceding Grijalva's call for an investigation was a statement issued in December 2002 by an activist group called the Border Action Network (BAN), which accused several civilian groups of having a racist, anti-immigrant agenda and having ties to hate groups outside Arizona. The network demanded that federal and state authorities, including Arizona Gov. Janet Napolitano, a Democrat, investigate the allegations.

Other state and federal leaders in Arizona and elsewhere have also called for a probe of these "border militias," as they are sometimes called. That included the city councils of Douglas and Bisbee, Arizona, which voted in 2003 to adopt resolutions opposing the formation of civilian militias and vigilantism to control illegal immigration along the border.[2,3] According to the background information that supported the resolution, "unsanctioned armed militias and vigilantism historically breed animosity among communities by propagating hate, malice and ill-conceived perceptions . . . untrained and armed individuals operating in pseudo-enforcement activities along our international border could lead to confrontations and violence for community residents."[4]

Most at issue, say those opposed to the border groups, "is the safety of people along the border and the legality of the so-called militia groups, formed out of frustration at the inability of U.S. border agents to slow illegal immigration from Mexico," the Arizona Daily Star reported in November 2002. But members and leaders of the groups say detractors are merely trying to deflect attention away from the real issues surrounding lax border enforcement: sticking American taxpayers for the health, welfare and safety of illegal immigrants, as well as the inherent security risk in open borders.

Publicly, the Border Patrol has adopted a pro-law enforcement stance regarding citizen border groups. "We discourage private parties from taking matters into their own hands," BP spokesman Mario Villarreal has said. But privately, the groups say Border Patrol field agents applaud their efforts, and realize they are not out there to disrupt BP operations, hurt border jumpers or "take matters into their own hands." In fact, some BP agents have credited these citizen groups with helping to curb illegal immigration and drug smuggling in areas where the groups are most active.

"We are a law-abiding group that is doing nothing else but protecting private property and the sovereignty of our borders, which are being invaded on a daily basis by drug dealers, criminals and illegal immigrants," says Chris Simcox, owner of Arizona's *Tombstone Tumbleweed* newspaper and founder of Civil Homeland Defense (CHD), a group he formed after calling for volunteers to help with armed patrols of the border on private property. He blames Mexico for much of the trouble along the border. "What is going on in Mexico? Why are we not turning our attention to Mexico's President Vicente Fox and questioning him about why his people are fleeing his country? It is time for the world to turn its attention to Mexico, a country that is obviously not caring for its citizens. Where are the human rights groups, and why are they not up in arms about the oppression and human rights violations being committed by Mexico's government?" Simcox also believes he has enemies on the U.S. side of the border. In January 2003, he was cited on three misdemeanor charges after he—accompanied by an associate—walked armed into Coronado National Memorial near the Arizona-Mexico border. He says he believes the citation was politically motivated by a ranger who didn't approve of his border anti-immigration activities.[5]

Jack Foote is a former Army officer who represents the Texas-based border group Ranch Rescue. With chapters in each state bordering Mexico as well as Oregon, Washington, Virginia and Minnesota, his group also participates in armed patrols, but always—and only—at the request of land owners, who must sign an agreement of understanding before any

Ranch Rescue member steps foot on private property. In separate operations during the fall of 2002, group volunteers—many of them former military and federal law enforcement (including Border Patrol agents) — managed to intercept drug mules from Mexico and confiscate hundreds of pounds of marijuana and other drugs, all of which were turned over to the proper law enforcement authorities. "Our border county landowners have been economically devastated by this ongoing crime wave, and live in fear for their lives from the thousands of criminals that cross their property every night. Our nation is being invaded, and these folks are on the front line of a silent war," he says.[6]

Members of border watch group Civil Homeland Defense keep an eye on several illegal aliens intercepted in Arizona, as they wait for Border Patrol agents to arrive.

Glenn Spencer of the Arizona-based American Border Patrol, however, takes a different approach. His group incorporates volunteer "hawkeyes," who set up video and audio equipment at crossing points along the border and record the border jumpers as they make their way north. Spencer shuns the use of armed volunteers, though sources who have worked with him on operations say armed personnel are never far away from him—for personal protection. Spencer's group, using technology, specializes in uploading live, real time video and audio feeds of their operations to the group's Web site (www.AmericanBorderPatrol.com) so that visitors—the general public as well as policy– and lawmakers—"can see for themselves the invasion that's taking place," he says.[7]

Despite what officials think of these groups, there is a growing body of evidence that the general public—more importantly, the general public that lives in the areas hardest hit by illegal immigration and drug running—support the creation of these citizen's groups. It's not that people support the kind of vigilantism that these groups are being portrayed as committing—the hooded, horseback-riding thugs who come drag helpless immigrants away in the middle of the night to hang them, burn them alive or shoot them. But clearly the attitude among the locals along the border is, "We've had enough."

According to an *Arizona Daily Star* survey in the summer of 2002, 94 percent of the 1,534 Internet visitors to the paper's Web site responded affirmatively to this question: "A California-based group that opposes illegal immigration is organizing a watchdog campaign in Southern Arizona to keep an eye on illegal border crossers and the U.S. Border Patrol agents assigned to stop them. Unlike the Samaritan Patrol, launched by Tucson religious groups with the goal of searching for border crossers in distress, the American Border Patrol will report illegal border crossers to the U.S. Border Patrol. Do you support or oppose this effort?" Only 3 percent of respondents said they did not support it, while 1 percent said they weren't sure. A separate *Star* survey showed that 90 percent supported the formation of a citizen's militia strictly for patrolling borders and thwarting illegal immigration, with 9 percent opposed. The paper reported more than 20,000 votes were cast; "the number of ballots cast in the militia poll is believed to be the most in StarNet's history of polling," the paper said. Meanwhile, respondents to a separate poll overwhelmingly (82 percent) said they did not support placing water jugs in the desert to aid illegal immigrants because to do so would only aid more illegal immigration.[8] Several other polls conducted by various media outlets online, asking whether residents approved of citizen involvement along the border, produced similar favorable results.[9]

In a June 25, 2003, online survey conducted by Lou Dobbs of CNN, more than 60 percent of 2,797 respondents said they would support the U.S. putting troops along the border to increase security.[10] In a Vote.com survey closed on September 6, 2002, 85 percent of the 30,504 respondents said "yes" to this statement: "Border security has become our nation's Achilles heel. Troops are needed to help keep terrorists from entering the U.S."[11]

While these surveys are not scientific, they clearly show that most people living in proximity to the U.S.-Mexico border want more done to ensure a safer, more secure environment and to curb illegal immigration. These surveys also show that ordinary people are willing to let ordinary people get involved in the process.

One of the reasons why civilians patrolling the borders resent the government's criticism is because they believe Washington is being hypocritical in putting military and other resources into guarding the borders of other nations.

"If the United States would deploy the half-million troops protecting other countries along its borders and deploy our army along the Mexican border, the nation would be secure," writes columnist Mike Blair. "American taxpayers have spent billions of dollars on military operations guarding the borders of countries around the world. However, America's borders remain open and porous to millions of illegal aliens. . . . Why does America today need to station 69,203 troops in Germany fifty-eight years after WWII and after the fall of the Iron Curtain? Why are 11,190 stationed in Italy? Another 11,207 stationed in Great Britain? Why does America need to have 40,159 in Japan, which, like the European nations, is as affluent as America and capable of defending itself? America has another 38,565 in South Korea to protect against intrusions from communist North Korea. There are 2,008 American troops in Turkey to help protect Turks against the Kurds of northern Iraq. However, there is not a single platoon of American soldiers in place along the American border with Mexico, which is almost regularly invaded by Mexican Army troops shielding Mexican bandits smuggling drugs and illegal aliens across the border."[12]

Adds veteran television and radio broadcaster George Putnam, who says he was put off by the United States' decision to defend Afghanistan's border from Taliban and al Qaeda-backed insurgents based in neighboring Pakistan in 2002: "The plan is to slow the flow of illegals, illicit drugs, terrorists and contraband into and out of Afghanistan. The United States will finance the construction and maintenance of 177 checkpoints, staffed by 12,000 border police in that far off land. The cost is staggering—each checkpoint and its facilities to cost an average of $300,000. It is to include offices, sleeping quarters, and, in some cases, clinics—this staggering expenditure to guarantee the sovereignty of Afghanistan. Contrast this with the fact that our country cannot and will not, control the flow of illegal aliens across our own porous borders—15 million illegals that have poured into the United States violating our sovereignty!" Putnam goes on to praise the citizens taking up positions along the border: "Where our government has failed us, several groups of patriotic citizens are taking up arms along the Arizona border with Mexico. . . . These armed civilian groups along our borders, providing civil homeland defense, are experiencing constant confrontations with illegals. There have been moments that bordered on extreme violence. It's bound to become more dangerous and, as one observer puts it, somebody is going to get killed. . . . The groups are growing. There are now more than a dozen known militia organizations—armed civilian groups—on the border. It's time Congress and the president become involved. If we can protect the porous border of Afghanistan, with 177 checkpoints and 12,000 border police, surely we can protect the border of the United States of America."[13]

Other residents along the border say they are increasingly becoming involved in tracking illegal immigration, reporting it to authorities when and where appropriate and participating more in the political and practical processes of the issue, because of what they feel is lax enforcement by the federal government. During one trip to the border, I was traversing open ground with some local Arizona residents while, in the near distance, a Border Patrol helicopter patrolled overhead. We never even got so much as a sniff from the chopper. "Here we are, the bunch of us, out in the open in broad daylight," complained one resident, "and they couldn't care less. They have no idea who we are or whether we're carrying anything illegal."

———————————

Is what these citizen border groups are doing—patrolling private property in an effort to thwart border jumping, drug running and other violations of the nation's sovereignty—really vigilantism in the true sense of the word? Not really, though there is such a thing as true vigilantism and it does have an ugly side, as witnessed by events that transpired in a small Missouri town in 1980.

The incident is recounted in a column by William L. Anderson, a professor and adjunct scholar at the Ludwig von Mises Institute:

> On a hot summer day in 1980, someone, perhaps more than one person, shot and killed Ken Rex McElroy while he sat unarmed in his truck in Skidmore, Missouri. Authorities arrested no one, and nobody admitted to the killing. The "prime suspects" told investigators they were "hiding under the pool table" in a nearby bar. Angered by the lack of speed with which local authorities were investigating the killing, the FBI muscled into the fray. Local residents were interviewed, threatened, and interviewed some more.

Anderson wrote that investigators "searched in vain" for a murder weapon, but when all was said and done, the shooting was officially deemed an "unsolved crime." Twenty years later, the perpetrator—or perpetrators—have never been brought to justice.

It is not as though Skidmore was a violent community, Anderson wrote. "To the contrary, it is quite law abiding," he said, "but the people there continue to refuse to talk about the killing of Ken Rex McElroy, and for good reason." It seems McElroy had made a life of terrorizing the community and surrounding area for more than ten years. His death, therefore, was seen as a blessing by most townsfolk—an act that "made life better for the majority of people living there," Anderson said. "Holding to the silence surrounding Ken Rex's death is worth keeping of the peace," local residents believe.[14]

While none of the citizen border groups is looking to gun down immigrants (though some do patrol armed because Mexican troops, drug smugglers and other unknown personnel routinely cross into the U.S. armed), their very existence is an outgrowth of government inaction. And, as Anderson describes, inaction by the duly appointed authority eventually leads people who are threatened to take matters into their own hands:

> One of the most pejorative terms one can use in reference to law and self-defense is "vigilante." Indeed, if one is called a vigilante, it is tantamount to being declared a criminal. Public officials, newscasters, and those in law enforcement solemnly tell us "there is no room in this country for vigilante justice." Instead, we must wait for the 'justice system' to work, and if it doesn't, well, that is simply a price we pay for having a free society.

Anderson bashes "the political classes," saying the "so-called threat" from vigilante justice is little more than the threat Americans face daily from private firms delivering mail or from home-schooling. The only "threat" he says the government is worried about is the fact that vigilantes challenge the government's monopoly on law enforcement. "If we permit people to 'take the law into their own hands,'" he says of the government's position, "we will have innocent people hurt or killed, and the proper wheels of justice will not be permitted to turn." But before debunking that, he says Americans first need to revisit the concept of "vigilante justice."

"The term 'vigilante' comes from the 'Committees of Vigilance' which dotted the western United States in the days following the California Gold Rush," he says. "Fortune seekers, some of whom looked to transfer it from others through robbery and murder, overran communities such as San Francisco. Because there were few law enforcement officials in California, local citizens banded together to fight crime. By all accounts, their actions worked and the crime rate in places like San Francisco was far lower than it is today. As one might also expect, some people abused their powers and government authorities later disbanded the committees. At this point, most people are ready to say that the prospect of private law enforcement is a guarantee that people will abuse their powers, thus making government-run police a necessity. This argument assumes, of course, that government law enforcement officers do not abuse their powers."[15]

Border groups denounce the term "vigilante" and, perhaps, rightfully so. Residents of Arizona, Texas and other increasingly lawless regions of the southwest say they are tired of being ignored by Washington and, as a matter of practicality and safety, are taking a measure of action—but only an *appropriate* measure of action. They see what they're doing as a civic duty. Border residents who don't belong to any group but who—gun in hand—still "patrol" their property in an effort to thwart the hordes, see what they're doing as a right. They believe that because they have vested interest in protecting their property and their lives, they should be permitted to defend it, in the very same way other Americans living in other parts of the country would defend their property and homes against intruders and invaders.

In many respects these people are prime examples of Americanism— they are demonstrating individualism, initiative and self-determination, just the kind of qualities Americans have heralded and fostered since the Revolutionary War and before. Yet the reaction of officialdom has often been pathetic, if not outrageous. Many times, rather than celebrate the fact that there are still people willing to help defend the sovereignty of the nation by putting their own lives at risk, authorities, officials and activist groups increasingly threaten and persecute them instead, all the while providing aid and comfort to the invaders.

For example, BAN, which is based in Tucson, Arizona, has consistently called for official investigations into the activities of citizen border patrol groups, even though there is nothing to prevent these groups from operating in their domain, on private property. In April 2003, the organization presented Arizona Attorney General Terry Goddard with 2,000 signatures on a petition calling for him to investigate the citizen's groups. "The Border Action Network is attacking us while at the same time helping to organize lawlessness on our border," says Glenn Spencer of American Border Patrol.

Besides citizen's groups, local officials have also tried to alert Washington's bureaucrats and politicians to deteriorating conditions along the borders. As the nation was engaged in global battle against al Qaeda and other terrorist organizations, and as war with Iraq loomed in mid-March 2003, a letter was published in a local newspaper—*The Enterprise*—by Sheriff Erasmo Alarcon Jr., of Jim Hogg County, Texas, that should have been a major security concern to Homeland Security officials in Washington, if not local residents themselves. It warned of "military type individuals" being spotted in "remote" sections of the county. Alarcon said it was unclear who the individuals were and what they were capable of, but it was obvious "these people are not the regular undocumented persons looking for a better way of life," he wrote.[16]

Newspaper accounts said officials in Washington, including the U.S. Border Patrol, were questioned about Sheriff Alarcon's warning but they indicated it was the first they'd heard about it. They then gave standard-issue promise to "check into the report."

The existence of such shadowy unknown paramilitary personnel inside our country is yet another reason concerned local residents have formed border groups, if even just to observe rather than interdict. As Sheriff Alarcon stated in his letter, he has no idea who these paramilitaries are. Worse, he notes, they have made numerous incursions into our country. With such an egregious, obvious and *repetitive* breach of our national borders—especially at a time when the nation embarked on a major war—is it really so outlandish for Americans to organize so they can protect themselves in a part of the country being overrun by incursions? Reasonable people think not, but there is a great deal missing from the debate over citizen border groups, rationality being one of the most important missing factors. Perhaps that's why the few folks who have been brave enough to stand up for themselves along the border have been chastised, ridiculed, threatened and even arrested.

Part of the problem isn't with law enforcement; it is with politicians who have adopted a self-serving approach to the problem of our porous borders. Part of it is fear; people who either don't know, understand or appreciate the gravity of the situation along the border—and have been accustomed by government and police to abdicate their right to self-defense—are scared and intimidated by people who have not abdicated that right. And so, absent the "proper" border enforcement authorities, Americans—until these groups came along—were expected to merely accept the abuse, mistreatment, victimization and threats of violence posed by our porous borders. Finally, however, a number of Americans just said no.

There are other local citizens groups besides the so-called vigilante militias, and while they are going about things differently, the goal is the same: to get government to be more responsible regarding border security. Groups of ranchers who own property along the U.S.-Mexico boundary, for instance, formed an organization in March 2003 called the Border Land Association, or BLA, "in an attempt to strengthen the cooperation with the U.S. Border Patrol and enhance the security of our nation's borders." The BLA's primary complaint? "Historically, border landowners have been citizen volunteers, working with the USBP and others to ensure that our nation is safe and secure," said Gene Walker of Laredo, Texas, a border county rancher and president of the BLA. "But over the past four years—long before September 11 [2001]—the USBP has begun to act like an 'occupation force,' ignoring, not only private property rights, but repudiating the assistance that landowners can provide—and have previously provided—to help control illegal entry into Texas" and other parts of the southeastern United States. "Unfortunately," he continued, "landowners have begun to fear the USBP's practices more than they fear the illegal aliens crossing their land."[17]

"Fear" the Border Patrol's "practices"? What practices? Walker names them: "Agents constructing roads and 'drag lines' and installing wireless monitors without landowner permission ("drag lines" are when Border Patrol agents hook tires that have been banded together and literally drag them behind their vehicles; the technique is effective at smoothing dirt roads so agents can detect fresh footprints made by illegal border crossers); agents and pilots, using helicopters, fixed wing aircraft and vehicles to chase and harass wildlife, livestock, property owners, ranch employees and commercial hunting clients; agents destroying private roads, fences and gates and replacing private locks on gates with government locks, barring owners, employees and guests from entering—and sometimes exiting—their own property; agents leaving gates open and cutting fences, allowing livestock to wander onto roadways or other pastures where they could mix with livestock of different ownership or genetics and causing enormous potential expense to ranchers; agents on horse patrol ignoring the [United States Department of Agriculture's] Fever Tick Quarantine Zone and regulations, endangering herds of livestock and placing significant ranch investment at precarious risk."[18]

Walker said many of the border landowners have tried to negotiate conduct agreements with Border Patrol sectors and agents, usually attempting to outline mutually acceptable practices for operations the USBP is conducting on private land. But, he says in a March 12, 2003 press release, the attempts have failed; they "have been ultimately rejected by USBP agents and supervisors." Landowners' response? To form the BLA and attempt to work things out via political action. "The Border Land Association was not created to dwell on past incidents, but to lay the groundwork for better cooperation and a stronger national security," Walker said. "With the . . . formation of the Homeland Security Department, we have an unprecedented opportunity to help restructure and reform the fundamental policies of the USBP, enlisting—instead of alienating—the citizens it is trying to protect." He also says it's "vital" for border action reform "to remove the disincentive that measures border patrol performance based on the number of apprehensions." Just the opposite should be the focus, Walker recommended.[19]

"Rewarding border patrol sectors for apprehending more aliens is backward. If a sector successfully deters crossings, its apprehension numbers go down, and the successful efforts of those agents aren't recognized. On the other hand, a high level of apprehensions indicates a high number of crossings, and the system rewards sectors that allow illegal aliens to enter the country initially," he said. "Regardless of motivation, illegal aliens have one thing in common—they cross an international border. Deterring them from entering the U.S. certainly seems more effective than having to catch them once they get here."

As civilian border groups gain more notoriety, it seems they also have drawn more ire from law enforcement. Border Patrol and Customs agents have privately expressed support for many of the groups' efforts, but other agencies are trying to intimidate them with thinly veiled threats of arrest and prosecution.

In October 2002, police near Red Rock, Arizona, announced they were investigating individuals the *New York Times* called "self-appointed guardians of the border" in connection with the killing of several illegal aliens.[20] The paper reported: "A 32-year-old man who was part of a group of a dozen migrants waiting to be picked up by smugglers at a pond just west of here last Wednesday told investigators that he escaped through the brush after two men wearing camouflage fatigues descended on the group, firing an automatic rifle and a pistol. Officers found two bodies riddled with bullets and no sign of the remaining nine migrants. It is not known whether they escaped or were loaded into vehicles and taken away, either dead or alive." The *Times* reported that at least two immigrants had been killed. It continued, "Mike Minter, a spokesman for the Pinal County Sheriff's Department, said detectives were looking into several possibilities, including a suggestion that the shootings were a result of a dispute between rival coyotes. . . . Conversely, [Minter] said, the possibility that vigilantes were involved 'hasn't been ruled out.'"

Later in the article, the *Times* quoted a local sheriff who denigrated efforts of the border groups: "Sheriff Marco Antonio Estrada of Santa Cruz County, where Lochiel is, said Ranch Rescue teams did not have the training to intercept drug traffickers and might lead such smugglers to believe that trafficking was easier, if they were not up against federal officers or local deputies. 'I have concerns that they're not really welcome, or really not needed,' Sheriff Estrada said of the citizens' patrols. 'They are not helping law enforcement, definitely not.'"

While these killings could have been the work of a few lone individuals—true "vigilantes," if you will—there is nothing, except the speculation of a few law enforcement agencies, to link them to any of the known border control groups. Indeed, after spending time on the border with two different such groups, it became apparent to me that their "mission" was closer to that of Walker's BLA—deterrence—than interdiction and detention or violence.

Another case of what some say was law enforcement intimidation occurred near the southern Texas town of Hebbronville in March 2003. A pair of Ranch Rescue volunteers was arrested after a Salvadoran couple, a man and a woman, caught in the U.S. illegally on the property of a local rancher, told Border Patrol and county deputies they were beaten. WorldNetDaily described the incident in a pair of stories.[21]

Two volunteers with border group Ranch Rescue—Casey Nethercutt of California and Hank Conner of Louisiana—had deployed to a ranch in southern Texas, to help the landowner there protect his property from a constant wave of illegal aliens. While in town on the second day of their deployment, the men were arrested by a Texas ranger and charged with two counts of aggravated assault with a weapon and two counts of unlawful restraint for allegedly pistol-whipping and detaining the Salvadoran couple. Witnesses to the alleged incident who spoke with WorldNetDaily said the charges were false; they said both men had discovered the Salvadoran couple on the rancher's property, but had treated them with care and respect. One of the witnesses was a French photojournalist on assignment in Texas.

Ranch Rescue spokesman Jack Foote, also a witness, said the arrest of the group's members was an ironic twist to the sad state of affairs on the border. "This is a massive travesty of justice," said Foote.[22] "These two [foreign] trespassers were treated with the utmost of kindness and respect." He also decried the fact that his volunteers were arrested doing a job federal, state and local law enforcement officials were failing to do. Eric Boye, the French photojournalist on the scene, told me he was very surprised at the charges. He said the Salvadoran man was smiling to his wife after the ranch owner, Joe Sutton, gave the couple food and water, along with a blanket. "They were treated with humanity," said Boye, who took photos of the event.

Nethercutt and Conner were part of a four-man detachment from Ranch Rescue—a property-rights activist group—which was led by Foote, the national spokesman for the group and the head of its Texas chapter. "The four-man contingent, at the request of rancher Joe Sutton, was here to prevent criminal trespassers from crossing Sutton's property," WorldNetDaily reported.[23]

Foote, in a follow-up interview told this author the Salvadoran couple was searched for weapons—to ensure the safety of them and his detachment—then driven by van to the front of Sutton's property. There they were to wait for the Border Patrol to come pick them up (a USBP inspection station was just seven miles south of Sutton's front gate). But after waiting forty-five or more minutes, Sutton ordered Foote's crew to release the couple—a mistake, Foote later admitted, because it broke the chain of custody. Nevertheless, Foote—a mild-mannered guy who deferentially answers "yes, sir," and "no, sir," to questions—said the couple was unharmed when they were released. Also, he said he didn't want them to remain hidden in the grass where they were found, at night, because of the danger of rattlesnakes and scorpions in the region.

In another incident, which occurred around April 2003, one member of Simcox's CHD said "virtually overnight" a local Border Patrol agent in the Tucson, Arizona sector became confrontational and hostile to him and other members of his group, even to the point of ignoring his pleas for medical attention for an illegal immigrant woman suffering from asthma. The CHD member said he and a few other volunteers were patrolling one sector of the border when they came across a few groups of illegals numbering about fifty in all. They small group summoned USBP agents, and when they arrived, one of the agents "gave us attitude" about their border activities. The CHD member said he informed USBP agents of the woman needing medical assistance, but several minutes later—possibly thirty to forty-five minutes—no professional help had arrived. "Who do you think will get blamed for denying an illegal immigrant medical treatment?" he asked sarcastically.

As many Border Patrol agents will testify, falsely accusing others of mistreatment is a staple in the repertoire of the illegal alien. BP agents, immigration inspectors, U.S. Customs officers—all of them constantly receive complaints of alleged mistreatment of illegal aliens, few of which are ever substantiated. In fact, agents say, illegals are coached by coyotes and pro-immigration officials in Mexico on what to say if captured in the U.S.; to demand medical treatment and food; and to demand access to Mexican consulate offices and attorneys.

It may be that American law enforcement officials are beginning to use similar tactics—leveling unsubstantiated charges—against the civilian groups, perhaps in an effort to shut them down. What is also odd is that the arrest of the pair of Ranch Rescue volunteers came only one week after the local sheriff of Jim Hogg County, Texas—Erasmo Alarcon, Jr. —publicly warned of "armed men dressed in military fatigues" that had been spotted traversing his county, as previously mentioned. Alarcon, in local reports, admitted he didn't believe the "troops" spotted were connected in any way to Ranch Rescue: "We know most of the local ranchers, and they don't have people like that . . . the sightings have been all over the county."[24]

Yet, the pair were arrested and held for days before making bail based only on the word of a pair of illegal aliens; the sheriff made little to no attempt, say witnesses to the alleged incident, to contact them for a statement before or after the arrests. "I've seen child molesters get less," said one local police officer, who asked not to be identified. "I would like to see an uprising by Texans and others over the arresting of these men and demand that they are freed and the charges dropped," added one local resident.

At the same time Alarcon was issuing his warning and Ranch Rescue volunteers were being arrested, the FBI was investigating a report that several Iraqi agents were attempting to gain access into the U.S. via Mexico into southern Texas, just as war with Baghdad had gotten underway.[25] *Newsweek* reported that agents began a "frantic search" for the group of Iraqis—at least a half-dozen—because an informant said they may be attempting to smuggle chemical weapons into the U.S. According to the informant the group of Iraqis allegedly paid a coyote $5,000 each to smuggle them in near Laredo. *Newsweek* said the informant was told the Iraqi's "may have some chemicals." Officials said the information was based solely on the word of a single Mexican informant, but it triggered alarm at the highest levels in Washington nonetheless; it was information included in a daily "threat matrix" given to President Bush:

> Mexican agents, working closely with the FBI, tracked down the Mexican smuggler who the informant claimed had provided him with the information. The smuggler denied the informant's claim and passed an FBI polygraph. But officials say the claim still had to be taken seriously because of fresh intelligence suggesting that terrorist groups are concentrating on the notoriously porous U.S.-Mexican border.[26]

In a similar time frame, 9-11 mastermind Khalid Shaikh Mohammed told interrogators he recently told U.S. officials that al Qaeda was planning to carry out a firebombing attack on Washington's Metrorail.[27] Also, one report said a group of al-Qaida terrorists planned to infiltrate the U.S. via Mexico.[28] Earlier, similar reports said terrorists infiltrating the U.S. may have chemical weapons. Besides chemical attacks, officials reportedly were worried that suicide terrorists could use conventional weapons against "soft" targets like shopping malls and sports stadiums.[29] Officials also said they were worried that shoulder-fired missiles could be employed against civilian airliners.[30]

All of these threats, U.S. intelligence officials say, could come through the porous southwestern border; such threats, some agents say, may already be in-country. This is the same border that is not, and cannot be, guarded effectively by the usual cadre of American and Mexican law enforcement officials, not that many of them aren't trying. But they are trying to do an impossible mission, and a number of federal, state and local law enforcement officials and politicians—rather than embrace the assistance from civilians volunteering their time—seem bent on destroying, discrediting and disbanding the civilian groups.

Other factors are working against these groups and the public's acceptance of them, and that includes plain old-fashioned propaganda, which is being employed effectively by pro-immigrant rights groups, politicians, bureaucrats and some law enforcement managers. For instance, a July 12, 2000, Council On Hemispheric Affairs press release titled, "Illegal Immigration: A Death Sentence?" warns that a "rancher's vigilante movement along the Arizona and Texas borders costs immigrant lives."[31] "No issue is more likely to bedevil U.S.-Mexican relations in the early days of the [Vicente] Fox presidency than the recent rise of the vigilante movement against illegal migrants trying to cross into Arizona and Texas. This new movement reveals the darker side of the U.S. immigration policy toward Mexico," the organization warns.

Activist organization BAN implied that immigrant deaths that have occurred in desert crossing corridors are the work of the border enforcement groups. "There's more than enough evidence, besides a moral imperative, to stop these groups," said Jennifer Allen, co-director of BAN. "People have already been killed, and it's only going to get worse."[32] In a report BAN delivered to Arizona Gov. Janet Napolitano (who has come out publicly against the border groups), BAN warned that "Arizona has become a fertile ground for outside vigilantes who are using national security concerns as an excuse to push their racist and anti-immigrant agenda and break numerous state laws," one newspaper report stated.[33] In its report, BAN demanded investigators examine alleged state land violations committed by border ranchers, as well as illegal citizens' arrests, some of which may have involved physical attacks on immigrants on public roads, as well as a spate of migrant shootings.[34] The report goes on to accuse the border groups of being fronts for neo-nazism, white supremacy and racism, and Allen said residents she interviewed in Cochise County, Arizona, while preparing the report opposed the border groups but were afraid to say so publicly out of fear of reprisal.

Many times the media and pro-immigrant organizations "investigating" border groups make little effort to be unbiased and fair in presenting "facts" about them to the public. Newspaper headlines regularly screech the term "vigilante" or "militia," for example, though none of the major, high-profile border groups are interested in law enforcement, detaining illegal immigrants or becoming paramilitary forces. Some press reports have even gone so far as to interview illegal migrants, giving them more "ink" than the American citizens volunteering to keep them out. In one news story titled, "Vigilantes Stir Fear at Border,"[35] The *Tucson Citizen* newspaper claimed that illegals fear border groups more than the Border Patrol, and that they believe the groups are there to shoot them if they see them. "They have bullets, they're not playing; they're going to kill," Juan Porras, a native of Chihuahua who waited four days to cross the border, told the paper. "We're just trying to cross, nothing more," the paper quoted Porras as saying, while failing to remind its readers that jumping the border is illegal or that there are simpler, easier, less dangerous and less costly ways to get permission to work in the U.S.[36]

What is also interesting about the unpopular attention being given civilian border groups is that, as of November 2003, not one member of any of them had been arrested or convicted of "executing" illegal immigrants, though such incidents are often discussed in the media by activists and some politicians as though they were established facts. Case in point: A *Washington Post* report written by Evelyn Nieves and published January 19, 2003, contains this paragraph: "Both the groups and their critics point to recent violence to prove their point—describing cases in which either U.S. citizens were kidnapped, invaded or shot by Mexican drug traffickers, or where migrants were shot by vigilantes."[37] No one in the major border groups—Civil Homeland Defense, American Border Patrol, or Ranch Rescue, the groups most commonly cited by media, politicians and bureaucrats—has, as of this book's publication date, been arrested and convicted of shooting migrants. But organizations opposed to armed citizens' groups trying to protect their homes, property and lives have created this lie in an effort to demonize, minimize and de-legitimize them.

Lost in the debate over civilian groups is the fact that these people, like law enforcement agents on the border, are putting their lives on the line as well, in defense of their property, their community and their nation—for free. And they are doing so without endorsement, without the powers of arrest and, often, without adequate protection. Granted, they aren't required to do this and indeed not everyone wants them to. But what is abundantly clear is that these volunteers are generally very conscientious, civic-minded people who simply want to assist U.S. law enforcement officials attempting to keep illegal invaders out.

Besides putting pressure on Washington, the mere presence of these volunteers—and the perceived need for them—also puts the onus on Mexico and whether its government is doing enough to curb illegal immigration. For instance, though Mexican migrant deaths quadrupled in 1998 to 350, the administration of President Vicente Fox has done little to discourage illegal migration.[38] Rather, President Fox has encouraged it by badgering the Bush White House to loosen U.S. immigration rules and by demonizing American citizens who are trying to prevent his people from invading and destroying their property as well as endangering the lives of their loved ones.

Immigrant rights groups and members of the media opposed to the citizen border effort are also succeeding in pitting one border group against another, in a sort of "divide and conquer" strategy. In late March 2003, for example, a local report in southern Arizona highlighted differences between Glenn Spencer of American Border Patrol and Chris Simcox of CHD. Spencer was upset by a statement Simcox issued publicly to Mexican citizens, which was picked up by U.S. and Mexican newspapers. Shortly after U.S. forces began military operations against Iraq, Simcox warned that any illegal border jumpers would be considered "enemies of the state" and would be treated as such. He advised them to remain in Mexico while encouraging the Mexican government to do all it could by heeding his warning. "We're at war," Simcox said. Mexico "should take that seriously."

According to the *Arizona Daily Star*, one border group is armed only with technology: a video camera, a computer and a portable satellite uplink. Meanwhile, members of other groups go with sidearms, rifles and "an attitude." Though both groups say they only want the government to do a better job of securing U.S. borders from illegal migrants and possible terrorists, there is division between Glenn Spencer's high-tech Sierra Vista-based American Border Patrol group and Tombstone Tumbleweed publisher Chris Simcox's Civil Homeland Patrol.

"The reason for the public bickering? A recent 'message to the world' Simcox issued with the warning: 'Do not attempt to cross the border illegally; you will be considered an enemy of the state; if aggressors attempt to forcefully enter our country they will be repelled with force if necessary!'"[39]

Spencer—a twelve-year veteran of the Proposition 187 and anti-illegal-immigration movements in California and creator of the popular Internet site AmericanPatrol.com—says that with statements like that, Simcox has attracted an "unsavory element." Also, he says such statements threaten the credibility of the anti-illegal-immigration movement Spencer has helped lead over the past decade. Spencer finally spoke out to the media in March 2003 because, he said, he was tired of the media continuing to portray him and his organization in the same [negative] light as others who he believes behave as genuine border vigilantes. "Spencer says he recently had a run-in with one of Simcox's volunteers that caused him to wonder about the stability and motivation of the people Simcox attracts," said the *Arizona Daily Star*.[40] "And this week—under a section of his Web site called the Rumor Mill—Spencer reported that Civil Homeland Defense volunteers had been seen drinking and firing weapons along the border with Mexico. 'It's called rabble rousing, isn't it?' Spencer said of the Simcox declaration, which was distributed to government officials and media contacts on both sides of the border last week at the start of the war with Iraq."[41]

"For years we've been dealing with an issue of lawlessness and we've said repeatedly, 'What part of illegal don't they understand? What part of illegal doesn't Chris Simcox understand?'" Spencer said. "The purpose is to put pressure on the government, to have governmental institutions that are there to enforce the law, not to go out and threaten people."[42] Spencer said he is more interested in filming, documenting and uploading to his Internet site violations of U.S. border integrity. He said he's not interested in confronting potential border jumpers with firearms. In fact, said the *Star*, Spencer said "he's . . . taken steps to avoid confusion by insisting that American Border Patrol volunteers belong either to his organization or Simcox's, but not both."[43] Simcox denies Spencer's allegations about drinking and shooting by his volunteers and attributes the dispute to media envy and sour grapes.

In the end, what the citizen border groups really represent is a grass roots rejection of poorly defined and executed immigration policies—policies that have largely been made by bureaucrats, politicians and leaders thousands of miles away. And, say the groups' supporters, the fact that more Americans are saying "no" to that kind of bad leadership and sanctioned incompetence is a good thing for our country and our communities, even if such attitudes make government officials on both sides of the border uncomfortable or nervous.

Does their *vigilance* constitute vigilante justice? Not at all. However, in extreme cases—perhaps when folks along the border feel so threatened they no longer have a choice—vigilante justice may be the only form of justice available. In the meantime, it's apparent that there is as much fear and loathing of illegal immigrants, drug runners and possible terrorist infiltrators by those Americans who are directly affected as there is by officialdom of citizens who are trying to stem the flow and limit the potential damage. Maybe both attitudes are a byproduct of the government's long-time monopoly on law enforcement.

But there are solutions—answers both citizen and official can live with. For one thing local, state and federal law enforcement agencies could and should take advantage of the growing number of Americans willing to help them guard our borders. If it's independent citizen's groups the feds and local cops don't like, fine—out West there is an old tradition called "gatherin' a posse," which was, in the old days, made up of citizen volunteers who want to help local officials keep law and order. Guarding the border is certainly a job that needs doing, and the cooperation between civilians and officials would eliminate misunderstandings and feelings of ill-will as much as it would actually offer a modicum of protection for illegal immigrants who are the focus of rights groups (which should make Mexico happy too, right?). It would also send the message to our southern neighbor that America is united in its efforts to end the destruction of her borders and plundering of her resources. Our borders have yet to become what reasonable people would call "secure," but by working together they can be.

NO RESPECT

There is no room in this country for hyphenated Americans. . . . The one absolutely certain way of bringing this nation to ruin, of preventing all possibility of its continuing to be a nation at all, would be to permit it to become a tangle of squabbling nationalities. . . . There is no place for the hyphen in our citizenship. . . . We are a nation, not a hodge-podge of foreign nationalities. We are a people, and not a polyglot boarding house.

—TEDDY ROOSEVELT

It was a somber scene as the blue hearse, adorned with red roses and white carnations, made its way slowly to the cemetery in Naco, Sonora, a town in Mexico. Inside, a silver casket was decorated with depictions of Mary holding Jesus in her arms after his crucifixion. Women wailed, especially the young widow, as dozens of mourners—some playing instruments from the back of a pick-up truck—trailed the hearse. The casket held twenty-three-year-old Jorge Luis Salomon, a U.S. Border Patrol agent who was killed by Mexican nationals because of his job.

According to news reports, Sonora state prosecutor in Cananea, Saul Ballesteros, said Salomon met Francisco Javier Rosas Molina, 18, earlier in the week near the border at Naco, Arizona, where Salomon had been stationed since late 2000, shortly after Rosas Molina's release from jail in Bisbee, Arizona, on drug trafficking charges. "He struck up a conversation and began a friendly relationship, giving him a ride and spending several hours drinking and talking with him and some of his companions," Ballesteros said. Salomon had initially confided in Rosas Molina that he was an agent, but later, when the conversation with the young man's companions turned to their involvement in drug and people trafficking, Salomon told the group he was a construction worker. "That's when Rosas Molina identified him to the others as a Border Patrol agent, and that appears to be the reason that they killed him," said Ballesteros.

Rosas Molina and three other suspects—Jose Arturo Arreola Lopez, Jesus Cesar Abusto Villa Villareal and Edna Yardis Montoya Medina— allegedly killed Salomon by repeatedly bashing his head with a fifty-pound boulder. It was an awful, gruesome way to die—as if there is ever a good way—but one that was precipitated solely because of the line of work this young man chose.

An album by comedian Rodney Dangerfield called *I Don't Get No Respect* exemplified a line he is most famous for, but very easily, the same could be said for federal agents and other American law enforcement personnel who risk their lives daily to guard America's borders.

For their efforts, they are killed and injured by cross-border criminals; they are constantly criticized, slandered and berated by politicians and pro-immigrant activists; they are shot at by foreign military members; they are vilified by the very citizens they are charged to protect. In particular, Border Patrol agents, like their federal law enforcement counterparts in the U.S. Forest Service, are among the most assaulted of federal officers. Yet most are hard-working, loyal and patriotic men and women trying to do a tough job under tough, if not impossible, conditions. Nevertheless, as demonstrated by a series of events and incidents that have happened to agents in recent times, they are among the least-respected authorities.

We've seen scores of examples throughout this book but those are by no means all of them:

- In January 2003, USBP agents reported being fired upon, as well as reporting a rise in the number of illegals they found who were armed.[1]

- In March 2003, a suspected alien smuggler rammed the van he was driving into a Border Patrol truck near Yuma, Arizona.[2]

- In January 2003, USBP agents came under gunfire from suspected drug smugglers near the Rio Grande River in the Del Rio, Texas, sector. About 7:50 P.M., officials said, agents—who were in a "still watch" position—saw several persons crossing the river carrying "large packages." When agents identified themselves, they began receiving gunfire. Agents had to return fire and take cover, but were not injured. Several bundles of marijuana were recovered. "It sounded like World War III," one witness told a local newspaper.[3]

- A USBP agent said he was fired upon by a Mexican soldier while he patrolled a portion of the Tohono O'odham Indian Reservation in southern Arizona in May 2002. The agent reported encountering three heavily armed Mexican soldiers who were riding in a military Humvee; he said he drove away but a shot ripped through his vehicle. Local Mexican military officials said it couldn't have been a soldier since they claimed none of the garrisons had troops in that area at the time; however, a Tohono O'odham police ranger reported being chased by similar-looking Mexican troopers earlier in the day, radioing USBP for back-up.[4]

- USBP agents in New Mexico reported being fired upon by Mexican troops allegedly on an anti-drug mission in March 2000.[5]

- In March 2002, a USBP agent near Naco exchanged gunfire with a suspected drug smuggler who fired about twenty rounds at the agent before stopping his Chevy truck just before the border and running into Mexico. Agents found drugs and a weapon in the vehicle.[6]

- Two shots were fired at USBP agents near El Paso, Texas, December 7, 2001, from Mexico, as they investigated a drug smuggling case.

- Within weeks of the 9-11 attacks, USBP, Customs and Immigration inspection agents reported being "overwhelmed" again by illegal aliens trying to get in through the San Diego sector from Tijuana, Mexico. "They are always testing us, scoping us out, trying to overwhelm our weakest point," says William Veal, chief of the US Border Patrol's San Diego sector.[7]

- In April 2001, a Border Patrol agent fired rounds from his handgun at illegal aliens who were pelting him with rocks; the agent was struck twice but did not require medical attention.[8]

- A Cochise County, Arizona, deputy was hospitalized with head and internal injuries after a pick-up loaded with illegals plowed into his patrol SUV in March 2001.

- In February 2001, a USBP supervisor in Douglas, Arizona, said attacks on agents were nearly double from the previous year. In 1999, said supervisor Fred Esquivel, agents reported thirty assaults; in 2000, that figure went up to fifty.[9]

- In January 2001, a USBP agent had to shoot an illegal alien because the alien was attempting to run him down with a stolen truck.[10]

- A Border Alliance Group agent was hospitalized in Cochise County, Arizona, after his patrol car was rammed as he used it for cover.[11] According to reports, a pair of BAG agents on routine drug interdiction patrol on a local highway, passed two white trucks with what appeared to be bundles in the back. Turning around with the intent of initiating a traffic stop to examine the bundles, the BAG officers attempted to get the vehicles to stop but they sped up instead. The drivers then turned their trucks around and began heading towards the BAG vehicle. The agent driving swerved off the road to avoid a collision, then both of them jumped out of the car to use it for cover. The second white truck then rammed the vehicle, causing one of the BAG officers to be injured. The second officer managed to squeeze off a couple of shots at the fleeing trucks, but hit nothing.

- A USBP agent had to fire his weapon three times at a mob of rock-throwing illegal aliens near Naco, Arizona, just to get them to stop before he was injured or killed.[12]

Agents nonchalantly speak of the dangers they face as being just part of the job. But with little doubt, those dangers occur far more frequently than in many other areas of law enforcement. "Smugglers trying to move a bumper marijuana crop across the fortified border are taking brazen risks and fighting violently with law officers—often on public roads," warned the *Arizona Daily Star*. "This hotter drug war in southern Arizona has put law officers on edge, rural school bus drivers on alert, and border travelers at some risk. In the last four months, smugglers facing a bigger gauntlet of law officers have shot at them, tried to run them down, sprinkled roads with spikes, and crashed vehicles through official ports of entry into the United States."[13]

The newspaper report continued, saying that a fifteen-year-old boy driving a Jeep filled with eight hundred pounds of pot sideswiped an innocent bystander's vehicle at the Douglas port of entry in January 2001; the same teen crashed the border eleven days earlier driving a Ford Crown Victoria filled with marijuana. And at least seven times since October 2000, vehicles filled with drugs raced northbound into the U.S. using the southbound lanes of traffic, endangering lives and snarling traffic. Other smugglers running from pursuing law officers have forced the officers and other traffic off of roads. Smugglers' weapons of choice, officers say, are small, concealable weapons—often automatic weapons with pistol-like features.[14]

Because of the realities of the terrain they must patrol, border officers often have to be creative in order to adapt to their harsh environment. They must also adapt to the violence. Park ranger Julie Horne, whose turf includes the Organ Pipe Cactus National Monument in Arizona, packs a pistol, a shotgun and a rifle while on patrol.[15] She says she encounters "hundreds" of illegals nightly, and she intercepts several drug loads per week as well.

Keeping their heads above water is a constant struggle for agents, requiring innovative tactics to close the competitive gap between them and the often better equipped drug smugglers. Reminiscent of the World War II Navajo code talkers, whose native-language-based cipher the Nazis couldn't crack, one U.S. Customs Service unit has adapted "ancient" Indian skills to modern times and modern crimes. The unit, called the Shadow Wolves, is made up of nineteen American Indians who track drug smugglers through the Arizona badlands. "Their job is to track their prey the old-fashioned way—through a broken twig, a hair snagged by a mesquite branch, a fiber left behind by a bulging burlap bag," says the *Arizona Daily Star*.[16]

In hauling loads of heroin, cocaine and marijuana across the border via foot, truck and horseback, smugglers leave behind clues. As there is no existing electronic or mechanical device that can detect the tracks of someone moving across the rugged borderland terrain, the Shadow Wolves earn their pay by tracking the traffickers like they would any other quarry. And they definitely earn their pay. This unlikely crew seizes "more than 70 percent of the drugs the agency finds on the three-million-acre Tohono O'odham Reservation west of Tucson. . . . The Indian trackers accounted for nearly a third of the 180,000 pounds of marijuana seized by Customs throughout Arizona [in 2000], including the border ports of entry."[17]

Four-member squad of "Shadow Wolves" U.S. Customs trackers.

There are also the Border Patrol search and rescue units. Called "BORSTAR"—BORder Search, Trauma And Rescue—teams, they were designed in conjunction with input from Mexican officials as a way to beef up safety along the borders. The agents, which must complete a grueling six-week course in San Diego, are taught many skills, ranging from reppelling to water survival.[18] The units, which are comprised of about eight agents apiece and are spread out among USBP stations along the border, are used for search and rescue and to provide medical assistance to illegals. "Each BORSTAR agent receives specialized training on conducting search and rescue operations in remote border areas. In addition, the agents learn how to provide the immediate medical assistance necessary to stabilize patients and transport them to areas accessible to paramedics, helicopters and other advanced emergency medical services," says a Bureau of Citizenship and Immigration Services description.[19] Teams share their expertise with Mexican law-enforcement officials.

As if the danger of the job weren't enough, everywhere border agents turn there are impediments to their jobs. "The better we do, the more complaining the activists do, and the less we're able to do," says one Border Patrol agent. As an example, he said his patrol sector in California was banned from "dragging"—smoothing dirt roads to make it easier to find fresh footprints made by illegals—because, agents were told, "it created too much dust." In reality, the agent believes "it is one of our most effective detection tools. That's why the activists complained and had it banned." Some landowners have also complained about the technique, however, saying it disrupts or destroys property and is a nuisance. But agents still maintain this low-tech method is ideal for tracking illegals.

Other agents say they are not permitted to work with local police and sheriff's departments, in part because their own supervisors prohibit it, but also because local departments, bureaucrats and politicians who take a pro-immigrant view disallow it. Border Patrol agents say despite federal rules that allow them to patrol bus stations, railways and other modes of public transportation in search of illegal aliens, cities and municipalities often pass local ordinances that prohibit such patrols; worse, many Border Patrol managers won't fight them, and, to be fair, many of Washington's bureaucrats aren't aware of such local ordinances.

Agents are also constantly harangued by official ignorance, enduring thoughtless and politically correct policy decisions made by bureaucrats with no border law enforcement experience. In April 2001, for example, the INS adopted a policy requiring Border Patrol agents to pick up trash while on patrol, and to stay out of "environmentally sensitive" areas. "We normally instruct our agents to pick up the trash once they've apprehended a group (of illegal aliens)," agent Jose Proenca said. "As they're making their trip north they begin discarding stuff."[20]

When not on trash duty, agents have to be careful where they walk— they must stay off of land that contains endangered plant and animal species as well. This burden directly affects their ability to do their jobs and could actually put them at greater risk; Park Ranger Eggle was killed while patrolling the environmentally sensitive Organ Pipe Cactus National Park, a region virtually devoid of any Border Patrol back-up, perhaps because of this INS policy. Bob Goldsborough of the Virginia-based American Immigration Control, summed it up well for Fox News: "If there's a bank robber and the police are called in, you don't tell the police to stay off the flower beds. This is the same thing. It is simply a misdirection of their time and their energy." Perhaps prophetically, Goldsborough predicted that smugglers and illegal aliens, upon learning of the INS' "green" policy, would simply find protected land on which to cross. They have; Organ Pipe is one of the most heavily trafficked regions along the border.[21]

The more serious the incident, the more harsh the criticism of USBP, Customs and Immigration agents. When shootings occur, for instance, agents and their supervisors endure a firestorm of criticism and probing— much of it irrational—from U.S. and Mexican officials and lawmakers, pro-immigration groups, and others critical of the agents' preventative roles. In one instance, Mexican consulate officials in El Paso cried for an official investigation of a USBP agent who shot and killed Juan Patricio Peraza Quijada, nineteen, of Mexicali, Mexico, after he threatened agents with a large metal pipe. "Our official point of view is we think it was abuse of lethal force," said Socorro Cordova, spokeswoman for the Mexican Consulate. "It was an excess of the use of force of these agents for the Border Patrol."[22]

Witnesses later reported seeing Peraza Quijada disappear into an alley as agents chased him, then reappear "ready for a fight." "Judging by the weapon that I saw, certainly if that agent had been hit, especially about head, it could have caused either serious injury or death to him," one witness to the shooting told KFOX-TV news out of Las Cruces, New Mexico. "There is nothing that says these agents must be injured before they can act. This person knew exactly who he was dealing with. They were Border Patrol agents. There was no reason, absolutely no reason for him to attack these agents," Border Patrol Chief Luis Barker said.[23]

A pair of Tampa, Florida., police officers were thankful to be alive after a near-deadly encounter with a pair of illegal aliens. According to reports, Officer Larry Mitchell and his partner, Richard "R.D." Pemberton, both sixteen-year veterans, were shot in January 2002 following a scuffle after they had stopped a van carrying three men after the driver ran a red light. The officers said the driver and front-seat passenger switched seats right after the stop, so Pemberton decided to detain the driver, later identified as twenty-four-year-old Saul Garcia. But Garcia attacked Pemberton, and when Mitchell tried to come to his aid, Garcia's brother, twenty-year-old Jose Hernandez-Garcia, struck Mitchell and began to beat Pemberton. While fighting both men on the ground, Pemberton said, he could feel Garcia pull the gun from his holster. Pemberton tried to warn his partner, but he was shot in the shoulder; Mitchell was shot in the hip before backup arrived and intervened. Garcia and Hernandez-Garcia were both in the U.S. illegally from Mexico.[24]

While intentional violence against immigrants is neither desirable nor tolerable, sometimes undocumented migrants are injured accidentally, or during the course of arrest (usually because of their own resistance). Instead of writing off the incidents as bad luck or just part of life trying to sneak into the U.S., often our own government rewards the illegal behavior by paying bogus injury or rights violation claims and/or punishing agents. In one case, the U.S. government paid $2 million of taxpayer money to the widow and son of a man killed in an accident involving a Border Patrol vehicle near Lordsburg, New Mexico. The family of Heriberto Parra Sr., twenty, filed suit against the agency in February 2000 in federal court in New Mexico, accusing the Border Patrol of acting negligently and with "disregard for human life" in placing five undocumented immigrants in the back of a Ford Bronco that had maintenance problems, was not equipped with seats or seat belts, and was usually used to transport dogs, plaintiff lawyers said. Border Patrol officials said they try to provide everyone they transport with seat belts; many vehicles used for transporting illegals are climate-controlled to offer heat in winter or air conditioning in summer months. But, officials added, sometimes offering seat belts to everyone isn't possible due to differences in Border Patrol vehicles or because of the sheer number of migrants that have to be transported. Four others also thrown from the vehicle settled for amounts ranging from $200,000 to $250,000. Yet, had these illegals not crossed improperly to begin with, they would not have been in the Border Patrol's custody.

Bullet holes in U.S. boundary sign. The indentation of the holes show that the bullets are coming from Mexico.

Agents say each case paid further legitimizes the role of the illegal migrant while further undermining their ability to do their jobs effectively, for which they also receive criticism. Such punitive actions also overshadow the much more numerous and selfless acts of heroism agents perform to defend and protect illegals, such as when Border Patrol agents risked their lives to save a Mexican national from the Colorado River in January 2002.

According to a report in the *Palo Verde Valley Times*, agents spotted the man in the river around 6 P.M. Believing he was likely trying to get into the U.S. illegally, the agents tried repeatedly to fish the crosser from the raging river, to no avail. Losing sight of him, agents called in Border Patrol Air Operations, along with other patrol rescue units. As darkness fell, and into the wee hours of the early morning, Border Patrol assets continued searching for the man. Finally, one agent found him under the searchlight of the patrol's air rescue helicopter. He was struggling and in obvious distress, but four agents fought through heavy brush to get to the river to save him. Though the water was icy cold, two agents entered the river nonetheless and managed to reach the man. In confusion, apparently from the shock of hypothermia, the man initially fought his rescuers, submerging beneath the surface and swimming away from the agents. But through persistence, the agents managed to catch up and pull the migrant to safety. On shore the man was too weak to walk on his own, so agents carried him to a waiting ambulance, where emergency medical personnel began immediate treatment for cold water exposure.[25]

Agents also endure constant media criticism and scrutiny—even from pseudo-media, like the following diatribe entitled "Border Bullies," from columnist Ryan Chirnomas, writing in the *Arizona Daily Wildcat*, a college newspaper:

While cruising down the interstate, we saw the body of an immigrant struck down by an oncoming vehicle. Whether they were running from la migra or toward America's financial opportunity, we'll never know. Regardless, all their hopes and worries died in a pool of blood at the hands of a Ford Contour hauling down Highway 8. Most disturbing, however, are the state border "inspection stations." Motorists used to stop at this station to protect California's agriculture industry. However, today's drivers are now rerouted to a makeshift Border Patrol check-point. All motorists are required to stop, then are waived through by a Border Patrol agent proudly decked in a green uniform, complete with a nightstick and inflated ego. That is, of course, provided you're white, for the protection of America's southern border is essentially legalized racism.[26]

———————

What is confusing to many agents is the hypocrisy of the public they are hired to serve. For instance, Border Patrol and Customs agents say that while they are endlessly harangued to beef up border security, they are also heavily criticized for doing so, especially if in the course of doing their jobs an illegal alien is hurt or, God forbid, killed.

The *San Diego Union-Tribune* reported March 11, 2003, for instance, that the deadly crash of a stolen pickup with twenty-two illegal immigrants crammed into its camper shell "has again put the spotlight on the dilemma facing authorities trying to stop smugglers desperate to escape." The paper said that agents and other law enforcement personnel—who had already broken off pursuit and were using a local sheriff's department helicopter to monitor the path of the truck—had laid out three sets of tire spikes, and when the pick-up swerved to miss the third set, it rolled violently, killing two immigrant passengers and injuring the other twenty. Who was at fault? "Critics say the deaths demonstrate the unconcern of U.S. law enforcement agencies about the threat posed by such pursuits to migrants already at the mercy of smugglers," the paper said. The local Mexican consulate blamed the Border Patrol and California Highway Patrol. "There is an alternative to stopping vehicles without using spike stripes," said consulate spokesman Alberto Lozano. "They could close off roads or wait till the car runs out of gas. They have to decide. But it's wrong to punch out the tires of a car traveling at eighty miles per hour knowing that an accident could occur." Law enforcement officials, always on the defensive, countered by rightfully blaming the driver-migrant of the truck and by pointing out that it was stolen in the first place.[27]

Catch the lawbreakers; don't catch the lawbreakers. Make the border more secure; don't make the border more secure. "I don't know how many times over the years that I asked myself, 'What the hell are we doing?' and, 'Does anybody out there know or really care what's happening to their country?'" a former Border Patrol supervisor wonders. "Agents are not allowed to do their jobs, and are, in fact, ordered not to. It got to the point that I couldn't take it any longer. I fully expected . . . an abrupt about face after 9-11. Obviously that didn't happen, and it doesn't appear that it will anytime soon. If most Americans actually knew what was being done to tie our hands, they would be appalled and demand that it end immediately."[28]

"I've been complaining for years about the patrols' operations, such as 'no city patrol', no pursuing of vehicles," another Border Patrol agent told me. "On September 12, the day after the attacks, many Border Patrol Agents (myself included) were detailed to New York. We stayed there working twelve hours on/twelve hours off helping to provide security at the three major airports until we left on October 12. We visited 'ground zero.' After standing there, seeing that, smelling it, looking at the faces on the New Yorkers, I knew that things were going to change. Policies, guidelines, operations—they're all going to change when we get home. They didn't. We're still told, 'You can't chase that car that just blew the port of entry,' and, 'You will not do city patrol. Stay right here and watch this fence rust and if they jump, push 'em back over' . . . so they can cross somewhere else undetected. Or cross though the mountains where they will die from lack of food and water because the guide that they hired told them that it will only be a few hours' walk. Then he robs them and leaves them in the middle of nowhere. This country is reactive and not proactive. [Supervisors] tell us we are not to pursue vehicles . . . until one of them is a bomb or a chemical agent and used against the U.S. I think the American people have had it. I know I have."[29]

For all the world it seems as if those who man our borders are being sabotaged. Americans spend millions training them, deploying them and providing them with the tools of their trade—only to allow agents to be undermined (officially and otherwise) in the process. "Mix politics with bureaucratic bungling and epic butt-covering, and this is what you get," wrote Steve Lopez of the *Los Angeles Times*.[30]

Morale is so bad in some Border Patrol sectors that when the Transportation Security Administration put out a call to hire thousands of new sky marshals following 9/11, some Border Patrol stations lost up to half their patrol staff. It's not that many of the former agents wanted to spend countless boring hours flying coast to coast, but they simply felt that despite their best efforts, they were unable to do their jobs properly because so much of the deck is stacked against them.

Even when agents try to do the right thing and clean up their own agencies they are often persecuted. A former U.S. Customs special agent, Diane Kleiman, who once worked as a prosecutor in New York, blew the whistle in 1999 about alleged drug trafficking and money laundering by airline workers. Kleiman also reported cash missing from drug seizures and drug overdoses by Customs employees. She also complained about a lack of proper employee background checks, but she said she was fired after exposing corruption and security breaches at New York's Kennedy Airport. "In January 1999, I had seized about $30,000 taped to the belly of a baggage handler who worked for American Airlines and who was an illegal alien," she said. "Upon doing a background check, I determined that this very same employee had been stopped only three months earlier for attempting to smuggle about the same amount of money. My boss refused to allow me to report this employee to security at American Airlines, and at the time of my firing, he was still employed at the airlines."[31]

Darlene Catalan, a former special agent for the U.S. Customs Service, says in her book *U.S. Customs: Badge of Dishonor* that U.S. borders are still wide open, not only to human migration, but to illegal drugs and terrorist weapons due to corruption by federal officials—payoffs, cronyism, fraud and abuse. She also said officials ignored her find of illegal drug trafficking.[32]

"I am sick of hearing border residents curse me for doing my job, then, in the same breath, curse me for all of the aliens that are destroying their property," said one Border Patrol agent, who posted comments to a union message board. "I am sick to death of my own agency giving more weight to the complaints of *smugglers* (you know who I'm talking about; the folks with the 4.78 acres of brush on the border that they threw a trailer on and a sign that says 'Rancho Del Scumbag', or 'Makin' Breakfast Ranch,' the ones that, when the dope or groups are crossing, you don't hear a peep out of them and, when the dope is past the old trailer and [USBP agents] are in pursuit, suddenly the thirty pit bulls get released, and the good citizens start a confrontation about how we are violating their property rights. Then they call the station, and the word comes down: 'Stay off of their property'). They can kiss my green ass. . . ."

BE MY GUEST

What does Cinco de Mayo mean to me? I don't need the reminder, but Cinco de Mayo reminds me of 9-11. It reminds me of America's immigration policies that threaten our form of constitutional government, policies that threaten American culture and our most treasured political traditions. It reminds me of third world cesspools spreading to America. The Rodney King rioters and looters weren't mostly blacks, they were mostly Hispanics. The corruption of American politics from unassimilated Mexicans streaming through our porous borders for half a century has undermined U.S. security. There is the real meaning of Cinco de Mayo.

—REX OSGOOD, INTERNATIONAL AFFAIRS CONSULTANT

In May 2001, President Bush asked Congress to revive an expired law that would grant amnesty to aliens who came to the U.S. on temporary visas—perhaps to work or attend school or as tourists—but then stayed to become illegal aliens. "The extension the president is asking for would offer a fourth chance to aliens who first overstayed their visas, then failed to take advantage of an initial amnesty, then failed to take advantage of a four-month extension of that amnesty that ended on April 30 [2001]," *Human Events* magazine reported.[1]

The program, known as Section 245(i) of U.S. immigration law, had already been extended for a year in 2000 by Congress after President Bill Clinton successfully lobbied lawmakers. "It remains in our national interest to legitimize those resident immigrants eligible for legal status, and to welcome them as full participants in our society," Bush wrote in a letter to congressmen and senators.[2] Bush said up to two hundred thousand people were eligible to take advantage of 245(i) who failed to do so by the deadline (at least, that was the figure of *known* aliens).

Earlier, in January 2001, Sen. Phil Gramm (R-Texas), along with Sens. Zell Miller (D-Georgia), Pete Domenici (R-New Mexico), Jim Bunning (R-Kentucky) and Mike Crapo (R-Idaho) met in Mexico City with President Vicente Fox to discuss a proposed worker amnesty program.[3] According to the Associated Press, the "program for Mexicans . . . would have the effect of granting amnesty to those currently working illegally in the country—up to 7 million people—while allowing others to apply for work from Mexico in the future."[4] And Zell Miller isn't the only Democrat who favors amnesty. "People in this country know they are benefiting from the work of undocumented workers," says Rep. Luis Gutierrez (D-Illinois). "Why not grant them the dignity and justice that comes with permanent legal residency?"[5]

Shortly after Republicans won the mid-term 2002 elections, the administration—careful not to discuss the unpopular subject prior to Election Day—began once again talking about amnesty. Tony Garza, the Bush administration's ambassador to Mexico, broached the subject in a newspaper interview with the Mexican daily *El Financiero*: "We should recognize the contribution of undocumented Mexicans and open the door for them to earned legalization."[6] He told the *Washington Times* the U.S. and Mexico should work towards "reaching an accord legalizing the status of Mexican immigrants—without giving them citizenship." He said that remained "a top administration priority," adding, "If we don't do something about their status, we will be admitting that our country has a permanent underclass."[7]

The notion of granting amnesty to the millions of illegal aliens residing in the U.S.—and the millions more family members they have living in Mexico—is favored by a number of powerful interests, including political, cultural and business interests, as well as the administrations of Vicente

Fox and George W. Bush. The reasons are varied but two are the most common: cheaper labor and better economics for business. Also, some immigrant-rights groups say granting amnesty will reduce illegal immigration. "It would be a national shame if, in the name of security, we were to close the door to immigrants who come here to work and build a better life for themselves and their families. The problem is not that we are letting too many people into the United States but that the government is not keeping out the wrong people," said Daniel Griswold, a scholar at the libertarian Cato Institute, which supports unlimited immigration.[8]

But granting amnesty for illegals has been tried before. So far, we haven't seen its promised benefits.

———————

Congress passed the Immigration and Reform Control Act (IRCA) in 1986. The bill gave amnesty "to all illegal aliens who had successfully evaded justice for four years or more or were illegally working in agriculture," according to an analysis by the Federation for American Immigration Reform (FAIR). By FAIR's count, seven separate amnesty programs have been passed since 1986, allowing some 2.8 million illegals to be counted as legal immigrants to the United States. "In addition, they have . . . brought in an additional 142,000 dependents."[9]

Quoting an INS study, FAIR said that after a decade, the average illegal alien who was granted amnesty in 1986 had only a seventh-grade education and earned an average of $9,000 a year. "Unlike immigrants with a sponsor who guarantees they will not become a burden on the public, when Congress enacts an amnesty, it makes the American public financially responsible for those amnestied," FAIR said.[10] Another immigration think tank, the Center for Immigration Reform (CIS), said the total net cost of the IRCA amnesty after ten years came to $78 billion.[11]

Critics of amnesty programs complain that politicians especially can't even be honest about such programs because of widespread voter opposition, a position summed up by Mark Krikorian, executive director of

CIS[12]: "If 'amnesty' means anything in the context of immigration, it means granting permanent residence to illegal aliens, as we did for [about 2.8] million illegals" since implementation of the 1986 amnesty law—"a move billed as the first and last amnesty in American history," he wrote in September 2001, before 9-11. In the previous month, when the Bush administration "floated its plan" to grant another amnesty to most or all of nearly four million Mexican nationals currently in the U.S. illegally, Krikorian wrote, "it met a firestorm of GOP criticism." Since that time, however, politicians who really favor amnesty have gone into overdrive to find an alternative plan, though such plans are "plainly" amnesties in disguise, he wrote.

"The White House mantra is that it opposes a 'blanket amnesty,'" said Krikorian. In the month prior to 9-11, President Bush even said, "There's going to be no amnesty," but he immediately backtracked, saying he favors a plan "that will legalize the hard work that's taking place now in America."[13]

"Presumably," Krikorian continued, "the point is that the only thing that can be called an amnesty is a grant of immediate legal status to all illegal aliens, without any standard to determine eligibility. By that reckoning, even the huge 1986 amnesty wasn't really an amnesty, since only about half the illegal aliens here at the time benefited from it, because of numerous residency and other requirements . . ."[14]

Of the attempt to cloud the amnesty issue, FAIR adds, "Apologists for illegal immigration have actually had the nerve to claim that, because the number of illegal immigrants living in the U.S. (between 8.7 and 11 million) is about the same as the number living here ten years ago, illegal immigration must not be that big of a problem. In doing so, they rely on the public's forgetting that, without the amnesty, there would be closer to 12 or 14 million illegal aliens in the country." FAIR said that thinking is the same as arbitrarily emptying every prison in the United States "then claiming there is no crime problem because the prisons are empty."[15]

Continually granting amnesty to illegal aliens sends the wrong signal—it teaches immigrants that U.S. laws don't mean anything and that it's okay to break laws you don't agree with. Suddenly giving legal status to illegal migrants is essentially offering a reward for breaking the law. It is also a slap in the face to legal migrants, those who play by the rules, wait in line, and go through the necessary legal hoops. With an amnesty for those who've broken the law, demonstrating you'll be a good citizen by following it now counts for exactly squat. Writes syndicated columnist Don Feder, "Illegal immigration benefits the people of this country the way treason enhances national security . . . Amnesties tell inhabitants of the impoverished Third World that if they can sneak past the Border Patrol, Uncle Softie will eventually welcome them with open arms. They also say to the foreigners who are patiently waiting for permission to immigrate (sometimes up to 18 years): 'Suckers!'"[16]

To add another troubling angle, experts say even talking about granting amnesty *encourages* more illegal immigration. The perception is like that of a base runner stealing home. You've got to make the plate before the catcher has the ball, but if you make it, you're home free. In this case, literally. Illegals think if they can hurry up and make it inside, lo their salvation draws nigh.

Granting mass amnesty could also present a massive security nightmare. "Aliens who apply in the home countries to become legal immigrants to the United States are screened by U.S. consular officials to weed out any criminals or likely terrorists," FAIR says. "Millions of illegal aliens in the U.S. have evaded this screening; amnesty would make them legal aliens without the necessary safeguards to ensure that they are not dangers to our national security."[17]

FAIR also points out that the current amnesty plans were devised when economic conditions were better in America. "The Bush/Fox concept was really a holdover from the economic expansion generated by the late '90s. Well, that period is over," said FAIR's executive director, Dan Stein, in the fall of 2002. "Even if you accept that we need large numbers of low-skilled workers to hold down wages, why should they be these workers? A billion people a year are trying to get into the United States, while Mexicans are just walking across the border."[18]

Given these realities, it should come as no surprise that there is little support among Americans for another amnesty. According to a Zogby
International poll in 2001, 55 percent say amnesty is a bad idea compared
to just 34 percent who support it.[19]

And among conservatives—the core of which are Bush administration supporters—the opposition is higher. Sixty percent think amnesty is
bad compared to 26 percent who support it. "Perhaps most troubling for
the president, almost one-third of all conservatives (32 percent) indicated
that they would be less likely to vote for Bush if he supported an amnesty,
while only 10 percent said they would be more likely to vote for him," said
a CIS analysis of the data.[20]

Democrats also oppose it. Fifty-five percent said they thought an
amnesty would be a bad idea; only 36 percent thought it was a good idea.

And, as the Zogby poll found, granting amnesty to illegals isn't necessarily a winner of Hispanic votes. Fifty-one percent said it was a bad idea,
Zogby said, while 49 percent said it was a good idea. Politically, it could
also hamper candidates; twice as many Hispanics—33 percent—said they
would be less likely to support President Bush in 2004 if he signed a law
granting another amnesty, compared to just 15 percent who said his
amnesty support would gain their vote.

Low-income voters usually side with Democrats, but they would
likely face the most job competition from an amnesty. According to the
Zogby poll, voters in households earning less than $35,000 did not sup-
port amnesty by a two-to-one margin over supporters. Also, the survey
said, more than one-third of low-income balloters said they would be less
likely to support a Democrat in Congress who also backed amnesty.[21]

Given the public pooh-poohing of outright amnesty, so-called "guest
worker" programs have also been considered as alternatives, but more
than three-quarters of those surveyed—77 percent—think guest workers
from Mexico would not return home when their time was up.[22]

Leniency for illegals—whether flying under the colors of an amnesty or a "guest worker" program—is a political snake pit. "Democrats support this dubious contribution to the general welfare, with a wink and a nod, because they directly benefit from the support of ethnic lobbies eager to increase their numbers," writes Feder. "Republicans lack the courage to do anything positive about the problem, though most in Congress oppose mass amnesties. They are convinced that by keeping a low profile they can do better with the Hispanic vote."[23] But there's trouble ahead. With voters taking note of who is busy supporting amnesty (or not opposing it), the conservative GOP base might register their displeasure by warming armchairs on Election Day instead of dimpling chads for their party. And while trying to woo Hispanic voters, Republicans might end up alienating huge swathes of moderates and swing voters. Despite appearances, Democrats are in no better position. They also run the risk of alienating moderates but, more importantly, also union members, a core constituency of the party. Low-income voters may also resist Democrat advances if they perceive their jobs threatened by an amnesty. It's a no-win situation.

Writes syndicated columnist and author Samuel Francis,

Americans have long since tumbled to the fact that we do have a "permanent underclass" and have it regardless of mass immigration, but they also know that mass immigration has merely imported yet another underclass even as those who peddled open borders claimed that immigration was a smashing economic success. They also know that legalizing the status of aliens who violated our laws to come here, so far from solving the problem of a "permanent underclass," will not only lock the new underclass into American society and economy forever but also will extend an open invitation to the numberless armies of other aliens waiting to immigrate.[24]

Nevertheless, the House of Representatives passed a modest amnesty bill as recently as March 2002, though it never went further. And amnesty supporters are trying hard to convince Americans it is a good idea. As is often the case, supporters are using different terms—"regularization," "legalization" and "normalization"—in an effort to redirect the debate away from the politically dangerous term "amnesty."

"If an amnesty has merit, then it should be debated as openly as possible. The results of [the Zogby] survey indicate that supporters of amnesty clearly have their work cut out for them across a broad range of the population," says Steven A. Camarota of CIS.

———————

Americans who live along the border realize most the failure of amnesty. They realize that the promises made by politicians and bureaucrats in approving the last amnesty—illegal immigrant traffic will subside—remain unfulfilled and the economic and social fallout ever-expanding.

Carey James, a former Border Patrol sector chief, says it isn't difficult to figure out why amnesties for illegal aliens don't work. And in doing so, he shatters other myths as well:

My ancestors were slaves. So, as I was growing up, one of the big things constantly thrown at me (by my parents) was, "Get your education, get out there, and do better. We don't want you going through what we went through."

After growing up and getting the job that I had [with the U.S. Border Patrol], I started making some correlations. I saw the results of the first amnesty, with the farm workers. Well, you take [an illegal alien] farm worker and you say, "Why are you a farm worker? Why are you doing this?" And they tell you, "Nobody else wants this job. If I went out and I tried competing for the good jobs or whatever, then people are going to turn me in and I'm going to get caught, and then I'm going be sent back. So it's better for me to take a low-profile job."

At the time of the first amnesty I was working in California, a lot of the farmers were talking about this amnesty thing and they were hollering, "Oh, you gotta do it and it needs to happen 'cause if it doesn't you're not gonna eat and we need these people." So a lot of the farmers were willing to step forward to say and do whatever was necessary to get these people legalized, so that they could have a source of [legal] labor.

[The lawmakers] did pass an amnesty, and guess what happened? As soon as they started legalizing these people and they didn't have the fear [of being caught] anymore, what did they do? They didn't want to work on the farm anymore. They wanted to go into the factories, to the offices—they wanted a better way of life. And it makes sense; that's what America is all about. You don't want to stay in a rut; you want to be able to pull yourself up and do something better. When you've got a fear that prevents you from doing that, of course you're going to stay down and do what's necessary.

What do we sell here? We sell the American dream. Everybody wants the American dream. So what are the grounds for amnesty? What else are you going to use [as incentive] for these people to do these jobs and tasks that nobody else wants? Once they get legalized, then you're going to have a mass exodus from what you were trying to do. . . . No matter how many times you try [amnesty], this is what's going to happen.

If you want to do anything like this, you do a guest-worker program; that way you can control these people and you know where they are. But trying legalization? They're never going to stay where you want them to be. And you can't legalize them just to tell them, "You gotta stay here." Next thing you know, they're going to start complaining, "This isn't what the American dream is all about."

James continued:

Farmers used to tell me, "If I don't get the cheap labor, and if I don't get someone to come and pick my crops, you're gonna go hungry!" That's bull. Nobody in this country's going to go hungry; it works on supply and demand.

If a farmer puts that crop out in a field, he's not going to let it rot. You might end up paying more for that corn or loaf of bread or that beef that you're eating, but he's not going to let it rot in the field. Somebody's going to come there (to pick it).

But, we in America are spoiled. We're used to cheap labor, we're used to cheap food, cheap gasoline prices, and in an effort to try and maintain those things, we have illegal immigration—which is a big draw, to fill in those voids, to keep those things that we're comfortable with and used to. To do that, the politicians and everybody else are exploiting these illegals, to get the cheap labor and cheaper products.[25]

Molly Ivins, nationally syndicated columnist, provides a specific example of James' thesis: "Thirty years ago, meatpacking was one of the highest-paid industrial jobs in the United States, with one of the lowest turnover rates. In the 1960s, employers broke the unions and brought in Mexican workers, and wages fell by as much as 50 percent. Today meatpacking is one of the nation's lowest-paid industrial jobs, with one of the highest turnover rates."[26]

A report in the *New York Times* in August 2002 revealed another, though little known, economic factor endemic to immigration. When the U.S. imports so many migrants, the country also imports a hefty amount of new poverty. "The surprising drop in median income in New York City that has puzzled demographers studying the results of the 2000 census appears to be traceable in large part to immigration," the paper said, using government figures. Income dropped the most in neighborhoods "where longtime residents have moved out and been replaced by immigrants."[27]

A similar pattern occurred in nearby New Jersey, where the biggest jump in income came in Hunterdon County, "a heavily white county at the heart of what has been called the state's flourishing wealth belt. Meanwhile, median incomes dropped in Newark, Paterson, and Trenton, and in smaller cities where less educated, less skilled immigrants have moved in." Additionally, teenage Latino girls "have the highest teenage birthrate of all major racial and ethnic groups in the nation."[28]

And the *Los Angeles Times* has reported: "Recent immigrants make less money, own fewer homes and are less likely to become citizens than foreigners who came to the United States in decades past. . . . The rate among California Latinas, though down, remains stubbornly high at 90.5 births per 1,000 girls ages 15 to 19, compared with 59.9 for black teenagers and 20.7 for whites."[29]

"It should have been obvious that masses of such people would not only not assimilate to a culture (including an economic culture) in which they remained, literally, alien, but also that the presence of millions of them would simply replicate their old culture here," writes Sam Francis.[30] "The reason it wasn't obvious is that the Open Borders lobby has cleverly exploited the myth of Economic Man to insinuate into the American mind the unexamined premise that immigration today means Asian computer geniuses and Korean store owners. There are such immigrants, obviously, but they're not typical of the millions who have entered this country during the last 30 years."[31]

In a major study by the Public Policy Institute of California, researchers found that amnesties have unexpected repercussions that echo for years. The study, "Understanding the Future of Californians Fertility: The Role of Immigrants," concluded that the 1986 amnesty for illegals set off a big baby boom among its beneficiaries, which worsened public health services, overcrowding in schools and other problems.

"Between 1987 and 1991, total fertility rates for foreign-born Hispanics [in California] increased from 3.2 to 4.4 [expected babies per woman over her lifetime]. This dramatic rise was the primary force behind the overall increase in the state's total fertility rate during this period. Were it not for the large increase in fertility among Hispanic immigrants, fertility rates in California would have increased very little between 1987 and 1991," wrote study authors Laura E. Hill and Hans P. Johnson.[32]

"Why did total fertility rates increase so dramatically for Hispanic immigrants? First, the composition of the Hispanic immigrant population in California changed as a result of the Immigration Reform and Control Act (IRCA) of 1986. In California alone, 1.6 million unauthorized immigrants applied for amnesty (legal immigrant status) under this act. The vast majority were young men, and many were agricultural workers who settled permanently in the United States. Previous research indicates that many of those granted amnesty were joined later by spouses and relatives in the United States. . . . As a result, many young adult Hispanic women came to California during the late 1980s. We also know that unauthorized immigrants tend to have less education than other immigrants and that they are more likely to come from rural areas. Both characteristics are associated with high levels of fertility. As a result, changes in the composition of the Hispanic immigration population probably increased fertility rates. Another possible reason for the sudden increase in fertility rates for Hispanic immigrants is also related to IRCA. Because many of those granted amnesty and their spouses had been apart for some time, their reunion in California prompted a 'catch-up' effect in the timing of births. . . ."[33]

Peter Brimelow—author of *Alien Nation*, a British immigrant to the U.S. who founded the Center for American Unity and publishes the immigration-reform news and opinion site, Vdare.com—says the problems inherent with illegal immigration and amnesty aren't popular among the nation's business and political elite, so they are often overlooked by many academics. "As a leading (neo-conservative) education expert said to me once, when I asked what studies have been done on the impact of immigration on the performance of native-born Americans in impacted schools: 'None. And none are going to be done. Because no one wants to know the answer.'"[34]

"It is obviously easier, for the short run, to draw cheap labor from adjacent pools of poverty . . . than to find it among one's own people. And to the millions of such prospective immigrants from poverty to prosperity, there is, rightly or wrongly, no place that looks more attractive than the United States," George F. Kennan, former U.S. ambassador to the former USSR, has said of immigration. "Given its head, and subject to no restrictions, this pressure will find its termination only when the levels of overpopulation and poverty in the United States are equal to those of the countries from which these people are now so anxious to escape."[35]

CIS head Krikorian is more candid: "Whatever one thinks of amnesty, the debate over such a sweeping measure should take place in plain English. If an amnesty does have merit, supporters should be able to make the case for it without evasion and obfuscation."[36]

To do so, supporters will have to explain why it is in our nation's best interest to employ the world's impoverished, at the risk of underemploying Americans. They will have to justify the enormous expense of providing benefits to so many who can't, don't or won't contribute to their own maintenance. They must explain why opening our nation's borders isn't a huge security risk—especially in a new age of domestic terrorism—and why the deployment of U.S. military assets to enhance homeland and border safety of countries overseas is a better use of American defense forces than to guard our own nation. And, ultimately, they will have to explain the vicious cycle of amnesty—why more of them will be needed once the current crop of low-wage foreign-born workers, newly legitimized, moves on to jobs with better working conditions and higher pay.

So far, anyway, they have not.

ACKNOWLEDGMENTS

Undertaking a book project is not an easy endeavor. It is tedious and all-consuming, but the reward—a great finished product—is worth the effort.

As always, though, a task as great as this is made easier with a cadre of wonderful family and friends offering words of advice, encouragement and, when needed, critique. With that in mind, I first want to thank my lovely bride, Shelly, for believing in me, coddling me when I needed it, kicking me in gear when that was appropriate, loving me through thick and thin and most of all for staying by my side. You truly are a rarity, sweetheart—my soulmate for life.

I also want to thank my children—Ashley Lynn Bates, Heather Leigh Dougherty, Heather Rae Burton, Lindsey Nicole Dougherty and Zachary Taylor Dougherty, for minding the fort while I was traveling conducting research for this project.

I want to thank my Moms—Diana McClelland and Deborah Dougherty—and my Dads—Louis McClelland and Ted Dougherty—for each contributing to make me the person I am today.

Thanks to Joel Miller, Wes Driver and the other editors at WND Books for their insight, humor and patience.

Thanks to my gym rat friends—Don "Dex" Dixon, Julia "Ms. Hollywood" Cassmeyer, Michelle "No Pain, No Gain" Kliethermes, Jay "Gunther" Cassady, Josh "The Quiet Man" Bax, Curtis "C-Dog" Williams, Brian "Big Stud" Beanland, and Brooke "Kickin' Booty" Pace—for your encouragement, perspective and helping me stay fit physically and mentally throughout this project.

Last but certainly not least, thanks also to Robin Kaigh, a wonderfully talented, refined lady and fellow Scorpio who, as a recovering literary agent and lawyer, was good enough to give the time of day to a hayseed writer from mid-Missouri.

Jon E. Dougherty
November 2003

NOTES

Chapter 1: Crisis Approaching

1. "Agents left in comas after border sting," Associated Press, 14 September 2002.

2. Joseph Farah, "The shooting war on the Mexican border," WorldNetDaily.com, 27 June 1997.

3. Farah, "The shooting war on the Mexican border."

4. Farah, "The shooting war on the Mexican border."

5. Robert Halpern, "Redford teenager killed by U.S. Marine," *Big Bend Sentinel*, 22 May 1997.

6. Farah, "The shooting war on the Mexican border."

7. Farah, "The shooting war on the Mexican border."

8. Farah, "The shooting war on the Mexican border."

9. Jon E. Dougherty, "Border accident or bounty hunting?" WorldNetDaily.com, 28 March 2000.

10. Dougherty, "Border accident or bounty hunting?"

11. Jon E. Dougherty, "Make a gun for the border," WorldNetDaily.com, 4 June 2000.

12. Jon E. Dougherty, "Border Patrol encounters Mexican soldiers," WorldNetDaily.com, 16 March 2002.

13. Jon E. Dougherty, "Mexicans shoot at Border Patrol," WorldNetDaily.com, 1 November 2000.

14. "Border Patrol officer discovers Mexican soldiers," Associated Press, 11 March 2002.
15. "U.S. demands probe of border 'act of war,'" WorldNetDaily.com, 24 May 2002.
16. "U.S. demands probe of border 'act of war,'" WorldNetDaily.com.
17. "Porous U.S. Border a 'war zone,'" CBSNews.com, 26 May 2003.
18. "Porous U.S. Border a 'war zone,'" CBSNews.com.
19. "Border Patrol reports increase in smuggling arrests," Associated Press, 20 May 2003.
20. Jerry Seper, "Border war: Mexican police join drug lords," *Washington Times*, 25 September 2002.
21. Brian Mitchell, "Public and elite part ways on U.S. immigration policy," *Investor's Business Daily*, 31 December 2002.
22. Poll was based on 2,800 telephone interviews from across the nation. The council also surveyed nearly 400 opinion leaders, including members of Congress, the administration, leaders of church groups, business executives, union leaders, journalists, academics and leaders of major interest groups.
23. Mitchell, "Public and elite part ways on U.S. immigration policy."
24. Mitchell, "Public and elite part ways on U.S. immigration policy."
25. Roy Beck and Steven A. Camarota, "Elite vs. Public Opinion," Center for Immigration Studies, December 2002.
26. "Illegal immigration is a crime," issue brief published by the Federation for American Immigration Reform, 2000 congressional season.
27. Thaddeus Herrick, "Do Americans want troops on the border?" *Houston Chronicle*, 16 November 1997.
28. Zogby International poll of 1,015 likely voters in the U.S. from 28-30 May 2001.
29. Jon Dougherty, "Hispanic women voice support for Tancredo," WorldNetDaily.com, 3 October 2002.
30. Press release, October 8, 2002.
31. *O'Reilly Factor*, Fox News, 7 November 2002.
32. Bill McAlister and Michael Riley, "Tancredo wants troops now along U.S borders," *Denver Post*, 19 June 2002.
33. Jon Dougherty, "Border killing points up security lack," WorldNetDaily.com, 13 August 2002.
34. Pamela Hess, "Soldiers at U.S. border posts to be armed," United Press International, 26 March 2002.
35. "U.S. arms some border guards," United Press International, 27 March 2002.
36. Jerry Seper, "Dangerous liaison: On the front line against illegal immigration," *Washington Times*, 25 September 2002.
37. Seper, "Border war."
38. President Abraham Lincoln, letter to Col. William F. Elkins, Nov. 21, 1864, in Archer H. Shaw, *The Lincoln Encyclopedia* (New York: Macmillan, 1950).

39. Samuel Gompers, letter to Congress, March 19, 1924, available at http://www.num-bersusa.com/about/sup_sgompers.html.

40. Alex Pulaski, "Farm union decries guest-worker hires," *Oregonian*, 30 October 1998.

Chapter 2: It's a Sieve

1. Interview with author.

2. Center for Trade Policy Studies, Cato Institute, available at http://www.freetrade.org/issues/immigration.html.

3. J. Zane Walley, "Arab terrorists crossing border," WorldNetDaily.com, 19 October 2001.

4. Chilton William Jr., "Do illegal immigrants have more rights than Americans?" Vdare.com, 9 November 2001.

5. Brian Blomquist, "Feds zap alien smuggling ring," *New York Post*, 8 January 2003.

6. Glenn Custred, "Alien crossings," *American Spectator*, October 2000.

7. Custred, "Alien crossings."

8. Dan Baum, "Patriots on the borderline," *Los Angeles Times Magazine*, 16 March 2003.

9. Interview with author.

10. "Estimates of unauthorized immigrant population residing in the United States: 1990-2000," U.S. Citizen and Immigration Services (formerly Immigration and Naturalization Service), January 2003.

11. U.S. Census Bureau data, available at http://www.census.gov.

12. U.S. Census Bureau data, available at http://www.census.gov.

13. U.S. Census Bureau data, available at http://www.census.gov.

14. NumbersUSA projection and analysis of current population trends and data, available at http://www.numbersusa.com/overpopulation/headed3.html.

15. Jacob H. Fries, "Business of human smuggling slowed only briefly after 9/11," *Denver Post*, 5 January 2003.

16. Steven Camarota, "800,000+ illegals entering annually in late 1990s," Center for Immigration Reform, February 2003; "Estimates of the Unauthorized Immigrant Population Residing in the United States: 1990 to 2000," U.S. Citizen and Immigration Services (formerly Immigration and Naturalization Service), January 2003.

17. Diane Smith, "Immigration views now focus on security, poll says," *Dallas Fort Worth Star-Telegram*, 20 February 2003.

18. Paul Craig Roberts, "An immigration dictatorship," TownHall.com, 18 February 2003.

19. Michelle Malkin, "Illegal alien scandal—at White House!" Vdare.com, 2 January 2003.

20. Kelly Patricia O'Meara, "Civilians patrolling the border," *Insight*, 20 January 2003.

21. Fries, "Business of human smuggling slowed only briefly after 9/11."

22. Fries, "Business of human smuggling slowed only briefly after 9/11."

23. Interview with author.

24. Tom DeWeese, "The Outrages of the Mexican Invasion," American Policy Center, 22 February 2003.

25. Dane Schiller, "Death still stalks those crossing the border," *San Antonio Express-News*, 9 January 2003.

26. Samuel Francis, "Mexican government sends illegal immigrants to death—knowingly," Creators Syndicate, 28 May 2001.

27. Francis, "Mexican government sends illegal immigrants to death."

28. Francis, "Mexican government sends illegal immigrants to death."

29. Ernesto Zedillo, speech televised on C-SPAN, 23 July 1997.

30. Interview with author.

31. William Norman Grigg, "Our 'friend' to the South," *New American*, 16 December 2002.

32. Grigg, "Our 'friend' to the South."

33. Joe Guzzardi, "View from Lodi, CA: Letter to American schoolchildren," Vdare.com, 21 February 2003.

34. Guzzardi, "View from Lodi, CA."

35. David Walsh, "Immigrant crime: Who wants to know?" Vdare.com, 18 June 2001.

36. Jon E. Dougherty, "Critics: U.S. borders still porous as sieves," WorldNetDaily.com, 6 August 2002.

37. Dougherty, "Critics: U.S. borders still porous as sieves."

38. Samuel Francis, "Immigration is ceasing to be controllable," Vdare.com, 20 February 2001.

39. Will Lester, "Political parties court Hispanic vote," Associated Press, 14 March 2003.

40. Lester, "Political parties court Hispanic vote."

41. Lester, "Political parties court Hispanic vote."

42. Robert H. Goldsborough, "The disastrous consequence of buying votes," *Immigration Watch,* Americans for Immigration Reform, n.d.

43. David Schippers with Alan P. Henry, "Schippers: Gore pressured INS to win in '96," WorldNetDaily.com, 28 August 2000.

44. Schippers and Henry, "Schippers: Gore pressured INS to win in '96."

45. Schippers and Henry, "Schippers: Gore pressured INS to win in '96."

46. Art Moore, "Is Mexico reconquering U.S. southwest?" WorldNetDaily.com, 4 January 2002.

47. Moore, "Is Mexico reconquering U.S. southwest?"

48. Moore, "Is Mexico reconquering U.S. southwest?"

49. Moore, "Is Mexico reconquering U.S. southwest?"

50. See Aztlan.net for details.

51. Art Moore, "Is Mexico reconquering U.S. southwest?"

52. Art Moore, "Is Mexico reconquering U.S. southwest?"
53. Baum, "Patriots on the borderline."

Chapter 3: Enemy of the States

1. Interview with author.
2. "Illegal immigration and crime," Pacific Research Institute, 2 September 1997.
3. Joseph Farah, "The shooting war on Mexican border," WorldNetDaily.com, 27 June 1997.
4. INS *Detention and Deportation Officers' Field Manual.*
5. Michelle Malkin, "Who let Lee Malvo loose?" TownHall.com, 25 October 2002.
6. Tim McGlone and Matthew Roy, "Migrant worker held in eastern shore raid," *Virginia-Pilot*, 6 February 2003.
7. "Officials worry over al Qaeda 'sleeper cells,'" Agence France Presse, 11 January 2003.
8. Bill Gertz, "Inside the Ring," *Washington Times*, 18 September 2002.
9. The International Court of Justice, a 15-judge panel in the Hague, Netherlands, known popularly as the World Court, issued a ruling in January 2003 instructing the United States to delay the execution of all Mexican nationals until a lawsuit filed by the Mexican government, which says its citizens on death row were never offered their "consular rights" as guaranteed by the Geneva Convention. The World Court has no power to enforce its rulings and the U.S. has ignored them in the past. As of February 2003, two U.S. states—Texas and Oklahoma—announced they, too, would ignore the court's "order."
10. Lisa J. Adams, "Mexico asks Hague court to intervene on behalf of Mexicans on death row in U.S.," Associated Press, 9 January 2003.
11. Virginia Hennessey, "World Court delays executions," *Monterey Herald*, 10 February 2003.
12. Charles Rabin, "Guatemalan man with three ill children faces deportation," *Miami Herald*, 10 February 2003.
13. Generally, Border Patrol policy is to follow but not give high-speed chase to suspected illegal immigrants fleeing in vehicles on highways.
14. Gregory Alan Gross and Irene McCormack Jason, "2 killed as truck crashes in Border Patrol pursuit," *San Diego Union-Tribune*, 10 January 2003.
15. Jacques Billeaud, "Immigrant kidnappings on the rise," Associated Press, 23 January 2003.
16. Billeaud, "Immigrant kidnappings on the rise."
17. "US taxpayers subsidize Mexico's theft of water," United Press International, 29 January 2003.
18. "US taxpayers subsidize Mexico's theft of water," United Press International.
19. Jon E. Dougherty, "Texas farmers plan blockage of bridges," WorldNetDaily.com, 10 May 2002.

20. "Mexican army herds invaders north," AmericanPatrol.com, 4 February 2003.

21. Carl F. Horowitz, " An examination of U.S. immigration policy and serious crime," Center for Immigration Studies, April 2001.

22. Horowitz, "An examination of U.S. immigration policy and serious crime."

23. Horowitz, "An examination of U.S. immigration policy and serious crime."

24. David Walsh, "Immigrant crime: Who wants to know?" Vdare.com, 18 June 2001.

25. Walsh, "Immigrant crime."

26. Kenneth Ma, "Police arrest seven in series of farmworker robberies," *North County Times*, 6 February 2003.

27. Classification by the National Park Rangers Lodge of the Fraternal Order of Police.

28. Ralph Vartabedian, "The law loses out at US parks," *Los Angeles Times*, 23 January 2003.

29. Vartabedian, "The law loses out at US parks."

30. Vartabedian, "The law loses out at US parks."

31. Tom Clynes, "Arizona park 'most dangerous' in U.S." *National Geographic*, 13 January 2003.

32. Clynes, "Arizona park 'most dangerous' in U.S."

33. Information relayed to author by a resident of Arizona, who claimed to be familiar with the incident.

34. Vartabedian, "The law loses out at US parks."

35. Vartabedian, "The law loses out at US parks."

36. Vartabedian, "The law loses out at US parks."

37. Julia Malone and Eliot Jaspin, "INS fails to send ex-cons home," Cox Newspapers, 15 December 2002.

38. Malone and Jaspin, "INS fails to send ex-cons home."

39. Malone and Jaspin, "INS fails to send ex-cons home."

40. Malone and Jaspin, "INS fails to send ex-cons home."

41. Malone and Jaspin, "INS fails to send ex-cons home."

42. Malone and Jaspin, "INS fails to send ex-cons home."

43. Susan Carroll, "Series of killings tied to people smuggling," *Arizona Republic*, 6 January 2003.

44. Billeaud, "Immigrant kidnappings on the rise."

45. Billeaud, "Immigrant kidnappings on the rise."

46. "Police bust house with 61 immigrants held against their will," Associated Press, 30 January 2003.

47. "Latino cultural differences result in scrapes with law," Associated Press, 22 February 2003.

48. "Latino cultural differences result in scrapes with law," Associated Press.

49. "Latino cultural differences result in scrapes with law," Associated Press.

50. Tom DeWeese, "The Outrages of the Mexican Invasion," American Policy Center, 22 February 2003.

51. Don Feder, "Tighter borders now!" *Boston Herald*, 22 October 2001.

Chapter 4: It's the Economy, Stupid

1. Jon E. Dougherty, "Mexicans to collect Social Security?" WorldNetDaily.com, 19 December 2002.

2. "The cost of immigration," Federation for American Immigration Reform, July 2003.

3. Donald Huddle, "The net national costs of immigration: Fiscal effects of welfare restorations to legal immigrants," Rice University, 1997.

4. Huddle, "The net national costs of immigration."

5. Figures supplied by Americans for Immigration Reform.

6. Figures supplied by Americans for Immigration Reform.

7. "The cost of immigration," Federation for American Immigration Reform.

8. "The cost of immigration," Federation for American Immigration Reform.

9. Tom DeWeese, "The outrages of the Mexican invasion," American Policy Center, 22 February 2003.

10. George Borjas, "The impact of welfare reform on immigrant welfare use," Center for Immigration Studies, July 2002.

11. Philip Martin, "Illegal immigration: Numbers, benefits, and costs in California," *Migration News*, May 1994, available at http://migration.ucdavis.edu/mn/more.php?id=298_0_2_0.

12. Figures supplied by the Center for Immigration Studies.

13. Nadia Rubaii-Barrett, "Disproportionate costs of illegal immigration," New Mexico State University news release, 8 February 2001.

14. "Costs," Center for Immigration Studies, available at http://www.cis.org/topics/costs.html.

15. Jerry Seper, "Bail out requested for ailing hospitals treating illegal immigrants," *Washington Times*, 27 September 2002.

16. Jessica Cantelon, "Congressman: 'Parasitic' illegal aliens burden U.S. hospitals," CNSNews.com, 16 July 2002.

17. Press release, 10 January 2003.

18. Jerry Seper, "Officials seek aid for border hospitals," *Washington Times*, 27 September 2002.

19. Seper, "Officials seek aid for border hospitals."

20. Haley Nolde, "Border hospitals on the brink," *Mother Jones*, 21 June 2000.

21. Nolde, "Border hospitals on the brink."

22. Nolde, "Border hospitals on the brink."

23. "Medical liability and lawsuit abuse along the border: Circling the drain," Texas Medical Association, 13 June 2002.

24. "Medical liability and lawsuit abuse along the border: Circling the drain," Texas Medical Association.

25. "Medical liability and lawsuit abuse along the border: Circling the drain," Texas Medical Association.

26. James Pinkerton, "Health care: Crisis at the border," *Houston Chronicle*, 5 May 2002.

27. James Pinkerton, "Doctors to protest rising insurance," *Houston Chronicle*, 24 March 2002.

28. Joe Guzzardi, "Americans subsidizing their own dispossession," Vdare.com, 31 January 2003.

29. Michelle Malkin, "Tough questions about Jesica's transplants," Creators Syndicate, 21 February 2003.

30. Malkin, "Tough questions about Jesica's transplants."

31. Malkin, "Tough questions about Jesica's transplants."

32. Brenda Walker, "Tax immigrants to support border hospitals," *Washington Times*, 2 December 2002.

33. Lois K. Solomon, "S. Florida schools see number of Venezuelans rising," Fort Lauderdale *Sun-Sentinel*, 10 February 2003.

34. "Education official says state shouldn't teach undocumented immigrants' children," TheKansasCityChannel.com, 12 March 2003.

35. Committee on Education and the Workforce statistic.

36. U.S. Department of Education statistics.

37. Data from Americans for Immigration Control.

38. Committee on Education and the Workforce statistic.

39. Jerry Seper, "We are overwhelmed," *Washington Times*, September 2002.

40. Seper, "We are overwhelmed."

41. Joe Guzzardi, "View from Lodi, CA: Federal immigration failure wrecking the Golden State," Vdare.com, 24 May 2002.

42. Matt Hayes, "Medical benefits for non-citizens," FoxNews.com, 5 March 2003.

43. Mark Bixler, "Colleges grant degrees of danger," *Atlanta Journal-Constitution*, 16 October 2002.

44. Tom DeWeese, "The outrages of the Mexican invasion," American Policy Center, 22 February 2003.

45. "More in-state tuition for illegal immigrants," Associated Press, 22 May 2003.

46. "Some states give illegal immigrants tuition breaks," National Center for Policy Analysis, 7 September 2001.

47. "Groups urge second look at immigration proposal," CNN.com, 10 April 1996.

48. Robert Gehrke, "Congress cuts aid for jailing aliens," Associated Press, 15 February 2003.

49. Billy House, "Jail tab for illegals could fall to states," *Arizona Republic*, 23 January 2003.

50. Robert Gehrke, "Border governments alarmed at reduction in aid for jailing criminal aliens," Associated Press, 15 February 2003.

51. Gehrke, "Border governments alarmed at reduction in aid."

52. Julia Malone, "Bill slashes funding to jail criminal aliens," Cox Newspapers, 14 February 2003.

53. Malone, "Bill slashes funding to jail criminal aliens."

54. House, "Jail tab for illegals could fall to states."

55. Federal budget statistics published by the Religious Task Force on Central America and Mexico newsletter, February 2002.

56. Joe Guzzardi, "Illegal aliens: The health cost dimension," Vdare.com, 24 January 2003.

57. Phyllis Schlafly, "Dealing with the high costs of health care," TownHall.com, 13 August 2002.

58. Schlafly, "Dealing with the high costs of health care."

59. Schlafly, "Dealing with the high costs of health care."

60. Schlafly, "Dealing with the high costs of health care."

61. Cantelon, "Congressman: 'Parasitic' illegal aliens burden U.S. hospitals."

62. National Academy of Sciences, 2002 figures.

63. "The cost of immigration," Federation for American Immigration Reform.

64. Statistics supplied by Drug Enforcement Administration.

65. DEA Chief of Operations Harold D. Wankel, statement before House Judiciary Committee regarding drug control along the southwest border, 31 July 1996.

66. "Greenspan cites war risks to economy," CBSNews.com, 11 February 2003.

67. Joe Guzzardi, "Health, college: Americans subsidizing their own dispossession," Vdare.com, 31 January 2003.

68. Paul Craig Roberts, "Was it all hype?" TownHall.com, 12 February 2003.

69. International Union for the Scientific Study of Population, XXIV General Population Conference, Salvador da Bahia, Brazil, Plenary Debate no 4., 24 August 2001.

70. International Union for the Scientific Study of Population, XXIV General Population Conference.

71. U.S. Department of Commerce figures.

72. William R. Hawkins, "NAFTA: A decade of failure," TradeAlert.org, 2 January 2003.

73. William R. Hawkins, "Has NAFTA been a good deal for the average worker in the United States?" *Insight*, 21 January-3 February 2003.

74. Tessie Borden, "Mexican farmers say NAFTA ruins lives, forces migration," *Arizona Republic*, 14 January 2003.

75. Hugh Dellios, "NAFTA sprouts Mexico woe," *Chicago Tribune*, 10 January 2003.

76. "Economic costs of legal and illegal immigration," The Colorado Alliance for Immigration Reform, n.d., available at http://www.cairco.org/econ/econ.html.

Chapter 5: One Toke over the Line

1. "Chaos along the border," *Washington Times*, 6 October 2002.
2. "Chaos along the border," *Washington Times*.
3. Bill Hess, "Increase in drug and people traffic: Drug smugglers fired at BP agents Sunday, Monday," *Sierra Vista Herald Review*, 13 January 2003.
4. Hess, "Increase in drug and people traffic."
5. National Park Service Morning Report, 14 January 2003.
6. "Marine helicopters crash on Mexico border, 4 dead," CNN.com, 23 January 2003.
7. Steven C. McCraw, Deputy Assistant Director, Investigative Services Division, FBI, statement before the House Judiciary Committee, subcommittee on crime, 13 December 2000.
8. "Terrorists using tunnels to come to U.S.?" WorldNetDaily.com, 9 January 2003.
9. "4 tunnels found under Mexico-Ariz. Border," Associated Press, 13 January 2003.
10. "4 tunnels found under Mexico-Ariz. Border," Associated Press.
11. Tom Clynes, "Arizona Park 'Most Dangerous' in US," *National Geographic*, 13 January 2003.
12. Jerry Seper, "Border war: Mexican police join drug lords," *Washington Times*, 25 September 2002.
13. Terrence P. Jeffrey, "Mexican military drug-running at border?" *Human Events*, 1 July 2002.
14. Jeffrey, "Mexican military drug-running at border?"
15. Interview with author.
16. Jose Antonio Jiminez, "Mexico soldiers probed for drug ties," Associated Press, 15 October 2002.
17. Seper, "Border war."
18. Jeffrey, "Mexican military drug-running at border?"
19. Seper, "Border war."
20. Interview with author.
21. "Key figure in Mexican army drug scandal murdered," Reuters, 31 July 1997.
22. "Mexican military caught in drug scandal," Reuters, 28 July 1997.
23. "Mexican military caught in drug scandal," Reuters.
24. Margaret Swedish, "Mexico certified in the war on drugs," *Central America/Mexico Report*, February 1999.
25. Swedish, "Mexico certified in the war on drugs."
26. White House press secretary statement, 31 January 2003.
27. Eric Swedlund, "SUVs not what they seem," *Arizona Daily Star*, 20 February 2003.
28. Eric Swedlund, "SUVs not what they seem."
29. "Drug lords hire ex-GI's," *El Paso Times*, 19 August 1997.
30. "Drug lords hire ex-GI's," *El Paso Times*.

31. Some estimates say Mexican cartels produce as much as $100 billion a year in drug sales.

32. "The slippery slope: Unmasking the drug war;" GlobalExchange.org, 6-12 May 1996.

33. Tom Barry, ed., *Mexico: A Country Guide* (Albuquerque, NM: The Inter Hemispheric Resource Center, 1992), 56.

34. Barry, 56.

35. "The slippery slope: Unmasking the drug war;" Global Exchange.org.

36. George Gedda, "Clinton vows more anti-drug aid to Colombia," Associated Press, 10 November 1999.

37. Pierre Thomas, "U.S.-Mexico trade may outweigh anti-drug concerns," *Washington Post*, 23 February 1997.

38. Tim Weiner and Ginger Thompson, "U.S. guns smuggled into Mexico aid war," *New York Times*, 19 May 2001.

39. Mexico has a gun homicide rate of about 10 per 100,000 people, compared to 7 per 100,000 people in the U.S., according to 1997 U.S. Centers for Disease Control figures.

40. Lora Lumpe, "U.S. arms both sides of Mexico's drug war," *Covert Action Quarterly*, Summer 1997.

41. M-2 rifles are World War II-era carbines similar to the M-1 carbine used by Mexican police, except that the M-2 has a selector switch which allows the user to fire fully automatic.

42. American citizens may own fully automatic weapons, but must first obtain an annual, renewable special license from the Bureau of Alcohol, Tobacco and Firearms. As you might guess, such licenses are rare.

43. Amparo Trejo and Niko Price, "Mexican drug lords seeking new cartel," Associated Press, 9 April 2001.

44. Trejo and Price, "Mexican drug lords seeking new cartel."

45. Trejo and Price, "Mexican drug lords seeking new cartel."

46. Trejo and Price, "Mexican drug lords seeking new cartel."

47. Trejo and Price, "Mexican drug lords seeking new cartel."

48. Trejo and Price, "Mexican drug lords seeking new cartel."

49. Deborah Amos, "Drug warriors win one," ABCNews.com, 28 September 2002.

50. Deborah Amos, "The hydra effect," ABCNews.com, 29 September 2002.

51. Amos, "The hydra effect."

52. The *Los Angeles Times* reported 15 Nov. 2001 that drug use has also increased in Mexico and throughout Latin America.

53. S. Brian Wilson, "The slippery slope: Unmasking the drug war," Global Exchange.org.

54. L. Jacobo Rodríguez, "Time to end the drug war," Cato Institute, 3 December 1997.

55. Rodríguez, "Time to end the drug war."

56. John Rice, "Fox talks drug legalization," Associated Press, 20 March 2001.

57. Rice, "Fox talks drug legalization."

58. Steven C. McCraw, deputy assistant director, FBI, statement before the House Judiciary Committee subcommittee on crime, 13 December 2000.

59. Jon E. Dougherty, "Make a gun for the border," WorldNetDaily.com, 4 June 2000.

60. Eva Bertram and Kenneth Sharpe, "Drug war money brings ever more corruption," *Los Angeles Times*, 12 December 1999.

61. Bertram, Sharpe, "Drug war money brings ever more corruption."

62. Bertram, Sharpe, "Drug war money brings ever more corruption."

63. Bertram, Sharpe, "Drug war money brings ever more corruption."

64. Kieran Murray, "Mexico disbands anti-drugs force in drive against corruption," London *Independent*, 18 January 2003.

65. Murray, "Mexico disbands anti-drugs force in drive against corruption."

66. Rob Krott, "America's border war," *Soldier of Fortune*, March 2003.

67. Krott, "America's border war."

68. Alison Gregor and Bonnie Pfister, "Mexico: Violence increases on the border," *San Antonio Express-News*, 16 July 2001.

69. Chris Kraul, "3 killings may signal battle for Tijuana drug corridor," *Los Angeles Times*, 20 March 2002.

70. Kraul, "3 killings may signal battle for Tijuana drug corridor."

71. U.S. Department of Justice, National Drug Intelligence Center, New Mexico Drug Threat Assessment, April 2002.

72. Miriam Davidson, *Lives on the line: Dispatches from the U.S.-Mexico border* (Tucson: Arizona University Press, 2002).

73. H.G. Reza, "Drug runners arrested at border often go free," *Los Angeles Times*, 13 May 1996.

Chapter 6: Incursion!

1. William Norman Grigg, "The border war," *New American*, July 2002.

2. Grigg, "The border war."

3. Grigg, "The border war."

4. Grigg, "The border war."

5. Grigg, "The border war."

6. Grigg, "The border war."

7. Grigg, "The border war."

8. Grigg, "The border war."

9. Terrence P. Jeffrey, "Mexican military drug running at border?" *Human Events*, 1 July 2002.

10. "Texas sheriff warns of unidentified troops," WorldNetDaily.com, 17 March 2003.

11. Jon E. Dougherty, "Border accident or bounty hunting?" WorldNetDaily.com, 28 March 2000.

12. "Activist denies making bounty announcement," Associated Press, 10 June 2000.

13. Jon E. Dougherty, "Border Patrol encounters Mexican soldiers," WorldNetDaily.com, 16 March 2002.

14. Dougherty, "Border accident or bounty hunting?"

15. Dougherty, "Border accident or bounty hunting?"

16. Dougherty, "Mexicans shoot at Border Patrol."

17. Jon E. Dougherty, "Mexicans shoot at Border Patrol," WorldNetDaily.com, 1 November 2000.

18. Dougherty, "Border Patrol encounters Mexican soldiers."

19. Dwight Daniels, "Mexican troops stray over border," *San Diego Union-Tribune*, 18 January 2003.

20. Daniels, "Mexican troops stray over border."

21. Tim Johnson and Jennifer Babson, "Protecting borders a complex challenge," *Miami Herald*, 8 February 2003.

22. Johnson, Babson, "Protecting borders a complex challenge."

23. Jon E. Dougherty, "Pressing Reno for body armor," WorldNetDaily.com, 7 June 2000.

24. Dougherty, "Pressing Reno for body armor."

25. Dougherty, "Pressing Reno for body armor."

26. Joseph D'Agostino, "Mexican official confirms border crossings," *Human Events*, 13 May 2002.

27. "Mexico, US discuss border problems," United Press International, 8 June 2000.

28. "U.S. demands probe of border 'act of war,'" WorldNetDaily.com, 24 May 2002.

29. Terrence P. Jeffrey, "Mexican military drug-running at border?" *Human Events*, 1 July 2002.

30. D'Agostino, "Mexican official confirms border crossings."

31. Joseph Farah, "Mexico: The next Lebanon?" WorldNetDaily.com, 22 June 2001.

32. Tim Steller, "Mexican troops enter N.M., shoot, go free," *Arizona Daily Star*, 27 March 2000.

33. Jon E. Dougherty, "Mexico cries 'red alert,'" WorldNetDaily.com, May 19, 2000.

34. Dougherty, "Mexico cries 'red alert.'"

35. Dougherty, "Mexico cries 'red alert.'"

36. Sergio Bustos, "Agencies unite to guard border," *Gannett News Service*, 31 January 2003.

37. Bustos, "Agencies unite to guard border."

38. "President wants $41 billion for homeland security," Associated Press, 31 January 2003.

39. Samuel Francis, "Abolishing America: Mexican army, police ignore border," Vdare.com, 20 May 2002.

Chapter 7: Mission: Illegals

1. Bill Hess, "Resident finds backpack with Arabic notebook," *Sierra Vista Herald-Review*, 12 February 2003.
2. Hess, "Resident finds backpack with Arabic notebook."
3. Rep. Sam Graves, press release, 10 March 2003.

Chapter 8: Way Up North

1. The northern border figure includes Alaska's border with western Canada.
2. Jon Benné, "Huge gaps remain on northern border" MSNBC.com, July 2002.
3. Benné, "Huge gaps remain on northern border."
4. Benné, "Huge gaps remain on northern border."
5. Benné, "Huge gaps remain on northern border."
6. "Smart borders: U.S./Canada joint anti-terrorism actions," U.S. Customs Service, February 2002.
7. "Huge cocaine bust at Blaine crossing," *Bellingham Herald*, 6 March 2003.
8. "Huge cocaine bust at Blaine crossing."
9. Tom Godfrey, "Aliens fail in smuggle bid," *Toronto Sun*, 12 December 2002.
10. Interview with author.
11. "Arrest of Ressam at Canadian border," U.S. Customs press release, 14 December 2000.
12. The Department of Homeland Security, created in the wake of the September 11, 2001, terrorist attacks, now has the responsibility for all aspects of U.S. border security.
13. White House press release, 6 December 2002.
14. Olyvia Rodriguez, "Drugs and crime find nest on U.S.-Canada border," Council on Hemispheric Affairs, 29 July 1998.
15. Rodriguez, "Drugs and crime find nest on U.S.-Canada border."
16. Bill Miller, "Plugging a very porous northern border," *Washington Post*, 7 April 2002.
17. Mike Blair, "America guards world's borders but not our own," *American Free Press*, 2 March 2003.
18. U.S. Census Bureau Figures.
19. Council on Foreign Relations statistics, 2001-2002.
20. Bill Curry, "Business to push Manley, Ridge for joint perimeter," *National Post*, 1 April 2003.
21. Gary Martin, "Local lawmaker wants more secure borders," *San Antonio Express-News*, April 2, 2003.
22. "U.S. Security Measures Drive Asylum Seekers to Canada," Reuters, 1 April 2003.
23. "U.S. Security Measures Drive Asylum Seekers to Canada," Reuters.

Chapter 9: Bad Apples

1. Brent Gray, Department of Justice Civil Rights Division, "Former Border Patrol agent sentenced for civil rights violations," Justice Department news advisory, March 10, 2003.

2. Interview, March 2003.

3. Rep. Tom Tancredo, press release, 18 June 2002.

4. Tancredo, 18 June 2002.

5. Interview with author.

6. "Kolbe criticizes BP management," *Nogales International*, 28 February 2003.

7. Interview with author.

8. Interview with author.

9. Interview with author.

10. "The truth about employment-based immigration," Federation for American Immigration Reform, October 2002.

11. "Recommendations of the U.S. Commission on Immigration Reform," Federation for American Immigration Reform, June 2003.

12. "Recommendations of the U.S. Commission on Immigration Reform," Federation for American Immigration Reform.

13. "Border Patrol agents found not guilty in United States Federal Court," National Border Patrol Council 1613, 26 November 2002.

14. "Border Patrol agents found not guilty in United States Federal Court," National Border Patrol Council 1613.

15. Interview with author.

16. Interview with author.

17. Interview with author.

18. Interview with author.

19. Interview with author.

20. Interview with author.

21. Interview with author.

22. Interview with author.

23. Interview with author.

24. "Border Patrol agents arrested," *Tucson Citizen*, 1 February 2002.

25. "Border Patrol agents arrested," *Tucson Citizen*.

26. "Border Patrol agents arrested," *Tucson Citizen*.

27. "Border Patrol agents arrested," *Tucson Citizen*.

28. Susan Carroll, "Crossing the line: Discipline at Border Patrol criticized as 'spotty, uneven'; agency defends its procedures," *Tucson Citizen*, 1 February 2003.

29. Bill Straub, "The budget of broken promises," *Scripps Howard News Service*, 1 March 2003.

30. Brian Blomquist, Philip Messing and Bridget Harrison, "INS lunacy forces New York City to keep thugs," *New York Post*, 28 February 2003.

31. Blomquist, Messing and Harrison, "INS lunacy forces New York City to keep thugs."

32. Blomquist, Messing and Harrison, "INS lunacy forces New York City to keep thugs."

33. Jerry Seper, "2 agents targeted by INS in Maine," *Washington Times*, 27 February 2003.

34. Seper, "2 agents targeted by INS in Maine."

35. Seper, "2 agents targeted by INS in Maine."

36. John M. Broder, "INS shredder ended work backlog, U.S. says," *New York Times*, 31 January 2003.

Chapter 10: Vigilante Justice

1. Luke Turf, "Grijalva: Have FBI probe alleged militia-racist link," *Tucson Citizen*, 19 December 2002.

2. Cathy Murphy, "Bisbee council joins stance against militias on the border," *Sierra Vista Herald*, 8 January 2003.

3. Ignacio Ibarra, "Border militias claim success," *Arizona Daily Star*, 9 November 2003.

4. Murphy, "Bisbee council joins stance against militias on the border."

5. Tim Steller, "Simcox, companion cited by park ranger," *Arizona Daily Star*, 28 January 2003.

6. Statement attributed to Jack Foote, national spokesman for the property and border group Ranch Rescue; available at http://www.ranchrescue.com/arizona.htm.

7. Interview with author.

8. "StarNet poll: Act of mercy or misjudgment?" available at http://www.azstarnet.com/border/waterjugpoll.html.

9. Available at http://www.americanpatrol.org/POLLS/Polls.html.

10. Available at http://www.ranchrescue.com.

11. "Should President Bush deploy troops to protect both U.S. land, borders from terrorist infiltration?" Vote.com survey, available at http://www.vote.com/vResults/index.phtml?voteID=46806953&cat=4075633.

12. Mike Blair, "America guards world's borders but not our own," *American Free Press*, 3 March 2003.

13. George Putnam, "One reporter's opinion: Citizen militia on the border," NewsMax.com, 13 December 2002.

14. William L. Anderson, "Vigilante justice: A proper response to government failure," LewRockwell.com, 4 April 2000.

15. Anderson, "Vigilante justice: A proper response to government failure."

16. "Texas sheriff warns of unidentified troops," WorldNetDaily.com, 17 March 2003.

17. Jon E. Dougherty, "Ranchers decry U.S. 'occupying force,'" WorldNetDaily.com, 14 March 2003.

18. Dougherty, "Ranchers decry U.S. 'occupying force.'"

19. Border Land Association press release, 12 March 2003.

20. Nick Madigan, "Police investigate killings of illegal immigrants in desert," *New York Times*, 23 October 2002.

21. Art Moore, Jon E. Dougherty, "Ranch defenders arrested on accusation by illegals," WorldNetDaily.com, 20 March 2003; Jon E. Dougherty, "Border group members face felony charges," WorldNetDaily.com, 21 March 2003.

22. Moore and Dougherty, "Ranch defenders arrested on accusation by illegals."

23. Dougherty, "Border group members face felony charges."

24. "Texas sheriff warns of unidentified troops," WorldNetDaily.com, 17 March 2003.

25. Michael Isikoff and Mark Hosenball, "Terrorism: The hunt at home," *Newsweek*, 20 March 2003.

26. Isikoff and Hosenball, "Terrorism: The hunt at home."

27. Bill Gertz, "Terrorists said to seek entry to U.S. via Mexico," *Washington Times*, 7 April 2003.

28. Gertz, "Terrorists said to seek entry to U.S. via Mexico."

29. Shaun Waterman, "Analysis: Shopping mall terror training," United Press International, 17 July 2003.

30. Jon E. Dougherty, "U.S. airliners vulnerable to missiles," WorldNetDaily.com, 6 December 2002.

31. Council On Hemispheric Affairs, press release, 12 July 2000.

32. Hernán Rozemberg, "Group slams border 'vigilante' groups," *Arizona Republic*, 18 December 2002.

33. Rozemberg, "Group slams border 'vigilante' groups."

34. Rozemberg, "Group slams border 'vigilante' groups."

35. Luke Turf, "Vigilantes stir fear at border," *Tucson Citizen*, 9 December 2002.

36. Turf, "Vigilantes stir fear at border."

37. Evelyn Nieves, "Arizona groups target illegals on border," *Washington Post*, 19 January 2003.

38. Mexican government figures.

39. Ignacio Ibarra, "Battle of border enforcers heats up," *Arizona Daily Star*, 27 March 2003.

40. Ibarra, "Battle of border enforcers heats up."

41. Ibarra, "Battle of border enforcers heats up."

42. Ibarra, "Battle of border enforcers heats up."

43. Ibarra, "Battle of border enforcers heats up."

Chapter 11: No Respect

1. "Border Patrol: More undocumented immigrants arriving armed," Agencia EFE, 23 January 2003, available in English at http://www.quepasa.com/content/?c=104&id=96473.

2. Kerry Pohlman, "Smugglers ram Border Patrol agents' truck," *Yuma Sun*, 11 March 2003.

3. Karen Gleason, "Gunfight on the Rio Grande," *Del Rio News Herald*, 16 January 2003.

4. William Norman Grigg, "The border war," *New American*, July 2002.

5. Gregory Allan Gross, "U.S. agents are fired on at border," *San Diego Union-Tribune*, 16 March 2000.

6. "Border Patrol agent in gunfight with drug-smuggling suspect," Associated Press, 27 March 2002.

7. Daniel B. Wood, "At border, uptick in illegal crossings," *Christian Science Monitor*, 24 January 2002.

8. Xavier Zaragoza, "Border Patrol agent response to rock throwers by shooting at them," *Douglas Daily Dispatch*, 5 April 2001.

9. Xavier Zaragoza, "Attacks on agents increasing as smugglers getting more frustrated," *Douglas Daily Dispatch*, 14 February 2001.

10. Xavier Zaragoza, "BP agent shoots illegal entrant," *Douglas Daily Dispatch*, 26 January 2001.

11. David Rupkalvis, "Smugglers ram drug agents' vehicle," *Sierra Vista Herald*, 29 January 2001.

12. Xavier Zaragoza, "BP agent fires weapon after eight migrants throw rocks," *Douglas Daily Dispatch*, 20 January 2001.

13. Ignacio Ibarra, "Border battles escalating," *Arizona Daily Star*, 12 February 2001.

14. Ibarra, "Border battles escalating."

15. Luke Turf, "Still tense at Organ Pipe," *Tucson Citizen*, 7 February 2003.

16. Ignacio Ibarra, "Ancient skills, modern crimes," *Arizona Daily Star*, 22 March 2001.

17. Ibarra, "Ancient skills, modern crimes."

18. Bureau of Citizenship and Immigration Services Web Site description.

19. "INS expands search and rescue capabilities along southwest border," U.S. Citizenship and Immigration Services press release, 3 August 2001.

20. William LaJeunesse, "New, green INS divides time between catching aliens and corralling trash," FoxNews.com, 25 April 2001.

21. U.S. Border Patrol, U.S. Customs and National Park Service statistic.

22. Darren Meritz, "Mexico calls for shooting inquiry," *El Paso Times*, 25 February 2003.

23. Patricia Maese, "Man shot by Border Patrol agents," KFOX-TV News, 23 February 2003.

24. Amy Herdy, "Two officers recall night they were shot," *St. Petersburg Times*, 23 January 23, 2003.

25. "Border Patrol rescues man from Colorado river," *Palo Verde Valley Times*, 16 January 16, 2002.

26. Ryan Chirnomas, "Border bullies," *Arizona Daily Wildcat*, 30 November 1998.

27. Irene McCormack Jackson and Leonel Sanchez, "Crash that killed two puts focus on dilemma," *San Diego Union-Tribune*, 11 March 2003.

28. Interview with author.
29. Interview with author.
30. Steve Lopez, "Hunting terrorists, INS bags taxpayer," *Los Angeles Times*, 20 December 2002.
31. Martin Edwin Andersen, "Customs whistleblower sues Treasury secretary," *Insight*, 21 November 2002.
32. Darlene Catalan Fitzgerald, *U.S. Customs: Badge of Dishonor* (iUniverse, 2001).

Chapter 12: Be My Guest

1. Joseph A. D'Agnostino, "Administration wants to extend immigration amnesty," *Human Events*, 14 May 2001.
2. Statement by President Bush, 1 May 2001.
3. Jon E. Dougherty, "Anti-immigration group slams amnesty plan," WorldNetDaily.com, 18 January 2001.
4. Dougherty, "Anti-immigration group slams amnesty plan."
5. Michael Dorning, "Gutierrez bill proposes immigration amnesty," *Chicago Times*, 6 February 2001.
6. Joseph Perkins, "U.S. shouldn't hand over whole enchilada to Mexico," *Nashville City Paper*, 25 November 2002.
7. Jerry Seper, "Bush to push for amnesty," *Washington Times*, 23 November 2002.
8. Daniel Griswold, "Don't blame immigrants for terrorism," Cato Institute, 23 October 2001.
9. "Why amnesty isn't the solution," Federation for American Immigration Reform, October 2002.
10. "Why amnesty isn't the solution," Federation for American Immigration Reform.
11. David Simcox, "Measuring the Fallout: The Cost of the IRCA Amnesty After 10 Years," Center for Immigration Studies, May 1997.
12. Mark Krikorian, "Amnesty in English," *National Review*, 4 September 2001.
13. Sandra Sobieraj, "Bush: No amnesty for immigrants," Associated Press, 23 August 2001.
14. Krikorian, "Amnesty in English."
15. "Why amnesty isn't the solution," Federation for American Immigration Reform.
16. Don Feder, "Amnesties are a green light for illegal immigration," TownHall.com, 14 February 2001.
17. "Why amnesty isn't the solution," Federation for American Immigration Reform.
18. Kris Axtman, "Mexico prods U.S. on issue of illegals," *Christian Science Monitor*, 28 October 2002.
19. Zogby International from 25-29 Aug. 2001, nationwide poll of 1,020 likely voters. The margin of error is +/-3.2 percent. Margins of error are higher in subgroups.
20. Steven A. Camarota, "New Zogby poll on amnesty for illegal immigrants," Center for Immigration Studies, 4 September 2001.

21. Camarota, "New Zogby poll on amnesty for illegal immigrants."

22. Camarota, "New Zogby poll on amnesty for illegal immigrants."

23. Feder, "Amnesties are a green light for illegal immigration."

24. Samuel Francis, "Election over, Bush backing amnesty again," Vdare.com, 2 December 2002.

25. Interview with author.

26. Molly Ivins, "Meatpacking and the making of immigration policy," Creators Syndicate, 25 July 2001.

27. Janny Scott, "Immigration cut into income in New York, Census finds," *New York Times*, 6 August 2002.

28. Sue Ellen Christian and Teresa Puente, "Hispanic teen births up, defying U.S. trends," *Chicago Tribune*, 29 January 2001.

29. Carla Rivera, "Seeking to help teenage Latinas avoid pregnancy," *Los Angeles Times*, 19 May 2002.

30. Samuel Francis, "It's official: U.S. importing poverty," Vdare.com, 19 August 2002.

31. Francis, "It's official: U.S. importing poverty."

32. Laura E. Hill and Hans P. Johnson, "Understanding the Future of Californians Fertility: The Role of Immigrants," Public Policy Institute of California, April 2002; Steve Sailer, "Karl Rove, call your office: Amnesty triggered immigrant baby boom," Vdare.com, 15 December 2002.

33. Hill and Johnson, "Understanding the Future of Californians Fertility."

34. Peter Brimelow, Vdare.com, 14 February 2001, available at http://www.vdare.com/pb/feder_amnesty_bill.htm.

35. Rescue American Jobs, quotes available at http://www.rescueamericanjobs.org/info/quotes.html.

36. Krikorian, "Amnesty in English." *National Review*, 4 September 2001.

INDEX